US Coercive Diplomacy and the Global Order

US Coercive Diplomacy and the Global Order

A Critical Analysis of Post–Cold War Strategies

Richard Outzen

Rapid Communications in Conflict and Security Series
General Editor: Thomas G. Mahnken
Founding Editor: Geoffrey R. H. Burn

CAMBRIA PRESS

Amherst, New York

Library of Congress Cataloging-in-Publication Data

Names: Outzen, Richard H. M., author.

Title: US coercive diplomacy and the global order : a critical
analysis of post-cold war strategies / Richard Outzen.
Other titles: U.S. coercive diplomacy and the global order
Description: Amherst, New York: Cambria Press, 2025. |
Includes bibliographical references and index. |
Summary: "A central question in post-Cold War statecraft is why the United
States failed to create a coherent global order despite its unmatched power.
Initially optimistic, Washington used coercive diplomacy (CD) to shape
the international system. From 1991 to 2020, the U.S. employed military
force, economic sanctions, and diplomatic campaigns frequently but often
unsuccessfully. This book explores why Washington relied on CD and the
effects of its frequent failures. It reviews CD principles, major coercive episodes,
and regional impacts through case studies and expert interviews. The analysis
reveals inadequate planning, management, and coordination as key problems,
offering practical feedback for policy adaptation"-- Provided by publisher.

Identifiers: LCCN 2024030797 (print) | LCCN 2024030798 (ebook) |
ISBN 9781638573302 (library binding) | ISBN 9781638573487 (paperback)
ISBN 9781638573449 (pdf) | ISBN 9781638573456 (epub)

Subjects: LCSH: World politics--1989- | United States--Foreign
relations--1989- | United States--Foreign economic relations--
History--20th century | United States--Foreign economic relations--
History--21st century | United States--Military policy--History--20th
century. | United States--Military policy--History--21st century.

Classification: LCC JZ1480 .O87 2024 (print) |
LCC JZ1480 (ebook) | DDC 909.82--dc23/eng/20240813

LC record available at https://lccn.loc.gov/2024030797

LC ebook record available at https://lccn.loc.gov/2024030798

Table of Contents

LIST OF TABLES

US Coercive Diplomacy and the Global Order

CHAPTER 1

UNFULFILLED PROMISE: US COERCIVE DIPLOMACY AFTER 1990

US foreign policy from 1990 to 2020 was marked by significant fluctuations, resembling a roller coaster with many downward turns. The period began with a sense of optimism and relief as the US emerged from five decades of the Cold War, triumphant and unrivaled as a global power. With this newfound position, the US pursued an ambitious agenda focused on democratization, globalization, and convergence, aiming to unify the world around a common set of norms and institutions. However, this vision faltered in the face of multiple crises from 2001 to 2011—such as the ones faced in Afghanistan, Iraq, and Georgia—which undermined efforts at international cooperation and fractured even the common understanding of global challenges. The optimism of the early 1990s gave way to disillusionment, particularly as the Arab Spring led to further violence and repression in countries like Syria and Libya. Meanwhile, Great Power Competition reemerged as Russia, China, Iran, and the Bolivarian states openly challenged American primacy, and US policy elites were forced to scale back their expectations of what US foreign policy could and should achieve.

Shifts in global geopolitics have many causes, and the failure of US primacy to remake the international system cannot be attributed to any single factor. However, from the perspective of US policymakers and practitioners, it is evident that Washington's declining position of advantage partly resulted from its own policy missteps. The Cold War had fostered a set of adaptive skills, particularly in alliance formation and maintenance, that appeared to weaken as the post–Cold War era progressed.

This book explores the roots of the America's failure to remake— or even effectively manage—the international system in the early twenty-first century. It examines that failure through the lens of coercive diplomacy, one of the key tools of statecraft available to Great Powers. Written at a time that the asymmetric American advantage has given way to a form of multipolarity or Great Power Competition, it serves as both a cautionary tale and an object lesson for those who seek to see American leadership exercised with prudence and effectiveness.

The fall of the Soviet Union in 1991 and attendant end of the Cold War ushered in brief period of unquestioned American primacy. Writing in *Foreign Affairs*, Eliot A. Cohen described "an age of American hegemony," characterized by military, political, and cultural dominance that appeared to be "envied, resented, suspected, mistrusted, and, often enough, hated," yet inevitable.[1] Cohen contended that, given weak international institutions and the alternative of global chaos, hegemony was the only reasonable option, with the real question being whether it would be "exercised prudently or foolishly, consistently or fecklessly, safely or dangerously." Others argued that the US was, for the foreseeable future, in a position to shape the global order through its actions and decisions, setting the rules rather than being bound by them.[2] The notion that the US not only could, but was morally obligated, to enforce its interests and norms globally through various forms of leverage gained widespread acceptance in Washington.

There were opposing views. French policy elites, for example, rejected the inevitability of American supremacy. Jacques Chirac and Hubert Védrine called for France and the European Union to assiduously work toward a multipolar world order that would counterbalance US power. Védrine famously referred to Washington as a "hyperpower," rejecting its role as political, economic, and cultural arbiter of world affairs.[3] Russia and China also bristled at US unilateralism and its attempts to dictate global norms, increasingly rejecting and seeking to undermine US primacy.[4] Domestic critics of interventionism as an imperative initially came from firebrands such as Pat Buchanan on the right[5] and Noam Chomsky on the left,[6] but after the controversial US decision to coerce and ultimately invade Iraq in 2003, broader segments of American society came to reject the notion of a global-shaping role.[7]

A series of conflicts and crises—such as in Afghanistan, Iraq, Libya, Syria, Iran, North Korea, Cuba, Russia—exposed the limitations of Washington's policy solutions, undermining the notion of unilaterally imposed hegemony or facile coercion. While there had been early successes in Latin America and the Balkans, the rising economic power of non-Western countries diminished the ability of the US and its close allies to impose political outcomes through sanctions and other tools.[8] At the same time, the broadening scope of US coercion fostered growing skepticism among its allies.[9] After several decades of failed or inconclusive US attempts to coerce a wide range of countries for various reasons, it became clear that many targets were forming cooperative resistance networks to blunt the force of US pressure.[10] By 2013, public opinion polling revealed that a majority of Americans thought it best to "mind its own business internationally and let other countries get along the best they can," a sentiment not expressed since 1964.[11] The public was cooling to the idea that the US could, or should, broadly and frequently shape global outcomes, preferring instead to adapt strategically to changes as they arose.

By 2018 the US government formally acknowledged that the unipolar moment, to the extent that it existed, had given way to a renewed era of Great Power Competition. The 2017 National Security Strategy and 2018 National Defense Strategy acknowledged direct threats from competitors, both large (China and Russia) and mid-sized (North Korea and Iran), the weakening of US relative advantage and of international norms and institutions, the need to assume resistance and competition rather than convergence and compliance, and the imperative of shoring up US and allied capabilities.[12]

Coercive diplomacy (CD) provides a key concept for understanding the frustrations of US foreign policy and strategy during this period. CD involves state actions short of major military operations[13] to induce an international actor either to refrain from an action (deterrence) or to take an action they initially resisted (compellence).[14] CD has become a frequent and ubiquitous tool of American statecraft in the early twenty-first century, yet scholarly and public attention to it has not kept pace. Over time the United States has employed coercion more frequently, with more failures than successes, yet CD theory has not comprehensively examined this performance record. Nor has there been thorough, systematic analysis of US coercive episodes across presidencies and modes of coercion. This work aims to help bridge both theoretical and empirical gaps, offering practical insights to those shaping and influencing US foreign policy. In an era of Great Power Competition during which Russia, China, Iran, and others are conducting their own forms of coercion, a deeper understanding of US coercive praxis is particularly timely.

Having escalated the practice of CD during the asymmetric advantage of the 1990s, the US now finds itself at a crossroads in the 2020s. It is conducting overlapping CD campaigns that either lack impact, are impactful but fail to achieve a clear policy effect, or undermine coalition-building for critical cases by dispersing efforts on less important ones. This book seeks to situate coercive performance within a comprehensive public policy framework, providing a rigorous examination of its causes, outcomes, and potential remedies. The objective is to offer empirically grounded, actionable guidance for US policymakers, politicians, and citizens on effectively understanding, employing, and, when appropriate, refraining from the use of CD. It can be argued that CD was overused during the period of aspirational hegemony from 1990 to 2020. In the current era of Great Power Competition, the US can ill afford to conduct CD in a profligate or ineffective manner, making the questions examined here of significant present value.

ORIGINS OF COERCIVE DIPLOMACY AS A POLICY CONCEPT

CD as a policy concept predates the end of the Cold War, emerging in its early stages. Alexander George traced the origins of CD theory to President Harry S. Truman's desire to reassert presidential control of military escalation following General Douglas MacArthur's miscalculation on Chinese intervention in Korea, as well as the early atomic arms race with the Soviet Union.[15] The need for presidential control of acceptable costs and risks associated with nuclear or conventional conflict drove studies on deterrence, compellence, and the psychology of coercion. The strategic response to the Soviet threat was an early point of debate, with figures like John Foster Dulles advocating for massive retaliation to deter aggressors who might otherwise underestimate the likelihood of US intervention, while others, such as President Dwight D. Eisenhower and later President John F. Kennedy, favored flexible response. Proponents of the flexible response wanted a broader range of military capabilities than the single "big hammer" implied by the massive retaliation, allowing the president and his security team more options and discretion. Alexander George identified seven requirements for success: 1) presidential control of military options, 2) pauses in military operations, 3) clear and appropriate demonstrations, 4) coordination of military action with political-diplomatic action, 5) confidence in the effectiveness and discrimination of military operations, 6) military options that avoid triggering counter-escalation, and 7) preventing the impression of escalation toward full-scale warfare.[16]

After the Cold War, as the specter of global thermonuclear war receded, the challenges of a new international order emerged, and new theoretical approaches to CD developed. It soon became apparent that US military and economic primacy did not guarantee an easy ability to coerce. Issues such as the psychology of resistance, asymmetric coercion, and the use of non-military coercive tools took on new urgency as Washington struggled to translate its power advantage into leverage over outcomes in specific international crises.

The Forms of Increasing US Coercive Diplomacy

When the US adopts a coercive policy stance toward a target country, rather than either waging outright war or engaging in diplomatic bargaining, several distinct tools can be applied separately or in combination. These include military force short of major operations, economic pressure of various kinds, and diplomatic campaigns of isolation, exclusion, and condemnation. The use of each tool increased from 1990 to 2020.[17]

During this period, the US military "undertook a breadth, depth, tempo and duration of overseas activities that was historically unprecedented."[18] A variety of military actions—including deployments, demonstrations, exercises, security assistance, blockades and air restrictions—were employed to pursue a wide range of policy goals over three decades. One study identified 115 cases of military coercion from 1991 to 2018, though that number often reflects successive actions within ongoing coercive episodes.[19] The study concluded that US military coercion took place in a rapidly vanishing permissive environment and lacked the discipline and planning necessary for an increasingly competitive international landscape.

Economic sanctions also increased dramatically after the Cold War, particularly after 2010. Sanctions became a "policy instrument of choice," roughly quadrupling in number.[20] Sanctions have grown not only in quantity but also in complexity, with a rising use of secondary and sectoral sanctions—targeting both the primary target and those who do business with it, as well as banning transactions with entire industrial sectors, specific companies, or government entities. The broad application of US economic sanctions has led to significant unintended consequences, including regional market disruptions, harm to vulnerable communities, and efforts by a growing number of targeted countries to reduce their economic dependence on the US and circumvent the US financial system.[21] An increasingly integrated global economy, moderated in important ways by liberal powers, has not provided direct leverage over global competition. This situation calls for both greater study and more careful integration of economic sanctions with other policy tools than has typically been undertaken.[22]

US application of diplomatic sanctions has increased in a manner consistent with other coercive tools. Diplomatic sanctions— measures aimed at isolating and delegitimizing a target—complicate bargaining by degrading the quality of information available to the coercer about the target. Tara Maller assessed that the US has applied such "diplomatic sanctions" to about 30% of the cases in which economic sanctions were used and found that in such cases the rate of coercive success dropped. Steps have ranged from recalling an ambassador for consultations to closing an embassy (both of which qualify as cessation of diplomatic contact) and further to extended campaigns to impugning and denying the legitimacy of specific regimes. These sanctions come with costs; an on-the-ground presence provides access to local gossip, news, intelligence, and other crucial contextual information. The absence of regular personal relationships and communication between officials increases the risk of miscommunication and misperception, while reducing the ability to influence opinions on the ground through direct contact and public diplomacy campaigns.[23]

The concept of CD as applied in this study should not be narrowly understood as actions taken solely by diplomats—it includes actions by military and intelligence forces, bureaucrats in executive departments, senior civilians in the White House, legislators, communications professionals, and other actors. It encompasses all foreign policy activities directed at a given country that exceed the consensual bounds of traditional diplomacy through the application of open threats and escalatory actions but fall short of major military operations. This study considers all coercive tools of statecraft as subsets of the broader coercive policy aimed at a target, viewing them as integral components of coercive diplomacy.

It has been argued that CD "offers the possibility of achieving one's objectives economically, with little if any bloodshed, and with fewer political and psychological costs than warfare exacts and with less risk of conflict escalation."[24] The use of CD to achieve national policy aims at reduced cost can be justified both on utilitarian and moral grounds, but only if it is effective—and if we understand the conditions under which it is likely to succeed. Given the combination of its increasingly frequent application, a consistently high rate of failure, and long-term policy implications, the study of the conditions and factors necessary for success requires serious and detailed investigation. This study will contextualize US practices of CD, summarize insights from existing literature, and examine US CD through various methods, including case studies and expert interviews.

Towards Integrated Analysis of Coercive Diplomacy

This study unifies the analysis of coercive tools—military, economic, and diplomatic—that are often studied separately. It also examines the role of communications in coercive episodes, particularly the effects of framing, and assess their influence, alongside more traditionally studied variables, on the prospects for coercive success. The central goal is to provide a more comprehensive and practical empirical examination of US CD over the past three decades, integrating all major coercive tools and offering actionable feedback for adaptive policy.

A growing body of evidence—including statistical, expert views, and case studies—indicates that the US lacks adequate mechanisms, methods, and competence to effectively manage CD as both a cognitive contest and a tool of statecraft. A central theme in the record of failure is the lack of steps to plan, assess, manage, and adapt CD measures once an episode has been initiated. The inability to coordinate across government agencies and between presidential administrations further exacerbates this problem. Accordingly, the following chapters will outline the process and the problems associated with US CD.

Written from a practitioner's standpoint, this study is mindful of theoretical challenges but focuses on outcomes, empirical evidence, and a coherent analytic approach. While learning lessons from historical cases risks oversimplifying the context and contingencies that are crucial for individual cases and different regions, particularly when a large number of episodes are aggregated, cautious and probabilistic claims based on such studies can complement more nuanced single- or few-case studies, providing practitioners with a useful sense of trends.[25] The large-N portion of this study provides useful baseline data and context to guide those tasked with shaping and assessing future coercive efforts. Alongside regional case studies and expert views in later chapters, the summary statistics and descriptions shed light on CD. This study does not aim to be the definitive statement on coercive diplomacy theory or the specific cases studied. Rather, it seeks to foster a more comprehensive debate and drive improvements in the process. The policy approach recommended here—one that consistently accounts for, assesses, and adapts coercive efforts—serves as a foundation that future scholars can build upon through subsequent studies with more refined criteria, scoring, and in-depth case analysis.

Notes

1. Eliot A. Cohen, "History and the Hyperpower," *Foreign Affairs* 83, no. 4 (Jul/Aug 2004): 49–63.

2. G. John Ikenberry, "Power and Liberal Order: America's Post-war Order in Transition," *International Relations of the Indo-Pacific* 5, no. 2 (2005): 133–152, https://doi.org/10.1093/irap/lci112.

3. Sheryle Bagwell, "France bridles at US 'hyperpower," *Financial Review*, November 11, 1999, https://www.afr.com/politics/france-bridles-at-us-hyperpower-19991111-k93ul.

4. Deborah Welch Larson and Alexei Shevchenko, "Status Seekers: Chinese and Russian Responses to US Primacy," *International Security* 34, no. 4 (Spring 2010): 63–95.

5. Sam Tanenhaus, "When Pat Buchanan Tried to Make America Great Again," *Esquire*, April 5, 2017, https://www.esquire.com/news-politics/a54275/charge-of-the-right-brigade/.

6. Seumas Milne, "US foreign policy is straight out of the mafia" (interview), *The Guardian (UK)*, November 7, 2009, https://www.theguardian.com/world/2009/nov/07/noam-chomsky-us-foreign-policy.

7. Ivo Daalder and James Lindsay, "America Unbound: The Bush Revolution in Foreign Policy," *Commentary*, Brookings, September 1, 2003, https://www.brookings.edu/articles/america-unbound-the-bush-revolution-in-foreign-policy/.

8. Katharina Buchholz, "Continental Shift: The World's Biggest Economies Over Time," *Global Economy*, Statista, April 20, 2023, https://www.statista.com/chart/22256/biggest-economies-in-the-world-timeline/.

9. Daniel Byman, "Defeating US Coercion," *Survival* 41, no. 2 (June 1999): 107–120, DOI:10.1093/survival/41.2.107.

10. Hanna Notte, "Russia's Axis of the Sanctioned," *Foreign Affairs*, October 6, 2023, https://www.foreignaffairs.com/russian-federation/russias-axis-sanctioned.

11. Max Fisher, "American Isolationism Just Hit a 50-year High. Why That Matters," *Washington Post*, December 4, 2013, https://www.washingtonpost.com/news/worldviews/wp/2013/12/04/american-isolationism-just-hit-a-50-year-high-why-that-matters/.

12. Ronald O'Rourke, *Renewed Great Power Competition: Implications for Defense - Issues for Congress*, Congressional Research Service (CRS),

Washington, DC, May 29, 2020, https://www.airuniversity.af.edu/Portals/ 10/CMSA/documents/Required_Reading/MSN%20402B%20Read-Ahead %20Renewed%20Great%20Power%20Competition%20Implications%20for %20Defense.pdf?ver=Kzy1YPMyJ9Os7sKntoPlxg%3D%3D.

13. Milan N. Vego, "Major Joint/Combined Operations," *Joint Forces Quarterly* 48 (1st Quarter 2008), National Defense University Press, https://apps. dtic.mil/sti/pdfs/ADA516642.pdf.

14. Tami Biddle, "Coercion Theory: A Basic Introduction for Practitioners," *Texas National Security Review* 3, no. 2 (Spring 2020): 94–109.

15. Alexander George, *The Limits of Coercive Diplomacy* (Boulder: Westview Press, 1994).

16. Alexander George, *Forceful Persuasion: Coercive Diplomacy as an Alternative to War* (Washington: USIP, 1991).

17. Peter Viggo Jakobsen, *Western Use of Coercive Diplomacy After the Cold War: A Challenge for Theory and Practice* (London: Palgrave MacMillan, 1998).

18. Barry Blechman, Melanie Sisson, and James Siebens, *Military Coercion and US Foreign Policy: The Use of Force Short of War* (New York: Routledge, 2020).

19. Blechman, Sisson, and Siebens, 180.

20. Kathy Gilsinan, "A Boom Time for US Sanctions," *The Atlantic*, May 3, 2019.

21. Peter Harrell and Elizabeth Rosenberg, *Maintaining America's Coercive Economic Strength, CNAS Task Force on the Future of US Sanctions*, March 2019, https://www.cnas.org/publications/reports/maintaining-americas-coercive-economic-strength.

22. Soren Scholvin and Mikael Wigell, *Geoeconomics and Power Politics in the 21st Century* (New York: Routledge, 2018), 219–226.

23. Tara Maller, "Diplomacy Derailed: The Consequences of Diplomatic Sanctions," *The Washington Quarterly* 33, no. 3 (2010): 61–79.

24. Alexander George, "Foreword," in *The United States and Coercive Diplomacy*, edited by Robert Art and Patrick Cronin (Washington, DC: United States Institute of Peace, 2003), vii.

25. Joseph Stieb, "History Has No Lessons For You: A Warning for Policymakers," *War on the Rocks*, February 24, 2024 https:// warontherocks.com/2024/02/history-has-no-lessons-for-you-a-warning-for-policymakers/.

CHAPTER 2

HOW AND WHY COERCIVE
DIPLOMACY SHOULD WORK

CENTRAL PROBLEMS IN COERCIVE DIPLOMACY

There are two primary challenges for scholars and practitioners concerning CD in US statecraft. The first challenge is the lack of universally accepted definitions for its scope. Does CD encompass both compellence and deterrence, or only the former? Does it involve active military measures, or is it limited to threats? Should it extend to economic and diplomatic pressure, or does it pertain solely to threats of military action? Thomas Schelling, in his conceptualization of CD, included both compellence (forcing an actor to undertake an action they do not intend) and deterrence (preventing an actor from taking an action they intend) and positioned its practice in a liminal space between war and persuasion.[1] Alexander George, by contrast, explicitly distinguished CD from both deterrence and compellence. He argued that CD addresses encroachments that require reversal, whereas deterrence aims to dissuade actions in advance. He further contended that "blackmail" is a more appropriate term for offensive coercion, as CD intertwines persuasion and accommodation with threats, relying less exclusively on coercive measures.[2] For George, CD consisted of an ultimatum, accompanied by limited and demonstrative military pressure if any, and excluded any economic dimension. This conception contrasts with the broader and more sustained campaigns of economic, military, and informational pressure addressed by other scholars.[3] This narrowing of Schelling's concept is neither intuitively evident nor widely convincing; coercive attempts are not inherently less coercive to the target based on perceived offensive or defensive intent, nor on the timing of the encroachment. Consequently, other scholars—such as Phil Haun, Todd Sechser, Dianne Pfundstein Chamberlain, Rob De Wijk, and others—have included these categories in their analyses. George also refers to CD variously as a strategy or a concept that shapes strategy, rather than a policy, even while articulating multiple different strategies ("variants") for its implementation.[4]

Robert Art also narrowed the scope of CD by distinguishing it from "coercive attempts," with the key difference being that the latter involves the actual application of force, whereas CD relies solely on the threat of force.[5] This characterization portrays CD as an alternative to military coercion, rather than as a broader policy tool that may encompass diplomatic, military, and economic dimensions. Failure to recognize the connections among coercive implements—a common policy logic—complicates the assessment of coercive success or failure and overlooks the potential interactions among those instruments. De Wijk conceptualized CD as part of a continuum of force, where CD ends at the point military compellence begins, and military compellence ends at the point the total destruction or overthrow of the target commences. The distinction, according to De Wijk, lies in the objective relative to the target.[6] De Wijk's continuum is useful for characterizing levels of military commitment, but it overlooks the policy dimension that links CD involving force to CD involving economic sanctions or diplomatic pressure, and it fails to distinguish all of these from collaborative diplomacy. De Wijk later incorporated both diplomatic and economic measures into the escalatory ladder of coercion, despite having initially defined coercion as strictly military. He argued that economic and military pressure should be understood as complementary elements in a coherent strategy.[7] Barry Blechman, Melanie Sisson, and James Siebens similarly framed coercion as primarily a military task, only to later reintegrate economic sanctions back and diplomatic pressure as critical factors in determining the success of coercive efforts.[8] Robert Art and Patrick Cronin also excluded economic sanctions from CD in their initial definition of CD unless such sanctions were accompanied by force. However, they later incorporated economic coercion into nearly all of their case studies on post–Cold War CD. Haun differentiated between coercion involving limited military actions and CD, which involves only verbal threats or negotiations. However, he treated both as analogous cases within his model.[9] Robert Pape's rejection of diplomatic coercion and economic sanctions in favor of "denial" strategies centered on bombing campaigns represents perhaps the most restrictive scoping of all. However, this approach has been effectively critiqued for overlooking the interplay of various policy tools, disregarding the empirical record of successful coercion without bombing, and neglecting the relative scarcity of cases in which the US seeks to coerce and quickly resorts to bombing.[10] Given that scholars analyzing the strategic and policy dimensions of CD routinely integrate economic and diplomatic measures, even after positing CD as a purely military function, failing to measure and incorporate these elements introduces a significant confounding variable problem: coercive outcomes attributed solely to military force may conflate the effects of conceptually and practically distinct types of pressure.

A second major theoretical problem in the literature on CD is the absence of a generally accepted model outlining the conditions and variables necessary for coercive success. George's works on decision-making in CD—*The Limits of Coercive Diplomacy* (1971) and later *Forceful Persuasion* (1991)—offered a comprehensive set of conditions and variables involved in CD.[11] Defining CD as a "demand on an adversary with a threat of punishment for non-compliance that he will consider credible and potent enough to persuade him to comply with the demand," George identified the primary determinants of success or failure as the nature of the demand and the target's disinclination to comply.[12] He identified seven preconditions for success: clarity of coercer objective, strength of coercer's motivation, asymmetry of motivation favoring the coercer, sense of urgency, adequate domestic and international political support, the opponent's fear of unacceptable escalation, and clarity regarding precise terms of settlement.[13] Additionally, he noted that there were eight contextual challenges in operationalizing CD that vary by the "unique configuration" of crisis: the type of provocation, the magnitude and depth of interest conflict, the nature of a possible war, time pressure to achieve objective, presence or absence of coalition, strong leadership, target isolation, and the preferred post-crisis relationship with target.[14] In his 1994 edition of *The Limits of Coercive Diplomacy*, he cited four key variables: demand, means to create sense of urgency, threatened punishment for noncompliance, and possible use of incentives.[15]

While George referred to the evolving mixture of conditions, contextual variables, and key variables in his works as "the abstract model," he accepted that it was far from a functioning theory for two reasons. First, it did not address how political and psychological variables interact with environmental and operational conditions to translate to effects in the mind of the target. Second, it lacked sufficient integration of inductive elements—the empirical evidence of what actually proves effective in CD.[16] George acknowledged that while rational factors largely determine the outcome of coercive episodes in the abstract—a target evaluates the motivation and commitment of the coercing power, as well as the credibility and potency of threatened acts weighed against the interests at stake—differing values, cultures, and traditions can significantly influence these judgments in specific situations. Logically, clear and consistent demands, adequate motivation on the part of the coercer, the ability to instill a sense of urgency in the target, and the target's fear of escalation should lead to successful coercion. Yet because these factors are inherently psychological, abstract logic often fails to apply. He therefore urged policymakers to cultivate three "perceptual variables" in the mind of the target: first, the belief that an asymmetry of interest and motivation favors the coercer; second, that the threatened punishment is both credible and potent enough to compel compliance, and third, that there is an urgent need to comply.[17] While he emphasized the importance of carefully assessing psychological factors and context in specific episodes, he did not provide a framework for conducting such an assessment.

These two central problems are significant but not insurmountable. The present study addresses the issue of uncertain scope by adopting a broad definition of CD that views multiple policy instruments as options on a spectrum of coercive diplomacy, rather than as separate phenomena. This approach allows for the consideration of various strategies and activities as complementary modes within a comprehensive policy framework, without attempting to attribute a specific portion of coercive effect to a single instrument. What distinguishes CD in policy terms is what it explicitly excludes; namely, accommodation or the use of brute force. In this sense CD competes as a policy option with both open war and collaborative diplomacy, rather than with compellence achieved through either purely military or purely non-kinetic means. This approach aligns with that of Peter Viggo Jakobsen, who has defined CD as "threats to do harm (political, economic, or military) and action that would hurt the adversary in order to influence it to stop/undo its hostile activities...may involve political, economic, and military measures, but actual use of force must be limited and serve signaling and influencing purposes...to bring the opponent to the negotiating table, not to defeat it or render it incapable of continued resistance."[18]

The present study addresses the second central problem by employing a simplified model derived from George's 1992 framework and Jakobsen's 1998 conditions for coercive success.[19] George's four conditions—clear and reasonable demand, means to create sense of urgency, threatened punishment for noncompliance, and the possible use of incentives—largely overlap Jakobsen's "ideal policy," which includes a credible threat with escalation dominance, a deadline, assurances against future demands, and incentives, though Jakobsen's third condition (assurance against future demands) can be grouped with other incentives, while his omission of demand clarity requires remedy. In cases of effective coercion, these conditions form a cycle of sorts through which a coercing power can be expected to succeed by effectively meeting the stipulated criteria.

THE APPEAL OF COERCIVE DIPLOMACY

While this study focuses on US CD since the Cold War, the phenomenon itself predates not only the end but also the beginning of the Cold War. De Wijk argues that the motivations to coerce are rooted in Western political culture, including the belief—most explicitly articulated in Hobbes' *Leviathan*—that states have an obligation to protect the security and property of citizens, and when they fail to do so, other states may develop an interest in intervening.[20] After the Napoleonic Wars, states began to consider "values" in addition to practical interests as justifications for the use of force. Over time, the combination of power politics with moral and ideological motivations became characteristic of Western political culture. In the post–Cold War era, Western democracies were more likely than other powers to intervene forcefully in crises beyond their contiguous regions. Foreign policy traditions of realism and liberal internationalism have both been invoked to justify coercive diplomacy for different reasons: realism seeks to undercut potential threats, while liberal internationalism aims to protect a liberal international order. Democracies tend to possess greater economic resources, more allies, and greater ability to mobilize popular support, making them less likely to be coerced and more likely to engage in coercion themselves. Citing Hoffman, de Wijk lays out several liberal justifications for intervention: protecting populations when states are unable to do so, safeguarding populations from their own tyrannical governments, and preventing destabilization.

George's observation neatly summarizes the appeal.

Coercive diplomacy is an attractive strategy insofar as it offers the possibility of achieving one's objective in a crisis economically, with little or no bloodshed, fewer political and psychological costs, and often with less risk of unwanted escalation than does traditional strategy. But for this very reason coercive diplomacy can be a beguiling strategy. Particularly leaders of militarily powerful countries may be tempted to believe sometimes that they can, with little risk, intimidate weaker opponents to give up their gains and objectives. But, of course, the militarily weaker side may be strongly motivated by what is at stake and refuse to back down, in effect calling the bluff of the coercing power. The latter must then decide whether to back off, accept a compromise settlement, or escalate to the use of military force to gain its objective...[and] may encounter other constraints, risks, and uncertainties in attempting to make effective use of the strategy.[21]

POST–COLD WAR OPTIMISM ABOUT DEFT COERCION

During the first post–Cold War decade, George expressed a cautious optimism about the potential for CD to succeed. With careful attention to contextual factors and the use of CD only when conditions appropriately aligned, it appeared to be the ultimate tool of "smart power," a skillful blend of coercive and persuasive strategies.[22] Writing a decade after George, Art and Cronin examined the outcomes of US CD during the Bill Clinton and early George W. Bush administrations and found the path to success was indeed narrow. US CD succeeded to some extent in approximately one-third of its applications (32%, consistent with Gary Clyde Hufbauer et al and other studies of military and economic coercion). Military superiority over the target did not guarantee successful coercion; the use of positive inducements was helpful, but only when sequenced to follow threats and demonstrations. Demonstrative denial—a form of deterrence through military actions that clearly and credibly threaten something the target values—had a better track record than coercive punishment or efforts to reverse an action. In any case, the prospects for coercive success were sufficiently low that a prudent statesman should avoid CD unless prepared either to escalate to full-scale war or to back down gracefully. CD "on the cheap," with no recourse to war and no suitable off-ramp, gradually erodes the very credibility upon which its success depends.[23]

In 1999, Barry Blechman and Tamara Cofman examined many of the same cases, seeking to understand why a superpower, freed from the threat of peer escalation, struggled to employ threats and limited force successfully during the 1990s. They identified success or partial success in seven of eighteen cases (39%), but this outcome relied on a generous interpretation of "partial successes," which, in hindsight, more closely resemble failures (e.g., North Korean nuclear tests and Iraq's compliance with weapons inspections).[24] What might be termed the "erosion" of coercive success—a decreasing success rate depending on how long after the application of coercive measures the policy outcome is measured— suggests that coercive success is often temporary. Blechman's earlier work demonstrated that nearly half of the apparent coercive successes could no longer be considered successful after three years.[25] Libya serves as another example of fairly rapid erosion. In 2006, Bruce Jentleson described the "de-roguing" of Libya as a major success in coercive diplomacy, exemplifying proportionality, reciprocity, and credibility. However, just five years later, the West led a military intervention in Libya, a conflict from which the country has yet to recover.[26]

The concept of the US employing limited and demonstrative pressure to achieve political goals was profoundly affected by the September 11, 2001, terrorist attacks—a shift that has not yet been fully incorporated into the literature on coercive diplomacy. Largely in response to those attacks, the idea of the US as a predominant power with significant leverage to employ force in a nuanced manner to achieve policy goals lost currency. In its place emerged the perception of the US as a nation under proximate and sustained threat, necessitating the use of preemptive and continuous coercive power to counter that threat. To the mixture of compellence, deterrence, and coercion, preemption was added: the principle that defensive security increasingly requires anticipatory offensive action, often undertaken unilaterally.[27] The element of preemption, combined with a lingering belief in the effectiveness of "smart power" tools such as economic sanctions, diplomatic isolation, and strategic messaging, has transformed CD from a crisis-management methodology into a default position for US foreign policy. James Nathan argued that by the end of the twentieth century, Washington had come to view coercion as a central rather than exceptional tool of foreign policy, maintaining faith in it as the most direct and efficient mode of diplomatic communication. However, the increasingly frequent use of coercion was not consistently or rigorously tied to specific, achievable policy goals; instead, it began to follow its own internal logic.[28] Gareth Porter has described this form of CD as "a dangerous farce" because the absence of clear off-ramps and compromise solutions reduces CD to pure coercion, stripping it of any genuine diplomatic element. The growing reliance on CD as a routine tool for domestic political signaling closes off opportunities for resolving specific international disputes.[29] This has been especially true of economic coercion through the use of sanctions, which dramatically escalated after 2010.[30]

Does the Coercive Modality Matter?

Diane Pfund Chamberlain's study of US CD since the Cold War examined the efficacy of purely military means for coercion and demonstrated that, despite the absence of a near-peer military competitor, the prospects for military coercion had not improved over historical norms during and before the Cold War. Using Alexander George and William Simon's 29% success rate and Art and Cronin's 32% success rate as baselines, her dataset, which tracks US military CD from 1947 to 2007, revealed both more frequent use of military coercion and a less frequent success rate since 1991.[31]

The record of US economic coercion did not yield significantly better results. Huffbauer et al conducted the benchmark empirical study of economic sanctions as part of coercive policy, finding partial success in 34% of cases. A key determinative factor was the magnitude of policy change being sought.[32]

Diplomatic pressure, separate from military and economic measures, provides a third type of coercive tool but suffers from similar shortcomings. Tara Maller investigated whether diplomatic sanctions aimed at isolating and delegitimizing target states complement other coercive measures more effectively than engagement. The US has applied such "diplomatic sanctions" in about 30% of the cases where it also applied economic sanctions, ranging from the recall of an ambassador for consultations or closure of an embassy (both of which qualify as cessation of diplomatic contact) to extended campaigns to impugn and deny the legitimacy of specific regimes. Maller found that in cases of coercion over modest policy demands, the success rate dropped from 52% to 34% when diplomatic sanctions were added to economic sanctions. Diplomatic presence is ultimately necessary to craft an effective bargaining framework for sanctions to "work."[33]

FACTORS IN COERCIVE FAILURE: DEMAND

Coercion proves ineffective when the coercer's demands lack precision and specificity. In his study of asymmetric coercion—where powerful states exert pressure on weaker ones—Haun identifies a recurring issue: coercers frequently overreach by demanding excessive concessions, such as regime change or territorial surrender. These demands are politically untenable for the leaders of the targeted states, resulting in the failure of coercive strategies. Haun's analysis contrasts CD with alternative strategies like accommodation and brute force, revealing a "coercive range" of demands that are most likely to succeed. These demands should be sufficiently moderate to convey that the US favors a negotiated resolution and feasible enough for the target to comply without incurring losses comparable to those of war. At the same time, they must be substantive enough to offer a preferable outcome to mere accommodation.[34] Haun illustrates how both rational and non-rational factors shape a target state's response to coercive demands, often resulting in the rejection of demands deemed reasonable by the coercer. These factors include the target's perception of the coercer's weak commitment, resolve, and capacity to execute threatened actions; a stronger attachment to the contested issue than anticipated by the coercer; fears that concessions may provoke further demands; the concept of indivisibility, where the target state is so deeply attached to the object of coercion that it will not relinquish it under any circumstances; and concerns over regime survival.[35] For coercion to be effective, the coercer must carefully account for the unique psychology, history, geography, and strategic culture of the target state and its leadership, thereby calibrating demands with greater precision.

It may be rational for the US to pursue coercion even without a thorough analysis of the target or realistic expectations of compliance under certain conditions. First, if the costs of coercion are low and there is at least a minimal chance of compliance, coercion can serve as a preparatory step for more extensive military operations. Second, the international standing of states is partly influenced by the perception of their adherence to international norms, including the norm of attempting negotiations. Even a half-hearted attempt at coercion can bolster a state's legitimacy by demonstrating a nominal commitment to diplomacy.[36] An underexplored issue with this form of rational-but-sloppy coercion is the potential for second- and third-order effects that accumulate over time as a series of target states recognize certain patterns: 1) the US does not carefully formulate its demands 2) it lacks rigorous follow-through on threats or inducements and 3) it may, in fact, be indifferent to whether demands are actually met. As a result, target states may start to doubt the sincerity of the coercer's threats and assurances, viewing these demands as mere political maneuvering rather than genuine attempts at negotiation, or alternatively, as gestures intended primarily for domestic political consumption, with no real intention of compromise. Porter argues that the US often issues insincere coercive demands to maintain a perpetual crisis atmosphere that justifies large defense and intelligence budgets.[37] A more common interpretation, however, is that such non- or semi-serious demands serve as instrumental signals to both domestic constituents and coercive targets, often with only a loose connection to the likelihood of actual implementation.[38]

Michael Allen and Benjamin Fordham compared coercive demands under two different assumptions: first, that the target behaves as a rational unitary actor, and second, relaxing that assumption to consider the influence of domestic politics and unique national preferences. In the first scenario, they align with with James Fearon's view that coercive demands may be discounted due to private information—such as differing assessments of relative capabilities or resolve—or because of commitment problems. These commitment problems arise when conditions create incentives for either side to renege on the terms of an agreement or act on the belief that the other side will fail to uphold its commitments.[39] In the second scenario, Allen and Fordham acknowledge that domestic institutions can distort the interpretation of coercive demands and that national preferences may render certain types of demands unacceptable at any cost. They found that both rational and non-rational factors influence the leaders of target states—even those facing severe resource disadvantage—to resist demands they perceive as extreme or lacking credible backing.[40] These factors may drive target states to reject demands regardless of the coercer's calculations, reflecting a complex interplay between internal political dynamics, perceived threats to national identity or sovereignty, and the credibility of the coercer's commitments.

Coercive demands must be strategically aligned with a careful selection of targets. Alexander Downes argued that prior to the end of the Cold War, the United States—and most Great Powers generally—achieved higher success rates in CD because they chose targets that met three criteria: the targets were disproportionately weak in economic and military terms relative to the coercer, were diplomatically isolated without support from other great powers, and were geographically proximate to the coercer. Downes found that general compellence typically fails, with a success rate of only 35%, whereas deterrence is more successful, with a success rate exceeding 50%. Regime change compellence, however, succeeds in approximately 80% of cases tried, a success he attributes to the careful selection of particularly vulnerable targets. Although Downes' analysis centers on regime change, his findings have broader implications for CD: understanding which targets are vulnerable at specific times—an insight that requires deeply contextual knowledge—correlates strongly with coercive success.[41]

FACTORS IN COERCIVE FAILURE: THREAT

Even when a demand is carefully crafted and appropriately matched to its target, coercion can still fail if the accompanying threat is perceived as lacking credibility or potency. A threat may be deemed not credible if it is seen to exceed the perceived will or capability of the coercer to execute it. Similarly, a threat may be viewed as insufficient if it is not proportional to the demand—for instance, a severe demand backed by only a moderate threat or a moderate demand accompanied by a light threat. Chamberlain has argued that US often suffer from a lack of "ultimate" rather than "immediate" credibility: while targets may believe the US will impose some initial costs, they are skeptical that the US will enforce these threats and remain committed to them over the long term. In militarized disputes the US generally does not bluff; it relies on explicit rather than implicit threats and has often sought to build coercive coalitions, thereby adhering to best practices rooted in coercive diplomacy theory. However, this approach has been complicated by the tendency to make more expansive demands in the post–Cold War era. Chamberlain's research shows finds that while expensive threats—those made credibly and with a demonstrated willingness to incur long-term costs—increase the likelihood for success, the data reveals several challenges: US threats are frequent, do not produce quick results, incur higher enforcement costs than anticipated, and harm both the target and third parties in ways that undermine sustained commitment. Chamberlain's costly compellence theory posits that American compellent threats are likely to fail when they are cheap to issue and to execute because such threats do not convey a high level of US motivation to achieve its objectives against a persistently resistant opponent. Target states resist not due to doubts about the credibility of Washington's threats but rather due to skepticism regarding the United States' underlying motivation to secure its preferred outcome over the course of a prolonged conflict. Compellent threats have become comparatively cheap in the post–Cold War period precisely because the United States has developed ways to minimize the human, political, and financial costs associated with using military force. As a result, the decision to engage in military action no longer entails substantial casualties, significant political repercussions, or enduring fiscal sacrifice for the United States. This diminishes the credibility of such threats as a signal that the world's sole superpower is genuinely committed to persevering in order to compel compliance from a stubbornly resistant target. Without the high costs traditionally associated with military engagement, the threat of force lacks the weight needed to convince opponents that the US is prepared to endure a prolonged and potentially costly struggle to achieve its objectives.[42]

Blechman and Cofman argue that a threat's credibility depends on both the character of the threat—such as its urgency, tangible actions, communication of intent, and the presence of a clear deadline—and the broader context, including historical precedent, public support, international backing, and the president's reputation. They endorse George's maxim that "the threat must be potent relative to the demand" and find that potent threats are closely associated with coercive success. However, such threats are challenging to deploy because they entail significant domestic political risk. It is often easier for policymakers to issue less forceful threats that do not alarm domestic constituencies, even though these may fail to impress or intimidate coercive targets.

Blechman and Cofman also note that US threats since the Vietnam War have suffered from a persistent international perception that US military power, while technically formidable, can ultimately be withstood. This perception stems not from doubts about America's military capabilities but from the belief that the US lacks the political will to sustain prolonged conflicts.[43]

Threats can also fail due to second-order effects that arise during and after implementation. Hufbauer et al observed that such failures are particularly common with economic sanctions. Sanctions may provoke a reaction from the target state, such as reordering trade relations, which can diminish their intended coercive impact. Additionally, sanctions can prompt intervention by powerful outside forces, or "black knights," who are aligned with the target state and can offset or mitigate the effects of coercion. Moreover, if threats are not carefully prepared and coordinated with allies and domestic stakeholders, they risk clashing with domestic or allied interests, potentially generating backlash that further undermines their coercive effectiveness.[44] Ebrahim Mohseni Cheraglou's study of US CD against Iran provides a detailed illustration of these second-order impacts. Coercive diplomacy not only failed to persuade Iran to accept binding constraints on its nuclear activities but also triggered a series of reactions that reinforced Iran's resolve to advance, enhance, and expand its fuel cycle program. Cheraglou argues that CD literature often overlooks the critical role of perceived intent within the target state and the internal policy forces that "shape and drive its objectionable policy." If elites or the general public in a target state perceive that the coercer intends to destroy or severely cripple them, resistance becomes inevitable. Conversely, if they believe that the coercer's intent is to chastise or incentivize on narrower matters, the likelihood of success increases. This approach demands strategic empathy, which Cheraglou defines as an understanding of the target's perceived intent and domestic decision structures, leveraging this understanding to achieve desired changes.[45]

The perceived utility of threats, combined with the increasing technical ease of application, has led to their integration as a routine element of American foreign policy rather than an exceptional tool.[46] However, the ease of applying coercive threats and their versatile use may, paradoxically, undermine the ultimate success of any given coercive project. Even when a coercive strategy benefits from escalation dominance and a precise understanding of the target's vulnerabilities, it can still fail if there is an inadequate understanding of target's psychology—its interests, resilience, adaptability—leading to an unrealistic view of the target's cost-benefit calculation.[47] The target will conduct its own careful analysis of costs and benefits in a coercive episode, shaped by its unique perspectives and framing of the issue. Meanwhile, the frequent use of threats may prevent the coercer from engaging in a similarly careful analysis and framing for any specific coercive instance. As a result, coercive diplomacy—when viewed primarily as a signaling exercise or a matter of technical leverage —can, over time, erode its own effectiveness as a tool of statecraft.

FACTORS IN COERCIVE FAILURE: URGENCY

George placed psychological factors at the core of coercive outcomes through his analysis of strategic options in CD, focusing on the most effective ways to instill a sense of urgency within the leadership of the target state. He identified several options: "ultimatum," "tacit ultimatum," "try-and-see," "turning of the screw," and "carrot/stick."[48] An ultimatum generates urgency coupling a clear demand with a credible threat and a specified time limit. In a tacit ultimatum, urgency is created when the time limit is implied but not explicitly stated, or when the threat remains implicit. In the absence of a clear ultimatum, a "try-and-see" approach may be used, where a demand is issued without a defined threat or timeline, allowing the situation to unfold incrementally. Alternatively, the "gradual turning of the screw" approach involves a strictly incremental application of pressure without an explicit threat or timeline, conveying a sense of relentless and inevitable escalation. Lastly, urgency can be fostered through a "carrot and stick" strategy, which combines inducements (carrots) that are time-sensitive or perishable with the threat of punishment (sticks) should the inducements not be accepted. Each approach is designed to manipulate the target's perception of time, risk, and consequences to maximize the coercer's chances of achieving compliance.[49]

Coercive demands can often be perceived by the target as mere background noise or routine political maneuvering, particularly when issued by frequent coercers. In such cases, the target is likely to view the demand as routine blackmail, assuming that the coercer lacks the resolve or commitment to fully pursue or enforce it. The most effective way to distinguish a demand or threat as extraordinary—and therefore credible— is through the issuance of an unambiguous ultimatum. However, Paul Gordon Lauren's study of ultimata in coercive diplomacy highlights their double-edged nature. While ultimata provide clarity by clearly defining the demand, threat, and timeline, they also pose significant risks to the coercer's credibility. If the coercer is unable to enforce the ultimatum due to a weak coercive position—such as insufficient domestic support, limited capability to act, an overly ambitious demand, or the existence of viable alternatives for the target—the ultimatum can backfire, undermining the coercer's credibility and weakening its position in future diplomatic or coercive engagements.[50]

For coercive diplomacy to generate urgency within the target, a sense of vulnerability must accompany a clear demand and a credible, potent threat. Vulnerability is a psychological state that arises when decision-makers, operating within specific personal and institutional contexts, conclude, first, that a projected sequence of events must be avoided to prevent unacceptable loss, and second, that this sequence is highly likely to unfold unless the target concedes to the coercer's demands. Understanding when a target might experience such a sense of vulnerability is crucial to the success of coercion; however, this requires careful study and precise timing—elements that are often neglected in practice.[51]

This sense of vulnerability partly arises from a feeling of isolation, which can be deliberately cultivated by efforts to shrink the target's network of alignments and alliances. By reducing the target's support network, the expected costs for the target increase while those for the coercer decrease, amplifying the pressure on the target to concede. This strategic isolation undermines the target's confidence in its ability to resist, making it more likely to perceive compliance with the coercer's demands as the less costly option.[52] Vulnerability also arises from a consistent tempo in implementing coercive measures, designed to convince the target that pressure will escalate steadily rather than diminish if compliance is not achieved.[53] A failure to combine clear deadlines with demands, isolate the target, or maintain a consistent tempo of coercive actions undermines the creation of this sense of vulnerability within the target state's leadership. Without these elements, the target is less likely to perceive the coercer's threats as credible or urgent, reducing the likelihood of compliance.

Factors in Coercive Failure: Off-Ramp

The fundamental logic of coercive effect—that a rational challenger applies selective and credible coercion and ceases coercive actions upon capitulation—fails if there is no clear plan to lift coercive measures or poor record of doing so. Haun's study of US CD against Iraq in the 1990s illustrates this breakdown. The US continued to enforce sanctions even after Iraq made concessions, which eliminated incentives for further compliance and increased the target's incentive to resist. Stronger coercing powers retain the option to either escalate or accommodate, with accommodation often being preferable when the issue at stake is not vital or when the anticipated costs of escalation exceed the expected returns. Haun emphasizes that success in CD relies on two critical factors: the target's willingness to offer compliance and the coercer's readiness to accept it. He argues that CD and strategies of containment often work at cross purposes in US practice because easing coercive measures in response to concessions can undermine the broader strategy of containment. In a containment strategy, the target is viewed as an adversary to be continuously coerced, regardless of compliance or non-compliance, which contradicts the principles of flexible and responsive CD.[54]

Prominent scholars of CD have recognized the importance of incentives and positive inducements to successful resolution of coercive episodes. Jakobsen differentiated between two types of positive incentives: those that reduce the costs of coercive compliance for the target and assurances that compliance will not lead to new demands. He argued that both types must be combined with credible threats of harm to achieve the desired effect.[55] George similarly noted that the prospects for CD in specific situations often hinge on the careful integration of such assurances and incentives.[56] Art identified positive inducements as a crucial component of coercive success, though not a guarantee. He also emphasized that timing is critical; inducements should be introduced after the target has conducted its initial cost-benefit analysis of the demand and threat, in order to effectively influence their calculations and decision-making process.[57]

Matthew Cebul, Allan Dafoe, and Nuno Monteiro have argued that credible assurances are as vital to coercive success as credible threats. While overwhelming military and economic strength can enhance the credibility of threats, it can simultaneously undermine the credibility of assurances. They developed a theory of credible coercive assurance, which posits that a coercer must cultivate a reputation for restraint to issue credible assurances. Such a reputation can alleviate the target's fears of future coercive attempts and increase confidence in agreements reached during specific coercive episodes. Longitudinal opinion polling by Pew Research supports the notion that the US is developing a reputation for violence; between 2013 and 2018, the percentage of respondents in 22 countries who viewed US power as a threat to their country increased from 25% to 45%.[58] The concepts of credible assurance and a reputation for restraint may help explain the apparent contradiction between the

US's unrivaled economic and military strength since the end of the Cold War and its declining success in CD during the same period.[59]

Omitted Point of Failure: Frame Dissonance

The CD literature presents a picture of complex cognitive contests that are inherently challenging to manage or predict. Much of the post–Cold War literature has moved beyond the assumption of coercive actors, especially targets, as unitary and rational, seeking instead to explore the metaphorical "black box" of the decision-making processes behind compliance or resistance.[60] George cautioned that for the abstract model of coercion to function effectively in practice, it is essential to address critical psychological variables in detail. This involves replacing the assumptions of strict rationality with behavioral models tailored to the specific adversary and grounded in empirical study and contextual understanding.[61] Scholars including Lawrence Freedman and Jack Levy have used prospect theory to examine how a target's response to coercion is likely to deviate from the assumptions of strict rationality in non-random ways.[62]

The study of communicative frames offers potential as a tool for understanding and assessing unique considerations of target state in CD. Frame theory helps explain coercive failure by predicting a contestation of meaning between the coercer and the target, rather than a shared understanding, as assumed in rational actor models. Frame analysis originated from Erving Goffman's observation that people interpret new information by organizing it with images, metaphors, and terms that are already familiar to them and their interlocutors. This approach allows information to be more quickly comprehended and facilitates communication. In the context of CD, frame theory suggests that both the coercer and the target may interpret the same signals, threats, or demands differently based on their distinct cognitive frames, leading to miscommunication, misunderstandings, and ultimately, failure of the coercive effort.[63] A set of shared verbal and visual organizing concepts

—known as frames—develop over time within cultures and subgroups, making complex ideas and new information more intelligible and shaping responses. These cognitive schemas, or "deep frames," were further explored by George Lakoff and Mark Johnson, who referred to them as "metaphors we live by."[64] Lakoff and Johnson observed that we all operate within a conceptual system that we rarely consider explicitly—a system grounded in metaphor and thus highly variable by language and culture. Without understanding how framing, narrative, and the use of metaphor differ between different cultures, achieving mutual understanding can be difficult—particularly in the context of interstate crises and coercion, where clear communication is essential.

Framing operates at multiple levels relevant to coercion and international relations. The first is cognitive framing, as identified by Goffman, as well as R. D. Benford and D. A. Snow, and others—a kind of intellectual scaffolding upon which societies construct shared meaning, often without conscious or deliberate selection.[65] These shared societal systems of meaning shape both individual thinking and group decision-making. Alex Mintz and Stephen B. Redd, building on the work of Amos Tversky and Daniel Kahneman, refer to this as decision framing: "the decision-maker's conception of the acts, outcomes, and contingencies associated with a particular choice. The frame that a decision-maker adopts is controlled partly by the norms, habits, and personal characteristics of the decision-maker."[66] They further discuss "framing effects," referring to experimental findings that individuals react differently to various descriptions of the same problem. This concept is critically important in international relations because political leaders use information and rhetoric to influence decision-makers—including allies, adversaries, the public, media, constituencies, voters, and third parties—to highlight certain aspects of a problem and steer groups toward particular actions. Effective framing of one's own position and counter-framing of an adversary's position is especially crucial. Lakoff's later work, especially *The Political Mind*, focuses on this competition.[67] Robert Entman provided a four-part working definition of how politicians engage in message framing: first, defining the issue at stake and identifying the agents involved; second, diagnosing the causes and origins of the issue; third, making a moral judgement about the agents, structures, or processes involved, and fourth, proposing a remedy to address the problem and justify action.[68] The interaction between the messaging frame and the audience—along with the audience's cognitive frames—determines the influence on the audience and practical outcomes. If framing creates differences in how coercing states and target states assess coercive dynamics, or if it enables a deeper understanding of and influence over the decision-making processes of target states, it warrants careful examination as part of the "black box" of CD. This study incorporates framing effectiveness as a variable impacting the outcome of coercive episodes, as detailed in the next chapter.

NOTES

1. Thomas C. Schelling, *Arms and Influence* (New Haven: Yale University Press, 2020), preface and chapter 1.
2. Alexander George, *Forceful Persuasion: Coercive Diplomacy as an Alternative to War* (Washington, DC: USIP, 1991), 5.
3. Alexander George, "Introduction: The Limits of Coercive Diplomacy," in *Limits of Coercive Diplomacy*, 2nd edition, edited by Alexander George and William Simons (Boulder: Westview Press, 1994), 2.
4. George, "Foreword," vii–xiii and 8–9.
5. Robert Art, "Introduction," in *The United States and Coercive Diplomacy*, edited by Robert Art and Patrick Cronin (Washington, DC: United States Institute of Peace, 2003), 3–20.
6. Rob De Wijk, *The Art of Military Coercion: Why the West's Military Superiority Scarcely Matters* (Amsterdam: University of Amsterdam Press, 2014), 1–27.
7. De Wijk, 23, 103.
8. Blechman, Sisson and Siebens, *Military Coercion and US Foreign Policy*, 3–5.
9. Phil Haun, *Coercion, Survival and War: Why Weak States Resist the United States* (Stanford, CA: Stanford University Press, 2015), 1–10.
10. Patrick Bratton, "A Coherent Theory of Coercion? The Writings of Robert Pape," *Comparative Strategy* 22 (2003): 355–372.
11. Alexander George and William Simons, eds., *The Limits of Coercive Diplomacy*, 1st edition (Boston: Little and Brown, 1971); and Alexander George, *Forceful Persuasion: Coercive Diplomacy as an Alternative to War* (Washington, DC: USIP, 1991).
12. George, *Forceful Persuasion*, 4.
13. George, 80–81.
14. George, 69–71.
15. Alexander George, "Theory and Practice," in Alexander George and William Simons, *Limits of Coercive Diplomacy*, 2nd edition (Boulder: Westview Press, 1994), 16–21.
16. George and Simons, *Limits of Coercive Diplomacy*, 12–16.
17. George and Simons, 290–293.

18. Peter Viggo Jakobsen, "Coercive Diplomacy as Crisis Management," *Oxford Research Encyclopedia of Politics*, February 28, 2020, https://doi.org/10.1093/acrefore/9780190228637.013.1624.
19. Peter Viggo Jakobsen, *Western Use of Coercive Diplomacy after the Cold War: A Challenge for Theory and Practice* (London: Palgrave MacMillan, 1998).
20. De Wijk, *The Art of Military Coercion*, 16–22.
21. Alexander George, *Forceful Persuasion*, 6.
22. Joseph Nye, "Get Smart: Combining Hard and Soft Power," *Foreign Affairs* 88, no. 4 (July-August 2009), Council on Foreign Relations, New York, 160–163.
23. Robert Art, "Coercive Diplomacy: What do we Know?" in *The United States and Coercive Diplomacy*, edited by Robert Art and Patrick Cronin (Washington, DC: USIP, 2003), 401–410.
24. Barry Blechman and Tamara Cofman Wittes, "Defining Moment: the Threat and Use of Force in American Foreign Policy," *Political Science Quarterly* 114, no. 1 (Spring 1999): 1–30.
25. Barry Blechman and Stephen Kaplan, *Force Without War: US Armed Forces as a Political Instrument*, (Washington, DC, Brookings Institution Press, 1978), introduction and chapter 1.
26. Bruce Jentleson, "Coercive Diplomacy: Scope and Limits in the Contemporary World," *Stanley Center Policy Analysis Brief* (Muscatine, IA: Stanley Foundation, December 2006).
27. Thomas McMullen, *The Bush Doctrine: Power Concepts, Preemption, and the Global War on Terror* (Carlisle PA: US Army War College, 2004), 8–9, https://apps.dtic.mil/dtic/tr/fulltext/u2/a423927.pdf.
28. James Nathan, *Soldiers Statecraft and History: Coercive Diplomacy and International Order* (Westport, CT: Praeger, 2002), 130–136.
29. Gareth Porter, "Why Coercive Diplomacy is a Dangerous Farce," *The American Conservative*, January 12, 2018.
30. Kathy Gilsinan, "Boom Time for US Sanctions," *The Atlantic*, May 3, 2019.
31. Dianne Pfundstein Chamberlain, *Cheap Threats: Why the United States Struggles to Coerce Weak States* (Washington, DC: Georgetown University Press, 2016).
32. Gary Clyde Hufbauer, Jeffrey Schott, Kimberly Ann Elliot, and Barbara Oegg, *Economics Sanctions Reconsidered* (3rd edition) (Washington, DC: Peterson Institute for International Economics, 2019), 1–17 and 155–178.

33. Tara Maller, "Diplomacy Derailed: The Consequences of Diplomatic Sanctions," *The Washington Quarterly* 33, no. 3 (2010): 61–79.

34. Haun, *Coercion, Survival and War*, 7–8.

35. Haun, 26–31.

36. Dan Altman, "Review," in "Coercion, Survival and War: Why Weak States Resist the United States," *H-Diplo/ISSF Roundtable* IX, no. 16 (2017): 5–7.

37. Gareth Porter, "Why 'Coercive Diplomacy' is a Dangerous Farce," *The American Conservative*, January 12, 2018, https://www.theamericanconservative.com/articles/north-korea-iran-trump-why-coercive-diplomacy-is-a-dangerous-farce/.

38. James Fearon, "Signaling Foreign Policy Interests: Tying Hands Versus Sinking Costs," *Journal of Conflict Resolution* 41, no. 1 (1997): 68–90; see also Akisato Suzuki, "Audience Costs, Domestic Economy and Coercive Diplomacy," *Research & Politics*, July 2018.

39. James Fearon, "Rationalist Explanations for War," *International Organization* 49 (1995): 379–414, and Fearon, "Signaling Foreign Policy Interests."

40. Michael Allen and Benjamin Fordham "From Melos to Baghdad: Explaining Resistance to Militarized Challenges from More Powerful States," *International Studies Quarterly* 55 (2011): 1025–1045.

41. Alexander Downes, "Step Aside or Face the Consequences: Explaining the Success and Failure of Compellent Threats to Remove Foreign Leaders," in *Coercion: The Power to Hurt in International Politics*, edited by Kelly Greenhill and Peter Krause (New York: Oxford University Press, 2018), 93–114.

42. Chamberlain, *Cheap Threats*, 19–55.

43. Blechman and Cofman, "Defining Moment," 1–30.

44. Hufbauer et al, *Economics Sanctions Reconsidered*, 7–9.

45. Ebrahim Mohseni Cheraglou, "When Coercion Backfires: The Limits of Coercive Diplomacy in Iran," (PhD diss., University of Maryland, College Park MD, 2015), 1–3.

46. "Sanctions Are Now a Central Tool of Governments' Foreign Policy," *The Economist*, April 24, 2021, https://www.economist.com/finance-and-economics/2021/04/22/sanctions-are-now-a-central-tool-of-governments-foreign-policy.

47. Daniel Byman, Matthew Waxman, and Eric Larson, *Air Power as a Coercive Instrument* (Santa Monica, CA: Rand Corporation, 1999), 29–56.

48. Alexander George, *Forceful Persuasion: Coercive Diplomacy as an Alternative to War* (Washington, DC: USIP, 1991), 7–14.
49. George, *Forceful Persuasion*, 7–11.
50. Paul Gordon Lauren, "Ultimata and Coercive Diplomacy," *International Studies Quarterly* 16, no. 2 (June 1972): 131–165.
51. Jack Levy, "Deterrence and Coercive Diplomacy: The Contributions of Alexander George," *Political Psychology* 29, no. 4 (2008): 537–544.
52. Timothy Crawford, "The Strategy of Coercive Isolation," in *Coercion: The Power to Hurt in International Politics*, edited by Kelly Greenhill and Peter Krause (New York: Oxford University Press, 2018), 228–250.
53. Joshua Schore, "Hollow Threats: Why Coercive Diplomacy Fails" (PhD diss., Maxwell Air Force Base, AL: School of Advanced Air and Space Studies, 2015), 24–28.
54. Phil Haun, "Air Power, Sanctions, Coercion, and Containment: When Foreign Policy Objectives Collide," in *Coercion: The Power to Hurt in International Politics*, edited by Kelly Greenhill and Peter Krause (New York: Oxford University Press, 2018), 77–92.
55. Jakobsen, "Coercive Diplomacy as Crisis Management," summary.
56. George, *Forceful Persuasion*, 11.
57. Robert Art, "Coercive Diplomacy: What do we Know?" in *The United States and Coercive Diplomacy*, edited by Robert Art and Patrick Cronin (Washington, DC: United States Institute of Peace, 2003), 387–402.
58. John Gramlich and Kat Devlin, "More People Around the World See US Power and Influence as a 'Major Threat' to Their Country," *Fact Tank*, Pew Research, February 14, 2019.
59. Matthew Cebul, Allan Dafoe, and Nuno Monteiro, "Coercion and the Credibility of Assurances," *The Journal of Politics* 83, no. 3 (July 2021): 975–991.
60. For use of the term "black box" in social science to describe variables that are assumed or not examined in causal analysis, see Kosuke Imai, Luke Keele, Dustin Tingley, and Teppei Yamamoto, "Unpacking the Black Box of Causality: Learning About Causal Mechanisms from Experimental and Observational Studies," *American Political Science Review* 105, no. 4 (November 2011): 765–789.
61. George, *Limits of Coercive Diplomacy* (2nd edition), 19–20.
62. Lawrence Freedman, ed., *Strategic Coercion: Concepts and Cases* (Oxford: Oxford University Press, 1998); and Jack Levy, "Prospect Theory, Rational Choice and International Relations," *International Studies Quarterly* 42, no. 1 (March 1997): 87–112.

63. Erving Goffman, *Frame Analysis: An Essay on the Organization of Experience*, (Boston: Northeastern University Press, 1986).

64. George Lakoff and Johnson, *Mark Metaphors We Live By* (Chicago: University of Chicago Press, 1980).

65. R. D. Benford and D. A. Snow, "Framing processes and social movements: An overview and assessment," *Annual Review of Sociology* (2000): 611–639.

66. Goffman, *Frame Analysis*; Alex Mintz and Stephen B. Redd, "Framing Effects in International Relations." *Synthese* 135 (2003): 193–213; Amos Tversky and Daniel Kahneman, "Prospect Theory: An Analysis of Decision Under Risk," *Econometrica* 47 (1979): 263–291.

67. George Lakoff, *The Political Mind* (New York: Penguin Group, 2008).

68. Robert Entman, "Cascading Activation: Contesting the White House's Frame After 9/11," *Political Communication* 20, no. 4 (2003): 415–432.

CHAPTER 3

COERCIVE PERFORMANCE
AND OUTCOMES

A MODEL TO ASSESS COERCIVE PERFORMANCE AND OUTCOMES

Many social science scholars and policy analysts have struggled to measure and understand the practice of CD. For both observers and policymakers, the absence of a clear assessment model hinders effectiveness and the successful resolution of coercive episodes. A thorough examination of the US CD record requires a model with defined terms and assessment measures.

A model for testing propositions in foreign policy or any area of social behavior should adhere to scientific method principles, including specifying the unit of analysis, key variables, and hypotheses. The most effective unit of analysis for understanding success and failure in US coercive practices is the coercive episode, defined as one historical instance of a coercing state attempting to change or deter a target state's behavior. When a single coercer repeatedly pressures a single target, this is referred to as a coercive dyad (a single coercer-target pair over time) for case studies.

The explanatory (independent) variables in this model include the clarity of coercive demand, credibility of threat, urgency, quality of off-ramps, and framing effort, each explained in the following pages. The coercive outcome (dependent) variables—compliance, alternative conces-sion, trajectory in bilateral relations subsequent to coercive episodes, and domestic political goal satisfaction—were evaluated through media and historical accounts, as well as interviews, for 122 identified coercive episodes. These outcomes were scored as ordinal values by an expert panel based on the reporting. Multivariate regressions were conducted STATA, a common statistical program in the social sciences, to estimate the impact of the independent variables on the dependent variables. These tools offer rough, imperfect, but useful measures of how the coercive episodes unfolded.

Assessing the impact of communications within CD requires a working definition of frames, their cross-national interactions, and their role in coercive processes. Communicative framing operates at multiple levels.[1] This study adopts a tripartite taxonomy of framing:

- **Deep frames**: National cultures have specific organizing principles and experiences that act as cognitive scaffolding, known as schema or "deep frames."
- **Conceptual frames**: Politicians, scholars, and analysts interpret current events in ways that reflect or reinforce a particular deep frame.
- **Message frames**: Communications professionals create and tailor video, audio, and print materials to influence conceptual frames in alignment with a society's deep frames.[2]

For analyzing CD, this taxonomy suggests a need to measure the congruity or friction between coercer and target messaging across these levels. In any coercive episode, it is expected that the coercer and target will each issue conflicting messages at the most transient level (message frames). These messages create a framing competition within the minds of the public and elites within the target country. Such messages gain traction only if they align with the deep and conceptual frames dominant in the target culture. If the coercer's demands, threats, escalatory steps, and off-ramps conflict with these established frames, the target's public and decision-makers will likely ignore or reinterpret them. Thus, understanding why specific coercive episodes succeed or fail requires assessing how well the coercer adapts to the deep and conceptual frames dominant among the target audiences.

Drawing on Entman's framework of cascading activation, this study measures competitive framing as a core process in political activation and coercive outcomes.[3] Target country decision-makers engage in simultaneous framing competitions with domestic policy elites and media, as well as global media and their own public. Including framing performance as a variable acknowledges that the information environments in the coercing state, the target state, and third-party states can significantly impact coercive outcomes, regardless of strong technical performance on other coercive variables.

Each independent variable (IV) and dependent variable (DV) was operationalized by identifying evidentiary criteria for their presence in specific coercive episodes, assigning a numeric value, and having the expert panel assess the presence of all variables based on narrative accounts. The five independent variables—demand clarity, threat credibility, urgency, off-ramp, framing effort—were coded with scores ranging from 0 to 1. A score of 0 indicates a failure to meet the four success criteria derived from previous studies of coercive diplomacy, while a score of 1 represents fulfillment of all four criteria (the four criteria differ for each variable). For each criterion violated by the United States in a coercive episode, 0.25 was deducted from the initial or presumed score of 1. If there was no clear evidence of a violation, the score remained unchanged. The expert panel independently coded these four outcome variables, and the scores were averaged to determine a final score for each variable in each coercive episode.

The expert panel consisted of eleven experienced regional specialists, each with a minimum of ten years of experience as US diplomats, military officers, or civilian policy professionals, all with personal experience in shaping or implementing coercive episodes. The panel's purpose was to apply a specific rubric to operationalize the theoretical variables within the model. Unlike the sixty practitioners interviewed for qualitative commentary on CD episodes, the panel's task was to provide quantitative parameters across the entire set of cases, not to offer commentary or insights on particular cases. The scoring rubric provided to the panel for evaluating variables included the following:

Demand Clarity (independent variable):
a) The US issued a clearly defined demand.
b) The demand was communicated consistently over time and across different branches of government.
c) The demand was within the target's capacity to comply with.
d) The demand did not contradict a known, strongly held national narrative related to the demand (e.g. sovereignty, national identity, traditional threats).

Threat Credibility (independent variable):
a) The US threatened a harm that was within its capabilities to execute.
b) There was no recent record of failed coercion involving similar demands and threats.
c) The threat posed relative menace, making it costlier for the target to resist than to comply or concede.
d) Specific steps were outlined or taken toward imposing the full threat.

Urgency (independent variable):
a) The US isolated the target from significant hedging or mitigating options (e.g., "black knight" external powers)
b) The US assembled a broad external coalition to support the coercive effort.
c) The US demonstrated broad internal support or commitment to the coercive episode.
d) The US demonstrated prioritization of the episode through senior-level engagement (President, Secretary of Defense, or Secretary of State level).

Off-Ramp (independent variable):
a) The US engaged in re-approach or re-negotiation at some point during the coercive episode following the initial demand.
b) The US had a record of lifting coercive measures after previous coercive episodes involving similar demands and threats.
c) The US demonstrated delimiting behavior, signaling intent to avoid open-ended coercion or escalation to war.
d) The US offered incentives or compromises.

Framing Effort (independent variable):
a) The US articulated clear terms framing the episode and achieved repetition of those terms across multiple US press outlets.
b) Political and media actors in the target region adopted those terms to some degree.
c) Political and media actors outside the target region adopted those terms to some degree.
d) There were some indications of a change in public or media support for resistance within the target state followed the onset of the coercive episode.

The outcomes of coercive episodes were considered as four separate dependent variables. As with the independent variables, an expert panel reviewed a narrative description of the episode, then scored the final resolution of the episode as follows:

1. **Compliance with Initial Coercive Demand (dependent variable):** Compliance or non-compliance with the initial coercive demand, coded as 1 (comply) or 0 (resist).

2. **Alternate Concession on a US Foreign Policy Interest (dependent variable):** Whether there was an identifiable alternative concession on a US foreign policy interest other than the specific demand, coded as 1 (identifiable alternative concession) or 0 (no identifiable alternative concession).

3. **Bilateral Trajectory after the Coercive Episode (dependent variable):** Coded as positive (1), neutral (0), or negative (-1). A positive coding is assigned when there is evidence that bilateral relations between the US and the target country improved after the coercive episode or were damaged but recovered in the study's timeframe. Neutral coding is used where there is no evidence of a major impact on bilateral relations or insufficient evidence to assess. Negative coding is applied when there is evidence of damage to bilateral relations that does not recover withing the study's timeframe (e.g., alignment with a non-Western state or alliance, destabilization, deterioration of democratic norms and human rights, or increased anti-American sentiment).

4. **Domestic Political Satisfaction (dependent variable):** Coded as zero (0) where no domestic constituent activity (Congress, press, interest groups) supporting the coercion can be identified in press or academic coverage, and one (1) where some domestic constituent activity can be identified.

As with most social science analyses, scoring and measuring coercive performance and outcomes involve human assessment, which introduces risks of bias, omission, and other potential errors. Although the quantitative measures in this study are anchored to specific criteria, they ultimately rely on human judgment—even if by expert practitioners— and different set of experts or criteria could yield different scores and insights. As Fearon has pointed out, comparative case studies are particularly vulnerable to selection effects, where the factors influencing case selection also significantly affect case outcomes, potentially distorting inferences about cause and effect.[4] This study identifies cases based on the US initiation of coercive episodes but measures effect through US actions *within* those episodes to mitigate the risk of selection effects. While it may not be possible to produce an exhaustive set of cases or fully satisfying set of criteria for a phenomenon as complex as coercive diplomacy—and much effective coercion may occur below the threshold of public attention—rough measures still have heuristic value when the goal is better practice rather than absolute truths. These measures, reflecting how experts involved in the conduct and review of US coercive diplomacy gauge effects over time, enable a high-level policy discussion that would otherwise not be possible.

DESIGN: THEORETICAL MODEL AND STRUCTURE OF THE STUDY

Figure 1 presents a simplified model of the variables involved in the study. The quantitative analysis follows a two-step approach: first, estimating the impacts of variables frequently cited in scholarly works on CD, and second, integrating an additional variable (framing) that has been less studied in previous CD research. This analysis aims to empirically confirm the theoretical proposition illustrated in figure 1—that coercive performance, as reflected in the most frequently cited variables, explains only part of the outcomes. Framing effects account for another dimension: both the coercer and target receive and interpret coercive signals embedded in these variables differently. When the coercer fails to account for these differences, coercive success becomes even more elusive, even with perfect communication.

Figure 1. Variables in the Model of Coercive Effect.

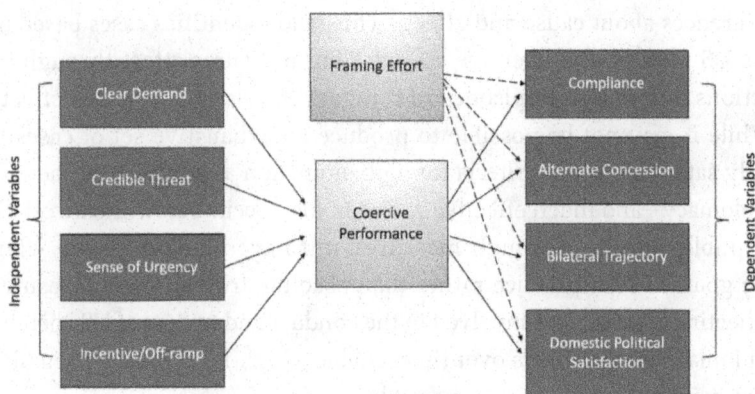

Methods

The data on coercive episodes were analyzed using a combination of descriptive and simple inferential statistics. Multivariate regressions were conducted using STATA, a statistical analysis program commonly used in policy research. This analysis offers valuable context for understanding the prevalence of and trends in US CD from 1990 to 2020, as well as insights into how theoretical variables influenced real-world outcomes during that period.

The analysis of framing effort in coercion utilized quantitative content analysis (QCA), a method previously applied in international relations research by scholars such as Ole Holsti, Abraham Kaplan, Harold Lasswell, Robert North, and Dinna Zinne.[5] This study used QCA to estimate the presence and impact of political frames in coercive messaging by sampling media coverage of coercive episodes in the target country and other stakeholder countries. It assessed whether US coercive message framing was broadly adopted or rejected regionally by counting instances of sympathetic or adversarial coverage in the sampled media. A purposeful sampling strategy of ten media outlets (five US media outlets and five non-US media outlets) per coercive episode was employed, with an emphasis on prominent outlets focused on foreign policy.

The research also employed case study method as described by Joachim Blatter and Markus Haverland, among others.[6] This method involved examining specific dyadic relationships over time between the US and a specific target, referred to as a coercive dyad. Analyzing the dynamics within a specific coercive dyad complements trend analysis derived from examining all 122 coercive episodes in aggregate. The case studies in this research integrated data from expert interviews with general descriptions from news media and historical accounts. The study presents five regions —the Americas, Europe, Africa, the Middle East and Central Asia, South and East Asia—as broad cases, with coercive dyads serving as more focused units of analysis within each region.

AGGREGATE QUANTITATIVE FINDINGS OF THE MODEL

The following quantitative descriptions measure how well theoretical variables from CD literature explain US coercion during the period under study. They help identify broad trends in US CD policy formulation and outcomes and provide a baseline for understanding specific cases examined in later chapters.

Table 1 categorizes the 122 identified coercive episodes by the coercive tools employed (leftmost column) and tracks each tool or combination of tools by their outcomes. An episode was considered to have resulted in compliance or alternative concession if the panel scoring for that episode was 0.5 or higher, indicating that half or more of the panel assessed it as leading to compliance or concession. An episode was considered to have significant domestic political interest if the average score from independent raters was 0.5 or higher. It was considered to have resulted in a negative trajectory if the average score from independent raters was negative. The coercive modality most likely to achieve compliance (41.7%)

was the combination of economic and military coercion, with purely diplomatic pressure (38.5%) and combined economic and diplomatic pressure (32.1%) the other approaches that succeeded over 30% of the time. These types of coercion achieved results consistent with other studies, which shows a roughly one-third success rate in coercive diplomacy when construed broadly.

Economic sanctions without additional military or diplomatic measures achieved compliance in 27.3% of the cases in which they were used. The broadest combination—diplomatic, military, and economic measures together—had a success rate of only 20%. Diplomatic and military pressure without economic leverage fared even worse, with a 16.7% success rate. In the only case in where military pressure was applied without economic or diplomatic measures, it failed. Overall, the US successfully coerced 34 of 122 targets during its 1990–2020 coercive diplomacy campaigns, resulting in a 27.9% success rate. Interestingly, the diplomatic tool used alone had a relatively high success rate, likely reflecting the modest demands typically pursued through such limited means. Military pressure short of war showed poor outcomes when combined with both economic and diplomatic pressure, paired with diplomatic pressure, or used alone. This may indicate that diplomatic sanctions reduce overall engagement, thereby limiting opportunities to leverage military pressure into tacit concessions. Military pressure combined with economic pressure—though not accompanied by broad diplomatic exclusions—seems to maximize the potential of military coercion, yet still succeeds less than half the time.

Similar patterns emerged in the achievement of concessions other than the primary demand, with two notable exceptions. Diplomatic and economic pressure together provided the same likelihood (32.1%) for obtaining an alternate concession as for compliance with the primary demand. Military force alone (0%), combined with the broadest suite of measures (30%), or used alongside diplomatic isolation (33.3%), underperformed compared to economic sanctions alone (36.4%) in securing alternate concessions. The advantage of combined economic and military measures over other modalities was even more pronounced for obtaining alternate concessions, achieving a 50% success rate. Overall, the likelihood of obtaining some concession through coercion was higher (39.3%) than the likelihood of achieving compliance with the primary demand (27.9%).

Table 1. Coercive Episodes by Tools Applied and Results Obtained.

Coercive Tools Applied	Compliance Achieved	Other Concession Obtained	Bilateral Trajectory Worsened	Domestic Satisfaction Involved	Escalation to War
Diplomatic Only (13)	5 (38.5%)	1 (8.7%)	2 (15.4%)	8 (61.5%)	0
Diplomatic and Economic (28)	9 (32.1%)	9 (32.1%)	14 (50.0%)	17 (60.7%)	0
Diplomatic and Military (6)	1 (16.7%)	2 (33.3%)	4 (66.6%)	2 (33.3%)	0
Diplomatic, Economic, and Military (40)	8 (20.0%)	12 (30.0%)	25 (62.5%)	29 (72.5%)	7 (17.5%)
Economic Only (22)	6 (27.3%)	8 (36.4%)	6 (27.3%)	6 (27.3%)	0
Economic and Military (12)	5 (41.7%)	6 (50.0%)	3 (25.0%)	7 (58.3%)	0
Military Only (1)	0 (0%)	0 (0%)	1 (100%)	1 (100%)	0
Aggregate (122)	34 (27.9%)	38 (39.3%)	55 (45.0%)	70 (57.4%)	7 (5.7%)

The long-term effect of CD on bilateral relations is shown in the results for bilateral trajectory in table 1. When diplomatic coercion (15.4%) or economic sanctions (27.3%) were used alone, only a few cases experienced serious, long-term deterioration after the coercive episode concluded. However, when military measures were employed alone (100%), as part of the broadest suite of sanctions (62.5%), or coupled with diplomatic isolation (66.6%), long-term deterioration was likely. Similarly, economic sanctions paired with diplomatic isolation had high incidence (50%) of long-term deterioration in bilateral relations. Interestingly, the most effective combination for achieving compliance and concession (economic and military measures together) had a relatively low rate for causing longer-term bilateral harm (25%). This may be because the use of economic measures implies a degree of interdependence that can quickly return to profitability once the episode concludes, whereas countries with minimal overlapping economic interests have little motive or benefit from imposing economic sanctions. The low success rate of economic or military tools combined with diplomatic isolation suggests that maintaining diplomatic ties during periods of economic or military coercion may help secure compliance or concession and prevent negative bilateral trajectory. This finding challenges the practice of diplomatically isolating target countries while applying economic and military coercive measures. Notably, across all coercive episodes, the incidence of long-term deterioration in bilateral relations (45%) exceeded both the rates of both compliance and alternate concessions. Frequent use of coercive diplomacy may therefore have serious and lasting negative effects, as the number of these deteriorating bilateral relationships accumulates.

Certain combinations of coercive modalities appear correlated with significant domestic political interest. When domestic political interest was an identified outcome, military means were often involved—either alone, combined with economic sanctions, or bundled with economic and diplomatic sanctions. Diplomatic sanctions alone, which have high symbolic value but cause little material harm, were also associated with high levels of domestic political satisfaction. In contrast, economic sanctions alone or military and diplomatic measures without economic pressure were linked to low levels of domestic political interest. Overall, domestic political satisfaction was an outcome in 57.4% of all coercive episodes examined, suggesting that coercive diplomacy often serves as a performative measure for the home audience rather than a reliable tool for achieving compliance, concession, or more favorable bilateral relations.

Coercive diplomacy is used as an alternative to major military operations, aimed at reducing the costs and risks of open war. However, in some cases, war ensues after failure to obtain compliance, concession, or other negotiated outcomes. This occurred in seven of the 122 episodes examined: Panama (1990), Iraq (1991 and 2003), Yugoslavia/Serbia (1995 and 1999), Afghanistan (2001), and Libya (2011). In each of these cases, a full set of coercive measures (diplomatic, economic, and military) was employed before the initiation of combat operations. While some coercive episodes may be intended, at least in part, to weaken a target in preparation for war, this study assumes that the coercer's preference for target compliance or concession over war is generally sincere.

DESCRIPTION BY PRESIDENTIAL ADMINISTRATION

Table 2 summarizes the coercive record of each presidential administration during the three decades examined. The Bush 41 administration best met the theoretical variables for coercive success, with an aggregate performance score of 3.04 out of a possible 4. Both Presidents Bush (41 and 43) engaged in coercion at the relatively low rate of two major episodes per year (eight for Bush 41 and 16 for Bush 43), achieving compliance in roughly 37.5% of cases. The Clinton and Trump administrations used coercion more frequently (37 cases over two terms for Clinton and 35 in one term for Trump) but underperformed compared to the Bush administrations in coercive performance scores (2.67 out of 4 for Clinton, 2.83 for Trump). Both Clinton and Trump also achieved compliance at slightly lower rates than the Bushes (32.4% for Clinton and 31.4% for Trump). The two-term Democratic administrations (Clinton and Obama) engaged in coercion more frequently than both Bush administrations (4.6 episodes per year for Clinton and 3.25 per year for Obama), though less frequently than Trump. The outlier is the Obama administration, which employed coercion at a moderate frequency (3.25-episode annual rate) but had the lowest coercive performance score (2.64 of 4) and the lowest rate for obtaining compliance (8.7%). Overall, Democratic administrations accounted for over half of the total coercive episodes (52%) but lagged behind Republican administrations in achieving compliance (17.5% versus 36%).

Table 2. Coercive Outcomes by Presidential Administration.

Presidential Administration	# Coercive Episodes / rate per year	Average Coercive Performance	Compliance Rate	Negative Trajectory Rate
Bush 41	8 (6.6%) / 2.0	3.04	37.5% (3 of 8)	25% (2 of 8)
Clinton	37 (30.3%) / 4.6	2.67	32.4% (12 of 37)	43% (16 of 37)
Bush 43	16 (13.1%) / 2.0	2.81	37.5% (6 of 16)	50% (8 of 16)
Obama	26 (21.3%) / 3.25	2.64	8.7% (2 of 26)	50% (13 of 26)
Trump	35 (28.7%) / 8.75	2.83	31.4% (11 of 35)	46% (16 of 35)

Another interesting trend is the failure of any administration after Bush 41 to achieve compliance or concessions at a higher rate than the deterioration in bilateral trajectory. Coercive episodes initiated by Presidents George W. Bush and Barack Obama resulted in a negative bilateral trajectory— deterioration for US interests in the country or region involved—in half of the episodes, far exceeding their compliance rate. Presidents Clinton and Trump fared slightly better (43% and 46%, respectively). Only Bush 41 achieved compliance more often than he experienced a negative bilateral trajectory, possibly due to his very low rate of engaging in such contests.

DESCRIPTION BY REGION

Table 3 shows patterns in coercive outcomes across different geographic regions. The highest rate of compliance (60%) was achieved in the Americas, followed by Africa (30%) and Europe (25%), with Middle East/Central Asia and South/East Asia both complying in only 14% of episodes. Generally, the closer a target country is to the US, the greater the prospects for coercive success. Several factors may explain this: proximate targets are often more economically integrated with the US and thus more vulnerable to its pressure, are less likely to have neighboring countries that can offset economic or military pressure through hedging strategies, and may have stronger motivations to maintain positive long-term relations with Washington. The likelihood of obtaining a concession other than the primary demand was similar (33–36%) across all regions except the Middle East/Central Asia, where concessions were obtained in only 14% of episodes.

The regions where US CD was most likely to result in a negative trajectory in bilateral relations were Europe (83%) and the Middle East/Central Asia (68%). In contrast, the negative impact on bilateral relations was more transitory in South and East Asia (39%), the Americas (35%), and Africa (23%). There is a correlation between the regions with high negative trajectory scores and the use of military pressure in the coercive approach; in Europe (50%, 6 of 12 episodes) and the Middle East/Central Asia (86%, 19 out of 22 episodes), coercive tools frequently included military measures. In regions with lower negative trajectory rates (the Americas and Africa), military tools were applied less often. South and East Asia is the exception to this trend, with a moderately high inclusion of military measures (57%, 16 of 28 episodes) but relatively low negative trajectory rate (39%).

Table 3. Coercive Outcomes by Region.

Region	Compliance	Concession	Negative Trajectory	Domestic Satisfaction	Escalation to War
Americas	12/20 (60%)	7/20 (35%)	7/20 (35%)	14/20 (70%)	1/20 (5%)
Europe	3/12 (25%)	4/12 (33%)	10/12 (83%)	10/12 (83%)	2/12 (17%)
Middle East and Central Asia	3/22 (14%)	3/22 (14%)	18/22 (82%)	18/22 (82%)	3/22 (14%)
Africa	12/40 (30%)	14/40 (35%)	9/40 (23%)	8/40 (20%)	1/40 (3%)
South and East Asia	4/28 (14%)	10/28 (36%)	11/28 (39%)	20/28 (71%)	0/28 (0%)

DURATION EFFECT

Another statistic of interest for the purposes of this study is episode duration. Many studies of CD have posited a connection between sense of urgency—escalation—and coercive success. The implies that once coercive measures become seen as routine, not escalatory, a key lever for compliance loses its effectiveness. If this theory holds, we would expect decreasing compliance rates as episodes extend in duration. The US experience from 1990 to 2020 supports this: 82% of the episodes resulting in compliance lasted four years or less, and 71% of the episodes yielding alternative concessions were resolved in the first four years. Episodes extending beyond four years had an aggregate compliance rate of 12.5% and an aggregate concession rate of 23%. Satisfaction of domestic political interests remained fairly constant after the first four years, as did the risk of escalation to war. In short, the desired specific results in coercive episodes—compliance or alternative concessions—typically occur within the first four years, with compliance particularly clustered in the first two. However, negative trajectory outcomes are more frequent (54%) in episodes that exceed four years compared to those that do not (41%). This pattern suggests diminishing returns in coercive diplomacy, yet it is unclear whether Washington has effective mechanisms for terminating episodes once the prospects for positive outcomes diminish.

Table 4. Coercive Outcomes by Duration of Episode.

Duration (years)	Compliance	Concession	Negative Trajectory	Domestic Satisfaction	Escalation to War
1-2	19/35 (54%)	10/35 (29%)	10/35 (29%)	21/35 (60%)	3/35 (9%)
3-4	9/39 (23%)	17/39 (44%)	19/39 (49%)	23/39 (59%)	3/39 (8%)
5-8	1/30 (3%)	8/30 (27%)	18/30 (60%)	18/30 (60%)	0/30 (0%)
9-12	4/13 (31%)	3/13 (23%)	6/13 (46%)	8/13 (62%)	1/13 (8%)
>12	1/5 (20%)	0/5 (0%)	2/5 (40%)	0/5 (0%)	0/5 (0%)

Trends in Outcomes

The quantitative record of US coercive diplomacy from 1990 to 2020 leads to several conclusions. First, coercive modalities matter. Coercive measures were rarely used in isolation; instead, diplomatic, economic, and military measures were applied in various combinations with differing success rates and drawbacks. Diplomatic sanctions alone were reasonably effective for limited demands and seldom caused negative bilateral trajectory but were less effective for achieving significant demands. Economic pressure had limited utility when used alone but was more potent when combined with military or diplomatic measures; however, when paired with diplomatic isolation, it often caused lasting damage to bilateral relations. Military pressure almost always led to long-term deterioration in bilateral relations, although this effect was somewhat mitigated if diplomatic sanctions were avoided and bilateral relations were maintained despite military and/or economic pressure. In short, the "kitchen sink" approach to pressure yielded disappointing results, frequently led to war, yet remained a common approach in part due to its appeal to domestic political sentiment.

Second, not all administrations performed equally or at the same pace. The Bush administrations (41 and 43) employed coercive diplomacy on a scale large enough to generate a substantial public record, averaging about two major episodes per year, and achieved compliance in more than one out of three cases. In contrast, the most frequent coercers (Clinton and Trump) succeeded less frequently and experienced sustained deterioration in bilateral relations more often than they succeeded. The Obama administration also employed coercion frequently but had a low success rate and shared the highest incidence of long-term bilateral damage. The clearest correlation here is that lower frequencies of coercion are associated with a higher likelihood of obtaining compliance.

Third, not all regions were equally vulnerable to US coercive diplomacy. Targets in the Americas warrant separate consideration, as their proximity and economic integration with the United States are correlated with relatively high rates of compliance or concessions and relatively low levels of negative bilateral trajectory. Coercive diplomacy offered greater rewards and lower risks in the Americas. In contrast, it had the weakest prospects in the Middle East and Central Asia, with low rates of compliance or concession (14% each) and a high rate of negative bilateral trajectory. Paradoxically, Africa was where the US coerced most frequently but most rarely satisfied a domestic interest or political value. Coercion of European targets occurred the least frequently but resulted in the most frequent lasting damage to bilateral relations.

Finally, the data reveal a pattern of diminishing returns. The likelihood of positive outcomes (compliance or concession) is higher in the first four years, while the likelihood of negative outcomes (resistance or non-compliance and non-concession, negative bilateral trajectory) increases after that period. Whether coercive diplomacy is pursued to avoid war or for to weaken an opponent before war, its effectiveness in achieving desired results declines over time, particularly after the first four years.

Inferential Statistics for US Coercive Diplomacy 1990–2020

When variables are operationalized as numeric values, regression techniques can help clarify the impact of independent variables on dependent variables. The following section summarizes a series of regressions that evaluate the effect of each independent variable on the dependent variables, based on the expert panel's scoring. Regressions were run using Stata.

Several values in the regression merit focused attention. The coefficient for each independent variable (IV) indicates the change the dependent variable (DV) observed for each unit change in the IV; a higher coefficient signifies a stronger effect. Positive coefficients suggest that an increase in the IV leads to an increase in the DV, while negative coefficients imply that an increase in the IV leads to a decrease in the DV. Significance testing uses a test statistic (t, z, or f depending on type of sample; the t-value is listed here) to indicate how far a point estimate falls from the parameter estimate under the null hypothesis, measured in standard errors. A higher test statistic value indicates stronger evidence against the null hypothesis of no effect. A t-value over 2 corresponds to a P-value under 0.05. The P-value reflects the probability that the observed result is due to random chance rather than being predictive. A low P-value, ideally under 0.05, suggests that the result is likely not random and thus has explanatory power. The R-squared is a goodness-of-fit measure that expresses the percentage of variance in the DV explained by the

IV (or collectively by several IVs). It ranges from 0 to 100%, with higher values indicating that the IV has a greater influence over the DV. Given the complexity of human behavior, achieving an R-squared over 50% is rare in social science research.

The impact of each independent variable (IV) on the dependent variables (DVs) was calculated using multiple regression in Stata, with the results summarized in the tables 5–8 for the four primary variables and tables 9–10 for framing. The R-squared value indicates the percentage of variance in the DV explained collectively by all the IVs.

Table 5. Obtaining Compliance.

IV	Coefficient	t-value	P-value	R-squared
Demand Clarity	.282	1.36	.175	-
Threat Credibility	.712	3.05	.003	-
Urgency	.160	0.85	.396	-
Off-Ramp	.331	2.67	.009	-
All IVs				.344

The results indicate that threat credibility and off-ramp had the strongest effect on compliance as measured by their coefficients. These two independent variables also had the lowest probability of their effects occurring by chance, as indicated by their t-values and P-values. Demand clarity and urgency were poor predictors of compliance by the target. Together, the four variables in the model together accounted for 34.4% of the variance in target compliance across the 122 cases, indicating a strong correlation.

Table 6. Obtaining Alternate Concessions.

IV	Coefficient	t-value	P-value	R-squared
Demand Clarity	-.147	-0.71	.481	-
Threat Credibility	.102	0.43	.667	-
Urgency	.212	1.12	.266	-
Off-Ramp	.403	3.23	.002	-
All IVs				.114

Demand clarity may negatively impact the offering of alternative concessions, though the P-value indicates a high degree of uncertainty about this
linkage. Threat credibility and urgency might both have a positive impact,
but neither meets the threshold (alpha-level of .05) needed to confidently
reject the null hypothesis of no significant effect. The clearest impact,
based on t-value and P-value, seems to be off-ramp; when an alternative
path to the primary concession was left open, alternate concessions were
often achievable. Overall, the variables collectively account for only 11.4%
of the variance in obtaining alternate concessions, which is far lower
than their estimated impact on achieving compliance.

Table 7. Bilateral Trajectory.

IV	Coefficient	t-value	P-value	R-squared
Demand Clarity	.733	2.24	.027	-
Threat Credibility	.277	0.75	.454	-
Urgency	-.017	-0.06	.953	-
Off-Ramp	.573	2.93	.004	-
All IVs				.196

Demand clarity demonstrates both a high coefficient and a high t-value
(over 2) and low P-value (less than 0.05), indicating that it significantly
contributes to a positive post-coercion bilateral trajectory and that the
effect is unlikely to be accidental. Threat credibility and urgency have
positive coefficients, but their t-values and P-values are too weak to
provide confidence in the strength of these relationships. The provision

of an off-ramp shows a high coefficient and a high t-value/low-P value, indicating both a strong influence over bilateral trajectory and a high level of confidence in the relationship. Together, these IVs account for roughly 20% of the variation in bilateral trajectory. The data suggests that if the US wishes to resume a positive bilateral trajectory with a target following a coercive episode, it should be clear about its demands and provide a mutually acceptable pathway to resolution. Conversely, vague demands without a clear resolution path are most likely to result in an extended downturn in bilateral relations.

Table 8. Domestic Political Satisfaction.

IV	Coefficient	t-value	P-value	R-squared
Demand Clarity	-.541	-2.44	.016	-
Threat Credibility	.493	1.97	.051	-
Urgency	-.035	-0.17	.863	-
Off-Ramp	.076	0.57	.568	-
All IVs				.059

Demand clarity correlates strongly, but negatively, with Domestic Political Satisfaction both in terms of coefficient (-0.541) and t-value (-2.44), suggesting that increasing specificity of demands decreases their utility in achieving domestic political goals. The low P-value supports the conclusion that this is not a random outcome. Threat credibility also shows a strong coefficient but falls just short of t-values and P-values that would provide strong evidence of the relationship. Urgency and off-ramp do not demonstrate strong correlations with success in achieving Domestic Political Satisfaction. Together, these IVs account for only 5.9% of the variation in such satisfaction. This suggests that factors outside the theoretical model for coercive success are more significant in determining whether domestic political goals and audiences are satisfied by coercive episodes.

The Impact of Framing Effort

The variables that determine coercive success considered thus far—demand clarity, threat credibility, sense of urgency, and off-ramp—have been central to previous studies of CD. This study introduces a less-examined causal variable: framing effort. Framing effort reflects the coercing power's efforts to clearly and consistently communicate the reasons for coercion, favorably influence the target's perception of the episode, shape regional and international narratives, and achieve shifts in action or opinion that support its framing. A content analysis of media framing was conducted in the US, target countries, neighboring countries, and other great powers by sampling stories from media outlets in each. Framing effort was scored from zero to one based by assigning 0 or 0.25 points for four criteria: the presence of clear and relatively uncontested official framing in US media, adoption or accommodation of US framing by media in the target country, adoption or accommodation of US framing by other countries in the region or by other great powers, and polling or events on the ground indicating shifts in public attitudes within the target that favor coercive success. The overall coercive performance of US administrations in terms of coercive framing is reflected in table 9.

Table 9. Framing Performance by Presidential Administration.

Administration	Negative Framing Effort (0)	Weak Framing Effort (.25)	Balanced Framing Effort (.5)	Strong Framing Effort (.75)	Ideal Framing Effort (1)
Bush 41 (8)	0	4	3	0	1
Clinton (37)	6	15	7	3	6
Bush 43 (16)	2	7	3	2	2
Obama (26)	1	7	12	3	3
Trump (35)	1	16	13	4	1
Aggregate (122)	10/122 (8%)	49/122 (40%)	38/122 (31%)	12/122 (10%)	13/122 (11%)

The record reveals a consistent pattern of poor performance by US administrations in developing coercive framing strategies that resonate effectively across domestic, target, regional, and international audiences. In 48% of the coercive episodes examined, the US framing efforts were marked by significant deficiencies, particularly in terms of message articulation or adaptation to key audiences. A moderate level of success was observed in 31% of the cases, while only 21% of episodes demonstrated strong or near-perfect framing efforts. Among the presidents whose administrations were covered in this study, three—Obama, Clinton, and Bush 43—achieved favorable framing outcomes in roughly a quarter of their coercive episodes, with rates of 23%, 24%, and 25%, respectively. In contrast, Presidents Bush 41 (12.5%) and Trump (14.3%) faced considerable challenges in crafting message frames that resonated effectively with relevant audiences.

The low rate of effective framing does appear to correlate with lower success in coercive episodes, as well as other variables of interest. Such a relationship would suggest that effective framing plays a critical role in determining coercive outcomes. Table 10 presents the results of simple regressions of framing effort against the four variables of this study: compliance, alternative concession, bilateral trajectory, and domestic political satisfaction.

Table 10. Impact of Framing Effort on Coercive Outcomes.

DV	Coefficient	t-value	P-value	R-squared
Compliance	.387	3.00	.003	.070
Alternative Concession	.146	1.26	.209	.013
Bilateral Trajectory	.357	1.90	.060	.029
Domestic Political Satisfaction	-.185	-1.56	.568	.020

A high framing effort score strongly correlates with obtaining compliance from the target, as evidenced by the positive coefficient, high t-value, low p-value, and higher R-squared relative to the other dependent variables regressed. Along with threat credibility and the provision of an off-ramp, as examined in the earlier regression, effective framing appears to play a significant role in securing target compliance during coercive episodes. In relation to avoiding negative trajectory in bilateral relations, effective framing narrowly misses a p-value that is low enough to reject the null hypothesis of no significant effect. With a p-value of .06, close to the alpha value (typically set at .05), we cannot entirely rule out the influence of framing on bilateral trajectory. Conversely, framing does not appear to significantly impact obtaining alternate concessions or achieving domestic political satisfaction, as indicated by low coefficients and t-values, high p-values, and low R-squared for both. In summary, effective framing seems to be a critical factor when the goal is genuine compliance and the maintenance of positive bilateral relations. Effective framing likely plays a lesser role in coercive episodes conducted as preludes to war or for primarily domestic political satisfaction, where compliance and bilateral relations are secondary concerns.

What Leads to Coercive Success?

It may be most useful to summarize the results of regressions analyzing the impact of independent variables on dependent variables in recent US coercive diplomacy as a series of "best practices" for policymakers. This approach assumes that, in most cases, policymakers genuinely aim for "work" by prompting target countries to comply or make concessions, while avoiding damage to bilateral relations, and ensuring domestic political approval. However, if in some instances the true intent behind coercion was disingenuous—such as seeking to weaken or overthrow the target rather than secure the stated demand—this would challenge the assumption. Proving the sincerity or disingenuousness of demands is complex, so it is preferable to take the coercing power at its word and assume sincerity in order to assess policy effectiveness.

What "Worked" (Positive Correlations):

- To secure compliance from a target during a coercive episode, the key factors in US experience between 1990 and 2020 were the alignment of credible threats with the target's interests and the provision of a viable off-ramp or path toward a mutually satisfactory resolution. While articulating a clear demand may contribute to success, it was not as pivotal. Moreover, generating a sense of urgency does not significantly improve the prospects for coercive success.

- The likelihood of securing concessions beyond the primary demand is significantly enhanced by offering a mutually acceptable off-ramp.

- Clear demands and workable off-ramps are effective in preventing serious and long-term deterioration in bilateral relations with the target.

- Credible threats can increase the likelihood of achieving domestic political satisfaction from coercive episodes.

- The descriptive statistics presented earlier suggest that compliance is significantly more likely when coercing geographically proximate targets, particularly within the Americas. The data also indicates that presidential administrations with the lowest frequency of coercive episodes (two episodes per year for both Bush presidencies) achieved the highest rates of compliance and experienced slightly lower rates of negative bilateral trajectory (10/24 or 42% compared to 45/98 or 46%).

- Effective framing by the coercing power contributes to successfully obtaining target compliance and may help prevent a negative trajectory in bilateral relations, following the coercive episode. However, framing does not appear to influence the likelihood of securing alternative concessions from the target or achieving domestic political interests.

What Did Not "Work" (Negative Correlations):

- Clear demands may actually reduce the likelihood of securing alternate concessions, although the confidence level of this linkage is low.

- Clear demands do not increase the likelihood of achieving domestic political satisfaction.

- Based on the descriptive statistics presented earlier, the Middle East and Central Asia emerge as the regions where compliance and concessions are most difficult to achieve, with a heightened likelihood of subsequent deterioration in bilateral relations. In Europe, the probability of sustained downturns in bilateral relations following coercive episodes are highest. Additionally, there appears to be a duration effect: as coercive episodes extend beyond four years, the rate of compliance or concessions declines, while the likelihood of a negative trajectory in bilateral relations increases.

- The combination of frequent coercion and poor coercive performance—most notably during the Obama administration—resulted in the lowest rates of compliance and the highest rates of negative trajectories in bilateral relations.

Effective framing aimed at audiences in the target state, region, and internationally correlate negatively with the satisfaction of domestic political goals within the coercing state (the US). Coercive framing and messaging crafted to influence the target and other stakeholders may not resonate with domestic audiences, as the saying goes, "it may not play well in Peoria." Conversely, coercive communications designed to appeal to domestic audiences often fail to gain traction with the target and its regional allies.

Data indicates that the dependent variables may represent competing policy goals, as each responds differently to changes in the independent variables. Specifically, increasing demand clarity enhances the likelihood of compliance and reduces the risk of a deteriorating bilateral trajectory, but it simultaneously limits the possibility for alternative concessions or domestic political satisfaction. Offering off-ramps facilitates compliance, concession, and improvements in bilateral relations, yet has limited impact on domestic political satisfaction. Prolonged coercion may sustain domestic political satisfaction and a negative bilateral trajectory for extended periods—sometimes a decade or more— though it fails to improve rates of compliance or concession over time. Notably, this data does not address the temporal dynamics of interactions as the frequency of coercive episodes increases. As coercion is applied to a growing number of states in extended episodes, the question arises: what types of hedging behaviors emerge among these targets? Anecdotal evidence suggests that nations are increasingly developing resistance economies to bypass economic pressure and deepening military ties with America's strategic competitors. Further research is required to explore the timing and criteria for terminating coercive episodes, as well as to assess the impacts of multiple, concurrent, and long-term coercive actions.

It is important to reiterate the caveat that quantitative scoring of episodes, and the subsequent statistical analysis, should be considered suggestive rather than definitive. The incorporation of human judgment in selecting and coding episodes introduces potential sources of error. Nevertheless, the correlations and trends identified offer a valuable framework for contextual case- and region-specific observations, providing US policymakers with insights to better evaluate the likelihood of success in future coercive initiatives.

NOTES

1. Michael J. Carter, "The Hermeneutics of Frames and Framing: An Examination of the Media's Construction of Reality," *SAGE Open* (April 2013), https://doi.org/10.1177/2158244013487915.
2. Athanassios Samaras, "Representations of 11/9 in Four Greek Newspapers: A Frames Perspective," *Questions de Communication* 8 (2005): 367–388.
3. Robert Entman, "Theorizing Mediated Public Diplomacy: The US Case," *Press/Politics* 13, no. 2 (April 2008): 87–102.
4. James Fearon, "Selection Effects and Deterrence," *International Interactions* 28, no. 1 (2002): 5–29.
5. Arash Heydarian Pashakhanlou, "Fully Integrated Frame Analysis in International Relations," *International Relations* 31, no. 4 (August 2017): 447–465.
6. Joachim Blatter and Markus Haverland, "Case Studies and (Causal-) Process Tracing," in *Comparative Policy Studies: Conceptual and Methodological Challenges*, edited by Isabelle Engeli and Christine Rothmayr (London: Palgrave MacMillan, 2014), 1–13.

CHAPTER 4

SWEET SPOT: US COERCIVE DIPLOMACY IN THE WESTERN HEMISPHERE

The most compelling evidence that US CD can be effective—when applied judiciously—comes from cases in the Western Hemisphere. As noted in chapter 4, instances of coercion in the Americas resulted in the highest rate of target compliance (60%) by a significant margin. The use of CD in this region was associated with relatively low risks of escalation to armed conflict, minimal long-term deterioration in bilateral ties or regional US interests, and a reasonable likelihood (35%) of securing alternative concessions, even in cases where full compliance was not achieved.

The following summary illustrates how three decades of US coercion played out across this subset of cases. Coercive performance scores range from 0 to 4, framing performance 0–1, Compliance and other outcome variables (alternative concession or AC, trajectory or T, and domestic satisfaction or DS) 0–1. Detailed episode scoring procedures and results are available in Appendix 1 online.[1]

US coercive performance in the Western Hemisphere averaged 2.77 on a 4-point scale, while framing performance scored .53 on a 1-point scale, surpassing results from other regions discussed in subsequent chapters. Correspondingly, the compliance outcome was rated higher in this region (0.6 out of a possible 1.0). Negative second-order effects, which were more prominent in other regions, were less pronounced in the Western hemisphere, with a low but positive score (0.02). Over a thirty-year period, the bilateral trajectory showed minimal impact from the application of US CD. Furthermore, domestic interest—and by extension, satisfaction of domestic political needs—was relatively high (0.67 from 1.0). In comparison to other regions, coercive efforts in the Western hemisphere coercion had a stronger likelihood of securing compliance, was more domestically popular, and resulted in fewer adverse consequences for US interests.

Coercive Dyads

Some of the most striking examples of effective US CD come from the Western Hemisphere during the early post–Cold War years. Notably, the Bush administration successfully pressured the Ortega government in Nicaragua, resulting in several decades of improved bilateral relations and enhanced US influence in the region. US coercion also played a key role in the return of civilian rule in Guatemala, Ecuador, Paraguay, and Haiti following military coups, the cessation of hostilities between Ecuador and Peru, the rise of a more US-aligned government in Colombia, and improved immigration enforcement by Guyana. These successes largely occurred within the first decade of the period under study, potentially influenced by the demonstrative effects of the Panama intervention and Operation Desert Storm. In many of these cases, the US benefited from strong regional backing, particularly from the Organization of American States (OAS) or Southern Common Market (MERCOSUR),[2] effective framing of the rationale for action both domestically and regionally, and in many instances, significant internal support within the target states.

A key element of this success was the provision of substantial post-coercion incentives, such as Plan Colombia or relief efforts for Haiti.[3]

The failures highlight the inherent challenges of executing successful CD, even under seemingly favorable conditions. In Panama (1989–1990), significant domestic skepticism within the United States regarding the removal of Manuel Noriega, coupled with weak framing of the rationale for action both domestically and regionally, contributed to Noriega's decision to resist US demands. As a result, coercive diplomacy failed, leading to full-scale military conflict. (One might argue that the attempt at coercive diplomacy ultimately bolstered the case for war, and in this sense, it could be viewed as a failure only in the technical sense). Similarly, in the case of Peru (1992–1993), US pressure failed to sway political elites or popular opinion to reverse Fujimori's autogolpe (self-coup), which retained widespread regional and domestic support. Instead, the US accepted alternate concessions in the Peruvian case, including compensation for the death of a US serviceman and the scheduling of elections.

Cuba
Coercive attempts involving Cuba serve as a distinctive example of the multiple purposes of CD. While they failed to compel Havana to comply with US demands, they succeeded domestically by fulfilling the public's desire for the appearance of assertive action.

1992–2000: The Cuban Democracy Act (CDA) of 1992 called for a "peaceful transition to democracy...through the careful application of sanctions directed at the [Fidel] Castro government,"[4] marking a new phase in US sanctions against Cuba. After the total embargo applied by Presidents Kennedy, Lyndon B. Johnson, and Richard Nixon, President Ford had allowed US subsidiaries abroad to sell to Cuba in an effort to avoid diplomatic friction with allies. While President Ronald Reagan tightened sanctions slightly, the collapse of the Soviet Union and subsequent contraction of the Cuban economy due to the loss of Soviet aid revealed a new vulnerability. The CDA terminated subsidiary sales to Cuba and was followed by the Libertad Act of 1996, which codified financial transaction bans and allowed civil suits over confiscated property. In both 1992 and 1996, President Clinton faced pressure from Republican rivals on Cuba policy, resulting in a tightening of sanctions despite earlier flirtations with incentives. However, following a papal visit to Havana in 1998, Clinton eased limits on humanitarian flights and remittances, and in January 1999, further relaxed sanctions after intelligence assessments concluded that Cuba posed no military threat to the United States.[5] By the end of the Clinton presidency, US Senators Tom Daschle and Byron Dorgan, along with the US Chamber of Commerce, visited Cuba to advocate for expanded trade. Nonetheless, pressure from Congress and Cuban-American interest groups constrained the extent of outreach.

2001–2008: President Bush entered office supporting the continuation of sanctions on Cuba but did not reverse the Clinton-era relaxations, which allowed for the import of medicine and, following the 2001 hurricane, some food. In 2002, Bush announced the Initiative for a New Cuba, which upheld economic sanctions and travel restrictions while expanding scholarships available for Cubans to study in the United States and enhancing Radio Martí's efforts.[6] By 2003, however, Bush moved to tighten the travel ban, rigorously enforce restrictions on cash transfers, intensify the US information campaign directed at Cuba, and establish the Commission for Assistance to a Free Cuba. The commission later concluded that regime change in Cuba was feasible. Following Fidel Castro's death in 2006, the largest Congressional delegation since 1959 visited Cuba, although they were denied a meeting with the new leader, Raul Castro. Raul subsequently indicated that he was open to improved relations but would only consider discussions after the US elections in 2008.[7]

2009–2016: In April 2009, President Obama lifted restrictions on family travel and remittances to Cuba. By the midpoint of his second term, his administration pursued more ambitious outreach, notably a 2014 prisoner exchange, swapping Alan Gross for three members of the so-called Havana Five.[8] In December of that year, Obama and Raul Castro announced a historic shift toward normalization. In early 2015, Obama further relaxed travel and trade restrictions, leading to a 36% increase in travel to Cuba by May 2015. Regular flight service between the US and Cuba resumed in February 2016, and in March, Obama became the first sitting US president to visit the island in eighty-eight years. US businesses also began operating in Cuba. While critics argued that this "normalization" involved unilateral concessions, supporters countered that the previous policy had failed to produce meaningful results.[9]

2017–2020: President Trump criticized the concessions, claiming they had benefited Cuba's repressive regime rather than the Cuban people, and reimposed some travel restrictions and bans on economic activity with military-controlled conglomerates. Following the emergence of "Havana syndrome"—suspected non-lethal electromagnetic attacks on US diplomats—Trump expelled several Cuban diplomats and reduced the US Embassy staff in Havana. National Security Advisor John Bolton labeled Cuba part of a "troika of tyranny," along with Venezuela and Nicaragua, and shortly thereafter Executive Order 13850 targeted Cuba-Venezuela trade. A series of new sanctions followed, restricting direct flights and tourism, and Cuba was reinstated on the list of State Sponsor of Terrorism (SST). These measures were met with opposition from Canada and the European Union.[10]

Panama

1989–1990: The Bush 41 administration increased pressure on Manuel Noriega to step down. Under the Reagan administration, a compromise had been sought in which Noriega would avoid prosecution, but Noriega rejected this offer.[11] After taking office, President Bush adopted a more assertive stance, publicly calling for Noriega to relinquish power in favor of the opposition. Despite this, prospects for military intervention were initially deemed low due to public and press opposition, as well as leaks from Pentagon officials.[12] In a major speech on May 11, 1989, President

Bush outlined various pathways for Noriega's removal. Admiral William Crowe, former Chairman of the Joint Chiefs of Staff, criticized Bush advisor Elliott Abrams as "reckless" for suggesting a military solution. Conversely, Senator Jesse Helms and other Congressional hawks derided Bush as "a wimp" and labeled his administration "Keystone cops" for not taking more decisive action. Congressional Democrats also criticized Bush as "timid" for not supporting a failed coup attempt against Noriega. Following escalatory behavior by Noriega supporters, including the declaration of a state of war and an attack on US forces that resulted in one death, President Bush ordered execution of Operation Just Cause, which ultimately led to the overthrow of the Noriega regime.[13]

Nicaragua

1989–1990: President Bush reversed eight years of Reagan's policy by seeking diplomatic solutions, rather than military force, to address the situation in Nicaragua. He halted lethal aid to the Contras and encouraged them to refrain from fighting. In response, Sandinista President Daniel Ortega declared an end to the ceasefire in October 1989.[14] This move unified Congress and President Bush in their support for renewed sanctions against the Sandinistas.[15] In January 1990, President Bush pointedly remarked that both Castro and Ortega should take heed of Operation Just Cause in Panama, stating that the "day of the dictator is over."[16] The cumulative impact of economic sanctions, diplomatic isolation, and the implied threat of military intervention significantly limited Ortega's options after the opposition's victory in the February 1990 elections, leading him to agree to transfer power to the opposition. Following this transition, US US aid flowed generously; between 1990 and 2006 the US forgave $390 million in debt, provided $175 million through the Millennium Challenge Account, and contributed additional aid in the tens of millions of dollars.[17]

2018–2020: Washington exerted significant pressure on President Ortega to end violent political repression in Nicaragua. Following the government's suppression of protests that began in April 2018, the US, the UN, and various human rights groups condemned the Nicaraguan government's actions. The US also called for free and fair elections. In November 2018, President Trump repeated the characterization of Nicaragua as part of a "troika of tyranny," alongside Cuba and Venezuela. Ortega rejected calls for early elections, originally scheduled for 2021, citing ongoing political unrest in July 2018. In response, President Trump issued EO 13851 in November 2018, which imposed property and visa blocking for the Nicaraguan vice president (Ortega's wife) and the national security advisor.[18] In December 2019, sanctions were extended to include Ortega's son, who was implicated in corrupt business dealings. The NICA Act, passed by Congress and signed into law by President Trump, further allowed for financial restrictions through multinational institutions. Meanwhile, in December 2018, the Nicaraguan parliament dissolved several NGOs accused of collaborating with the West to incite unrest between April and July, characterizing it as part of a "neo-imperialist coup attempt." Bolivia, Cuba, and Venezuela denounced what they perceived as US imperialism toward Nicaragua. Additional sanctions were imposed in early 2020 while Nicaragua and the other countries of the Bolivarian Alliance for the Americas (ALBA) deepened security and economic ties with Russia during this period.[19]

Haiti
1991–1994: On September 30, 1991, a coup overthrew President Jean-Bertrand Aristide, the first democratically elected president in Haitian history. The US, supported by several European and Latin American countries, pressured the junta, led by General Raoul Cédras, to relinquish power and restore Aristide to office. President Bush froze Haitian assets and supported mediation efforts by the OAS, though he opposed the use of military threats. Under the July 1993 Governor's Island Accord, the lifting of sanctions was made contingent on Aristide's return to power. However, as Cédras refused to step down, President Clinton spent much of 1994 escalating sanctions, enforcing an economic embargo and naval blockade, securing UN authorization for the use of force, and building

a diplomatic coalition in support of military action.[20] Clinton assembled an invasion force of approximately 20,000 troops, but former president Jimmy Carter brokered an agreement in which Cédras agreed to "retire." Cédras complied, leading to the lifting of sanctions in October 1994.[21]

Peru

1992–1993: In April 1992, following a series of major terrorist attacks, President Alberto Fujimori suspended Peru's constitution, marking a significant shift in the country's political trajectory. This decision came shortly after a tragic incident in which the Peruvian Air Force mistakenly shot down a US Air Force plane, resulting in the death of a US airman.[22] In response, the US suspended all military and development aid to Peru, maintaining only humanitarian assistance.[23] Furthermore, counter-narcotics cooperation was curtailed as US legislators emphasized the need to "hold Fujimori's feet to the fire" until constitutional order was restored.[24] While limited counter-drug collaboration resumed by June 1992, broader sanctions remained in place. Following an unsuccessful coup attempt by military officers, Fujimori organized congressional elections, which his party decisively won. His popularity surged with the capture of Abimael Guzman, the notorious leader of the Shining Path terrorist organization. In the years that followed, Fujimori solidified his grip on power, establishing what some have called an "authoritarian democracy," which persisted until his resignation in 2000.[25] US economic aid to Peru was reinstated in 1993, and further sanctions regarding compensation for the US airman's death were averted after successful negotiations, alongside the implementation of revised shoot-down precautions by the Peruvian Air Force.[26]

1995 (and Ecuador): The Clinton administration played a pivotal role in applying diplomatic pressure to end the border conflict between Peru and Ecuador during the Cenepa War of February 1995. The conflict arose over a poorly demarcated border area, where Ecuador established border posts in territories Peru claimed as sovereign. In response, President Clinton wrote to the leaders of both countries to cease hostilities. The

Rio Group, composed of the US, Argentina, Brazil, and Chile, worked out a proposal for a ceasefire, mutual withdrawal, demilitarization of the conflict zone, the deployment of multinational observers, and the establishment of a negotiating forum. As part of its efforts to de-escalate the conflict, the US suspended security assistance to both countries, with allied nations agreeing to take similar measures.[27] After several weeks of air and ground combat, during which Ecuador briefly seized and later lost control of the contested areas, the Montevideo Declaration was signed, bringing an end to the fighting and paving the way for arbitration.[28] By May 1995, the sanctions imposed during the conflict were lifted. In 1996 Secretary of State Warren Christopher highlighted the region's positive trajectory, attributing the peaceful resolution of the conflict to successful US intervention. By 1999, the two countries reached a formal agreement that established the Cordillera del Cóndor ridgeline as the official border. This agreement also included a ten-year border integration plan, with US troops and Rio Group observers continuing to monitor the border area to ensure lasting peace.[29]

Guatemala

1993–1996: In May 1993, Guatemalan President Jorge Serrano attempted an autogolpe, dissolving Congress, disregarding the judiciary, shutting down newspapers, and banning opposition political activity. This unprecedented move, aimed at consolidating his power over the very institutions he nominally led, sparked a severe political crisis. The following Monday, Serrano was ousted by a military coup and replaced on an interim basis by Vice President Gustavo Espina. However, Espina's tenure was short-lived, as he was swiftly repudiated by the Constitutional Court, which appointed Ramiro de León Carpio as the new president.[30] Throughout the summer of 1993, de León Carpio faced continuous challenges to his authority, with both Serrano and Espina making renewed attempts to reclaim power. This period was marked by significant violence between leftist and rightist factions, including the assassination of de León Carpio's brother. Despite the instability, elections were successfully held in November 1995, and relative political calm was restored by 1996. In response to Serrano's self-coup, the US suspended balance of payment support ($10.5 million) and development aid ($10 million), linking the restoration of assistance to the reestablishment of constitutional order. Furthermore, the US threatened to revoke Guatemala's preferential trade status if democratic norms were not restored. The European Community and Japan also suspended aid, while the OAS dispatched a fact-finding mission to assess the situation. Although US military aid had been partially reduced in 1990 following the murder of an American citizen, some forms of assistance continued. This included $113 million in International Military Education and Training (IMET) and other funding between 1993 and 1994). The Department of Defense (DoD) continued its engagement with the Guatemalan military, aiming to use its influence to promote stability within the country. However, by 1995, all military aid was discontinued in response to ongoing political and human rights concerns. While economic sanctions were lifted following the successful elections in 1996, no significant military aid was ever reinstated.[31]

2018–2019: President Trump threatened tariffs against Guatemala, which resulted in a two-year agreement to tighten immigration procedures within the country. The migration crisis came to the forefront in April 2018, when a caravan of migrants from the Northern Triangle headed toward the US border. In reaction, President Trump signaled a potential cessation of aid to these countries. Although the caravan eventually dispersed, Trump did not immediately follow through on his threat. However, by October 2018, Trump renewed his warning, citing lax border control. In March 2019, the administration formally notified Congress of its decision to suspend aid to Guatemala, Honduras, and El Salvador by reprogramming $450 million in funds earmarked for 2018.[32] This threat coincided with the signing of a Memorandum of Cooperation between the Department of Homeland Security (DHS) and the Northern Triangle countries. By July 2019, the US and Guatemala signed a key agreement, under which Salvadoran and Honduran migrants would remain in Guatemala while their asylum claims were processed. Only

Guatemalan and Mexican nationals would be permitted to proceed to Mexico for processing. The agreement had a two-year term and was subject to review every three months. Aid to the Northern Triangle was resumed in October 2019 after Guatemala, Honduras, and El Salvador each signed an Asylum Cooperation Agreement with the US. Guatemala demonstrated its commitment to the deal by halting a migrant caravan and pledging to collaborate regionally to reduce migration flows.[33]

Colombia

1996–1998: sanctions were imposed on Colombia in an effort to curb drug trafficking and address human rights abuses.[34] In early 1996, Washington decertified Colombia on counter-narcotics (CN) cooperation, impacting up to $1.5 billion in multilateral loans and its preferential trade status. This move came amid accusations that President Ernesto Samper had received campaign funding from drug cartels during his 1994 presidential bid, a charge from which Colombia's parliament eventually exonerated him. However, the US continued to support efforts to prosecute Samper. President Clinton emphasized that future bilateral relations would be evaluated solely on Colombia's CN cooperation, while the Department of State described that cooperation as being in a "sorry state." In the summer of 1996, the US further escalated pressure by suspending landing rights for Colombian airlines and threatening additional sanctions. President Samper's US visa was revoked, despite his attempts to initiate international dialogue on drug trafficking, including appeals to the United Nations (UN) and efforts to garner sympathy from France and Spain. Domestically, Samper's increasingly toxic reputation was effectively leveraged by the opposition Conservative Party in the 1998 elections, resulting in the defeat of Samper's Liberal Party and the election of President Andrés Pastrana. Under Pastrana's leadership, Colombia emerged as a key security partner of the United States. The two countries developed *Plan Colombia*, a $1 billion initiative with a 16-year timeline aimed at strengthening Colombia's CN efforts, enhancing military capabilities, and promoting development.[35] US government agencies played a critical role in helping

Pastrana's administration dismantle the Cali cartel, which led to the decentralization and reduction—though not the elimination—of drug production in Colombia.

Paraguay

1996: The US took action to deter a coup attempt.[36] In 1989, Paraguayan democrats, with support from the military led by General Andrés Rodríguez, overthrew long-time military dictator General Alfredo Stroessner. Subsequent elections brought civilian Juan Carlos Wasmosy to power as Paraguay's first civilian president. Over time, tensions between Wasmosy and Lino Oviedo, also a member of the ruling Colorado Party, escalated, with clashes over power and policy. By 1996 Wasmosy dismissed Oviedo, sparking a political crisis when Oviedo demanded the resignations of both Wasmosy and his vice president. Amidst rumors of a coup, the situation reached a breaking point in April 1996. The US, along with Argentina and Brazil, openly backed Wasmosy's government. Wasmosy was offered refuge at the US Embassy after Oviedo made veiled threats against the president. In a strategic maneuver, Wasmosy offered Oviedo the position of defense minister, on the condition that he resign from the military. Oviedo accepted and resigned, but Wasmosy then rescinded the offer, neutralizing Oviedo's threat. During this crisis, President Clinton personally called Wasmosy, expressing that the "entire hemisphere" supported his leadership. Clinton also ordered the brief suspension of US military assistance to Paraguay as a warning. The MERCOSUR regional group, including Brazil and Argentina, joined the US in backing Wasmosy and applied additional pressure on Oviedo, threatening Paraguay's expulsion from the bloc if Oviedo proceeded with the coup attempt. Facing mounting regional and international pressure, Oviedo eventually backed down. In 1998, Oviedo initially ran for president but was imprisoned and barred from running shortly before the election. His ally, Raúl Cubas Grau, ran in his place and defeated the opposition. Once in office, Cubas controversially pardoned Oviedo. Both

Oviedo and Cubas eventually fled Paraguay after the 1999 assassination of Vice President Luis María Argaña, further destabilizing the country.[37]

Ecuador

1999–2000: In 1999 President Jamil Mahuad's attempt to implement fiscal austerity measures and an International Monetary Fund (IMF) program sparked widespread protests, exacerbating an already severe economic crisis and leading to a partial debt default. By January 2000, protestors had besieged the capital, Quito, occupied Congress, and declared a People's Parliament. A junta composed of Indigenous leader Antonio Vargas, Colonel Lucio Gutiérrez, and former Supreme Court justice Carlos Solórzano sought to oust Mahuad, with Gutiérrez—a hero of the 1995 border war with Peru—playing a key role in the attempted coup. However, under significant pressure from the United States, General Carlos Mendoza withdrew his support for the junta, facilitating Vice President Gustavo Noboa's rise to the presidency. In the wake of the congressional occupation, the US State Department issued a stern warning to the putschists, cautioning that they could expect "political and economic isolation carrying with them even worse misery for the Ecuadorean people." Simultaneously, at an emergency meeting in Washington, the OAS passed a resolution condemning the coup. Following the ascension of President Noboa, the State Department described the transfer of power as "irregular" but expressed support for the new president.[38] By 2001, US military and economic programs to Ecuador resumed. However, in 2002, Noboa was voted out of office and replaced by the retired Colonel Gutiérrez, marking a shift in the Ecuadorean electorate toward leftist populism.[39]

Guyana

2001: In the wake of the *Zadvydas v. Davis* decision by the US Supreme Court, which required the US government to deport foreign criminals within six months of sentencing or release them, the Executive Branch faced heightened pressure to ensure foreign governments would accept their deported nationals and provide necessary travel documents. Guyana became the first case where diplomatic sanctions were applied to compel compliance. The Department of State, on behalf of the Department of Justice, employed several diplomatic strategies to secure documentation and repatriation for 113 criminally convicted Guyanese nationals. These efforts included issuing formal demarches, summoning the Guyanese ambassador, threatening visa bans, and publicly discussing potential economic sanctions through interagency consultations. Ultimately, visa sanctions were imposed on certain Guyanese officials under Section 243(d) of the Immigration and Nationality Act. Within two months, Guyana complied by issuing travel documents for 112 of the 113 deportees.[40] Such sanctions would not be used again until 2016.

Argentina
2012–2016: US hedge funds, with support from the courts, denied Argentina access to bond markets until they agreed to pay old debts, a victory that came after a protracted 15-year legal battle. Following Argentina's 2001 default, the Kirchner governments, led by Néstor and later Cristina, adopted a populist economic agenda that initially achieved growth but soon led to rising debt, inflation, and deficit spending. This economic approach resulted in price controls, followed by capital controls. Argentina offered foreign bondholders a debt restructuring deal with modest returns, which a majority of the creditors accepted ("hold-ins") but a small number of hedge funds ("vulture" funds or "hold-outs") rejected. The hold-outs' persistence was exemplified by their success in convincing Ghanaian authorities to seize an Argentinian naval training vessel as collateral for unpaid Argentine state debt. Despite Argentina's efforts to resolve the issue, the US courts maintained pressure. In 2014, the US Supreme Court rejected Argentina's appeal to overturn a Southern District of New York (SDNY) ruling, which contributed to the country's default later that year. The SDNY had ruled that Argentina could not repay the hold-in creditors without also settling with the hold-outs, forcing the country into default on $29 billion of debt in 2014. The situation

shifted with the election of Mauricio Macri in 2015, who moved quickly to resolve the long-standing debt dispute. In 2016, Argentina reached a settlement with the hold-out creditors, allowing those hedge funds to turn a solid profit.[41] Throughout this legal battle, the "comity principle" could have been invoked by President Obama to request that the SDNY defer to broader US national security and foreign policy interests, as President George W. Bush had done in similar cases. However, while Obama administration officials were critical of the vulture funds and expressed sympathy for Argentina's situation, President Obama ultimately chose not to invoke comity, allowing the court rulings to stand.[42]

Venezuela

2014–2020: Obama intensified pressure on President Nicolás Maduro, a strategy further escalated under Trump.[43] Opposition protests in February 2014 led to a violent crackdown that killed 43 during the year. In response, Congress passed the Venezuela Defense of Human Rights and Civil Society Act, which mandated asset freezes and travel bans for designated individuals. In March 2015, Obama sanctioned seven Venezuelan government officials. The Maduro-controlled Supreme Tribunal of Justice subsequently seized legislative powers, an action widely condemned by both the US and the OAS. Although these powers were briefly restored, Maduro convened a pro-government National Constituent Assembly in the summer of 2017, effectively displacing the opposition-controlled National Assembly. The European Union (EU) imposed a military embargo later that year. Trump heightened sanctions through a series of executive orders targeting financial transactions (August 2017), digital and cryptocurrency transactions (March 2018), debt and equity transactions (May 2018), gold transactions (November 2018), and dealings with government entities (January 2019), culminating in broader property-blocking measures (August 2019), all in support of interim President Juan Guaidó. Following Maduro's widely disputed re-election in 2018, Switzerland, Canada, and the EU imposed additional sanctions. Despite efforts by military and intelligence personnel inspired by Guaidó and backed by the US, attempts to dislodge Maduro in 2019 were unsuccessful. Maduro retained support from key international allies, including Russia, China, Cuba, and Iran, which continued to engage in trade and diplomatic relations. The Rio Group of Western Hemisphere countries aligned with Washington's sanctions but ruled out military intervention, despite speculation that Trump was considering such action to support Guaidó. The US condemned Venezuela's fraudulent parliamentary elections in late 2020 and continued to recognize Guaidó and the National Assembly as the country's legitimate authorities. This analysis also situates Trump's travel ban under Executive Order 13780 within this broader geopolitical context.

Mexico
2017–2019: Trump exerted tariff pressure in a broader dispute over trade and immigration controls.[44] Shortly after taking office, Trump criticized Mexican president Enrique Peña Nieto for the US-Mexico trade imbalance and border security, threatening a 20% additional tax on Mexican goods sold in the US (ostensibly to fund a border wall). In early 2018 he threatened to deploy National Guard troops to the border and to withdraw from the North American Free Trade Agreement (NAFTA); Peña Nieto said he was willing to work with Trump on such matters, but would not allow attacks on Mexico's dignity. In October 2018 Trump again threatened to send the military to the US-Mexico border. Following Peña Nieto's replacement in December 2018 by President Andrés Manuel López Obrador ("AMLO"), Trump again threatened a 5% tariff on Mexican goods unless Mexico took stronger measures to address irregular migrant flows. Trump suggested that this issue could derail ongoing negotiations to replace NAFTA with the US-Mexico-Canada Agreement (USMCA). In June 2019 Trump and AMLO reached an agreement to implement the "Remain in Mexico" policy, which aimed to reduce migrant flows from Central America. As a result, Trump rescinded the tariff threat. Mexico responded by bolstering its immigration enforcement efforts, hiring additional officers, increasing checkpoints, conducting more frequent

raids, and deploying military forces to assist with border enforcement. These measures led to an increase in apprehensions and deportations.[45] The "Remain in Mexico" policy remained in effect until it was suspended by President Biden in 2021. AMLO and Trump met in Washington in July 2020, reflecting continued dialogue between the two leaders despite earlier tensions.

Canada

2017–2019: Pressure on Canada over the USMCA deal to replace NAFTA intensified as negotiations unfolded. In May 2017, the US Trade Representative (USTR) formally notified Congress of the intent to renegotiate NAFTA, with talks scheduled to begin 90 days later. Negotiations between the US, Mexico, and Canada commenced in August 2017, culminating in the signing of the USMCA on November 30, 2018. However, before the trilateral agreement was finalized, the US and Mexico reached a bilateral agreement on August 27, 2018, leaving Canada under pressure to finalize its position. USTR Robert Lighthizer criticized Canada for filing World Trade Organization (WTO) complaints and offering a vague response to proposals regarding automobile content. In response, President Trump threatened to exclude Canada from the deal entirely and impose 5% tariffs on Canadian-manufactured cars sold in the US if Canada failed to align with the agreement.[46] Despite the heightened tensions, all three countries signed the agreement at the end of November 2018. Legal changes and the necessary implementing regulations were approved the following year, and in January 2020, the USMCA was signed into law. The agreement officially entered into force on July 1, 2020.[47]

EXPERT AND PRACTITIONER COMMENTS

Several senior retired US officials have cautioned against viewing 1990s-era coercive campaigns in Latin America as representative of broader US CD operations globally, or as ultimately successful. One retired US ambassador, who served multiple tours in Latin America and held senior national policy positions argued that

> ...especially in the post-9/11 period, the US used it [CD] far too frequently, and without clearly distinguishing the benefits of doing so and the benefits of each case. Too often applied with minimal benefits, though sometimes with existential stakes (North Korea, Iran, Iraq). At least you could argue in those cases that it required more than normal diplomacy. But when we started threatening over economic questions, or conditionalities on assistance that the target couldn't immediately bring change on, we weren't very good at assessing costs and benefits. This stems from a view born of our success in post-1989 world at democratizing Eastern Europe, Latin America, promoting global economic development, countering aggression in the Balkans, with the US in each case functioning as the indispensable nation. We were so powerful during the unipolar moment that it seemed the US had an obligation and interest to right things that were wrong. After 9/11 it became clear that we had spread ourselves too thin, and did not distinguish what was more and less important.[48]

Focusing on Venezuela, the ambassador added:

> In the case of Venezuela there were thoughts Maduro's support would crumble when 50 countries recognized the opposition government. Stakes were very high for Maduro. Yet Maduro is now stronger than he was when we started sanctions. I would suggest anticipating likely target response needs room for improvement. I am not questioning why CD was brought to bear—there were and are strong strategic reasons. But the executors must account for the domestic and regional environment and possible responses by the target and third parties.

A senior US military officer, who served as a military advisor and staff officer focused on Latin America during this period, described serious flaws in the communication process between policy shapers in Washington, those responsible for policy implementation, and decision-makers in the target countries:

Sanctions eventually gain a life of their own. The people executing them forget why they were put in place to begin with. Some do not understand our objectives (since they are usually not well defined) so there is no way to achieve them (if you don't know where you are going any road will get you there). Others don't care if we have achieved our objectives. Still others have an ideologically driven dislike for the target. I worked one country that was trying to get out from under sanctions. Their attaché asked me how to get off the 'bad boy' list. I asked my Department of State counterpart how they could get off the list. He literally said "they know". I pointed out that they would not have asked me how to get off the list if they knew. His only reply was still "they know" and he refused to tell me. He wasn't interested in them reforming, he just wanted to punish them.[49]

REGIONAL SUMMARY

While US CD in the Western Hemisphere was comparatively successful (at least in immediate and tactical terms), the region as a whole did not develop into the prosperous, democratic, and US-friendly region envisioned in the early post–Cold War years.[50] Instead, with the notable exception of Canada, many countries in the region remained cautious, tentative, and skeptical of US intentions. A number of countries hedged their bets by aligning with extra-regional powers.[51] Notably, an anti-US regional organization, the previously mentioned ALBA, emerged during this period as a response to perceived US imperialism.[52]

More concerning, perhaps, was the growing military cooperation between ALBA states and open adversaries of Washington—namely Russia, China, and Iran—during this period. While none posed a direct threat to US military supremacy in the region, such partnerships would have been unthinkable just a few years prior. However, there were also notable successes in US coercive diplomacy in the Western Hemisphere. The US was able to gain traction by securing robust multilateral support in several instances, working closely with regional organizations such as the OAS, MERCOSUR, or looser groupings of like-minded partners.

Effective policymaking hinges on asking the right questions. Washington could benefit from not only assessing whether a particular coercive episode achieved the desired or acceptable outcome, but also considering whether, over time, US statecraft in the region has improved or deteriorated in advancing national interests. In the case of Latin America and the Western Hemisphere more broadly, the answer remains far from clear-cut.

NOTES

1. See https://www.cambriapress.com/USCoerciveDiplomacy.
2. "MERCOSUR in Brief," *Mercosur.int*, https://www.mercosur.int/en/about-mercosur/mercosur-in-brief/.
3. Jacob Kushner, "Haiti and the Failed Promise of US Aid," *The Guardian* (UK), October 11, 2019, https://www.theguardian.com/world/2019/oct/11/haiti-and-the-failed-promise-of-us-aid.
4. United States Congress, *Cuban Democracy Act of 1992*, US Code Title 22, Chapter 69, October 23, 1992, https://uscode.house.gov/view.xhtml?path=/prelim@title22/chapter69&edition=prelim.
5. Maureen Taft-Morales and Mark Sullivan, *Cuba: Issues and Legislation in the 106th Congress*, Congressional Research Service, January 11, 2001, https://digital.library.unt.edu/ark:/67531/metacrs1786/.
6. Office of the Press Secretary, "President Bush Announces Initiative for a New Cuba" (fact sheet), The White House, May 20, 2002, https://georgewbush-whitehouse.archives.gov/news/releases/2002/05/2002052 0-1.html.
7. Mark Sullivan, *Cuba's Future Political Scenarios and US Policy Approaches*, Congressional Research Service CRS Report RL33622, September 3, 2006, https://crsreports.congress.gov/product/pdf/RL/RL33622.
8. Rachaell Davis, "13 Ways President Obama Historically Improved US Relations With Cuba," *Essence*, October 26, 2020, https://www.essence.com/news/ways-president-obama-improved-us-cuba-relations/.
9. Elliot Abrams, "Time to Tighten the Screws on Cuba?" *Expert Brief*, Council on Foreign Relations, April 2, 2018, https://www.cfr.org/expert-brief/time-tighten-screws-cuba.
10. Matthew Lee and Joshua Goodman, "Trump hits Cuba with new sanctions in waning days," PBS Newshour Politics, January 11, 2020, https://www.pbs.org/newshour/politics/trump-hits-cuba-with-new-terrorism-sanctions-in-waning-days.
11. Nathaniel Sheppard, "US Deal With Noriega Crumbles," *Chicago Tribune*, May 26, 1988, www.chicagotribune.com/news/ct-xpm-1988-05-26-8801020420-story.html.
12. John Broder, "Step Down, Bush Urges Noriega : Tells Panama's Ruler to 'Heed Call of People,'" *Los Angeles Times*, May 10, 1989, www.latimes.com/archives/la-xpm-1989-05-10-mn-2777-story.html.

13. Eytan Gilboa, "The Panama Invasion Revisited: Lessons for the Use of Force in the Post-Cold War Era," *Political Science Quarterly* 110, no. 4 (1995–1996): 539–562.

14. Ann Devroy and Lee Hockstader, "Bush Assails Ortega for Cease-fire Stand," *Washington Post*, October 29, 1989, https://www.washingtonpost.com/archive/politics/1989/10/29/bush-assails-ortega-for-cease-fire-stand/db136618-dfc6-4274-a3cd-dde6393fd64c/.

15. Robert Pear, "Anger With Ortega Unites Policy Makers in U.S.," *New York Times*, November 2, 1989, https://www.nytimes.com/1989/11/02/world/anger-with-ortega-unites-policy-makers-in-us.html.

16. Lori Santos, "Bush Warns Castro, Ortega to Note Democratic Changes," United Press International, January 20, 1990, https://www.upi.com/Archives/1990/01/20/Bush-warns-Castro-Ortega-to-note-democratic-changes/9475632811600/.

17. Maureen Taft-Morales, *Nicaragua: The Election of Daniel Ortega and Issues in US Relations,* Congressional Research Service (CRS) RL33983, April 19, 2007, https://crsreports.congress.gov/product/pdf/RL/RL33983/4.

18. Elisabeth Malkin, "Raising Pressure on Nicaragua, US Imposes Sanctions on Vice President," *New York Times,* November 27, 2018, https://www.nytimes.com/2018/11/27/world/americas/nicaragua-us-sanctions.html.

19. Ivelisse Gonzalez, *An Assessment of Russia's Military Presence in Latin America,* Foreign Policy Research Institute, June 18, 2019, https://www.fpri.org/article/2019/06/an-assessment-of-russias-military-presence-in-latin-america/.

20. Ann Devroy and John Harris, "Leave Now, Clinton Tells Haitian Rulers," *Washington Post*, September 16, 1994, https://www.washingtonpost.com/archive/politics/1994/09/16/leave-now-clinton-tells-haitian-rulers/e9428202-e323-4f3d-b9e9-54bbb707f2de/.

21. Office of the Historian "Intervention in Haiti 1994–1995," *Milestones in the History of US Foreign Relations,* US Department of State, May 9, 2017, https://history.state.gov/milestones/1993-2000/haiti.

22. "Peru Suspends Democracy, Citing Revolt," *New York Times,* April 7, 1992, https://www.nytimes.com/1992/04/07/world/peru-suspends-democracy-citing-revolt.html.

23. Barbara Crossette, "U.S., Condemning Fujimori, Cuts Aid to Peru," *New York Times,* April 7, 1992 https://www.nytimes.com/1992/04/07/world/us-condemning-fujimori-cuts-aid-to-peru.html.

24. House Foreign Affairs Committee (HFAC) *Situation in Peru and the Drug War* (Hearing of the Western Hemisphere Affairs Subcommittee), Federal News Service, May 7, 1992.

25. James Brooke, "Peru's Leader Clears a Path With Sharp Elbows," *New York Times*, February 22, 1993, https://www.nytimes.com/1993/02/22/world/peru-s-leader-clears-a-path-with-sharp-elbows.html.

26. Thomas Lippman, "Peru Pays Compensation for Attack on US Plane," *Washington Post*, December 10, 1993, https://www.washingtonpost.com/archive/politics/1993/12/10/peru-pays-compensation-for-attack-on-us-plane/2854811e-29e0-417c-924e-2f3f08b3d941/.

27. Sid Balman, "US Penalizes Peru, Ecuador," United Press International, February 10, 1995, https://www.upi.com/Archives/1995/02/10/US-penalizes-Peru-Ecuador/3306792392400/.

28. Montevideo Declaration, United Nations Digital Library, May 19, 1995, https://digitallibrary.un.org/record/204962?ln=en.

29. Anthony Faiola, "Peru, Ecuador Sign Pact Ending Border Dispute," *Washington Post,* October 27, 1998, https://www.washingtonpost.com/archive/politics/1998/10/27/peru-ecuador-sign-pact-ending-border-dispute/8e129a82-06a2-4034-9890-d41678accca5/.

30. Tim Golden, "Guatemala's Counter-Coup: A Military About-Face," *New York Times*, June 3, 1993, https://www.nytimes.com/1993/06/03/world/guatemala-s-counter-coup-a-military-about-face.html.

31. Meri Khananashvili, "Carpio Nicolle et al. v. Guatemala" (Case Abstract), *Loyola of Los Angeles International and Comparative Law Review* 36 (2014): 1741, https://iachr.lls.edu/sites/default/files/iachr/Cases/Carpio_Nicolle_et_al_v_Guatemala/Carpio%20Nicolle%20et%20al.%20v.%20Guatemala.pdf.

32. Tim McDonnell, "Trump Froze Aid to Guatemala. Now Programs are Shutting Down," *Goats and Soda*, NPR, September 17, 2019 https://www.npr.org/sections/goatsandsoda/2019/09/17/761266169/trump-froze-aid-to-guatemala-now-programs-are-shutting-down.

33. "Guatemala Signs Immigration Deal with US After Trump Threats," British Broadcasting Corporation (BBC), July 27, 2019, https://www.bbc.com/news/world-latin-america-49134544.

34. Russell Crandall, "Explicit Narcotization" US Policy toward Colombia During the Samper Administration," *Latin American Politics and Society* 43, no. 3 (Autumn 2001): 95–120, https://www.jstor.org/stable/3177145.

35. Michael Shifter, "Plan Colombia: A Retrospective," *Americas Quarterly*, July 18, 2012, https://www.americasquarterly.org/fulltextarticle/plan-colombia-a-retrospective/.
36. Robert Service, "Forestalling a Democracy Crisis in Paraguay," *The Foreign Service Journal*, American Foreign Service Association, November 2021, https://afsa.org/forestalling-democracy-crisis-paraguay.
37. Alex Bellow, "Paraguayan Fugitive Held for Political Murder," *The Guardian* (UK), June 12, 2000, https://www.theguardian.com/world/20 00/jun/13/alexbellos.
38. Stephen Buckley, "Civilian Rule is Restored in Ecuador," *Washington Post*, January 23, 2000, https://www.washingtonpost.com/archive/politics/2 000/01/23/civilian-rule-is-restored-in-ecuador/b75af2e0-1569-4db2-9f23 -1e7f49bced34/.
39. Duncan Campbell, "A Continent on the Edge of a Volcano," *The Guardian* (UK), November 27, 2002, https://www.theguardian.com/world/2002/ nov/28/brazil.argentina.
40. Jill Wilson, *Immigration: 'Recalcitrant' Countries and the Use of Visa Sanctions to Encourage Cooperation with Alien Removals*, CRS In Focus, Congressional Research Service, July 10, 2020, https://crsreports.congress. gov/product/pdf/IF/IF11025.
41. Alexandra Stevenson, "How Argentina Settled a Billion-Dollar Debt Dispute With Hedge Funds," *New York Times*, April 25, 2016, https://www. nytimes.com/2016/04/25/business/dealbook/how-argentina-settled-a-billion-dollar-debt-dispute-with-hedge-funds.html.
42. Andreas Kanaris Miyashiro, *Argentina vs. the Hedge Funds: the 2014 Argentinian Bond Default*, Seven Pillars Institute of Global Finance and Ethics, August 2, 2017, https://sevenpillarsinstitute.org/argentina-vs-hedge-funds-2014-argentinian-bond-default/.
43. Clare Ribando, Seelke, *Venezuela: Political Crisis and US Policy*, In Focus (IF) 10320, Congressional Research Service (CRS), Washington, DC.
44. Geoffrey Gertz, "Did Trump's Tariffs Benefit American Workers and National Security?" *Brookings Commentary*, Brookings, September 10, 2020 https://www.brookings.edu/policy2020/votervital/did-trumps-tariffs-benefit-american-workers-and-national-security/.
45. Todd Bensman, "Trump's 'Remain in Mexico' Policy Appears to be Working," Center for Immigration Studies, July 22, 2019, https://cis.org/ Bensman/Trumps-Remain-Mexico-Policy-Appears-Be-Working.

46. Doug Palmer and Adam Behsudi, "Trump's Trade Chief Clashes with Canada, Mexico in NAFTA Talks, *Politico*, January 29, 2018, https://www.politico.com/story/2018/01/29/trump-nafta-mexico-canada-374836.

47. M. Angeles Villareal, *The United States Mexico Canada Agreement (USMCA)*, CRS Report R44981, September 29, 2023, Congressional Research Service (CRS), https://crsreports.congress.gov/product/pdf/R/R44981/23.

48. Author interview, August 25, 2022.

49. Author interview, September 4, 2022.

50. P. Michael McKinley, *Inflection Point: The Challenges Facing Latin America and US Policy in the Region*, Center for Strategic and International Studies (CSIS), September 7, 2023, https://www.csis.org/analysis/inflection-point-challenges-facing-latin-america-and-us-policy-region.

51. Moises Rendon, and Claudia Fernandez, "The Fabulous Five: How Foreign Actors Prop up the Maduro Regime in Venezuela," CSIS Briefs, Center for Strategic and International Studies (CSIS), October 19, 2020, https://www.csis.org/analysis/fabulous-five-how-foreign-actors-prop-maduro-regime-venezuela.

52. Luis Suarez Salazar, "Cuba's Foreign Policy and the Promise of ALBA," NACLA, September 25, 2007, https://nacla.org/article/cuba's-foreign-policy-and-promise-alba.

Chapter 5

Process Over Progress: US Coercive Diplomacy in the Middle East and Central Asia

US CD in the Middle East and Central Asia achieved limited success in eliciting compliance or alternative concessions from target countries, with only 14% (3 out of 22) of cases registering a positive outcome by either measure. This tied for the lowest success rate among the five regions analyzed in the study, alongside South and East Asia. Conversely, the region recorded a high rate of long-term degradation in bilateral relations or a perceived decline in US regional standing, with 82% (18 out of 22 cases) falling into this category—the second-highest among the regions. Additionally, CD in this region led to outright war at the second-highest regional rate, occurring in 14% of cases (3 out of 22). Despite these mixed results, the application of CD remained popular domestically, with 82% of cases associated with significant political satisfaction within the US. Another distinguishing feature of US CD in the Middle East and Central Asia was the prevalence of long-running, multi-episode coercive engagements. Six countries were targeted iteratively, in contrast to only four that experienced "one-and-done" episodes of coercion.

The following summary illustrates how three decades of US coercion played out across this subset of cases. Coercive performance scores range from 0 to 4, framing performance 0–1, compliance and other outcome variables (alternative concession or AC, trajectory or T, and domestic satisfaction or DS) 0–1. Detailed episode scoring procedures and results are available in Appendix 1 online.

The data indicate that overall coercive performance and framing efforts were both weaker in the Middle East and Central Asia compared to other regions, such as the Western Hemisphere. Strikingly, the rate of compliance achieved in the Middle East and Central Asia was an order of magnitude lower than that in the Western Hemisphere, demonstrating that the US did not obtain anything close to the results it demanded or expected from targets in these regions. While alternative concessions and domestic political satisfaction were comparable between the two regions, the post-coercion trajectory was significantly worse in the Middle East and Central Asia. In this context, coercive efforts appear to have been far more damaging to the long-term standing of the US in the Middle East and Central Asia than in the Western Hemisphere.

COERCIVE DYADS

Iraq

1990–1991: The Bush 41 administration sought to deter Iraqi forces from attacking Kuwait and later to compel their withdrawal. Critics accused President Bush of appearing indecisive before Saddam Hussein's invasion in August 1990, citing the ambiguous message by his ambassador in Baghdad regarding a potential American response to an Iraqi attack on Kuwait, as well as a Congressional delegation led by Senator Bob Dole, which expressed sympathy for Iraq's grievances with Kuwait.[1] Following the invasion, the United States responded by imposing sanctions on Iraq and securing a series of United Nations Security Council Resolutions (UNSCRs) that condemned the invasion and demanded the withdrawal of Iraqi forces. Notably, UNSCR 678 authorized the use of force to expel Iraqi forces from Kuwait. President Bush publicly stated that Iraqi withdrawal would be sufficient to avoid war, yet also characterized Saddam Hussein as a "new Hitler," signaling a more aggressive posture. Meanwhile, Vice President Dan Quayle suggested that Iraq's military strength could not remain intact even if Kuwait were liberated. Despite Bush's continued messaging to Saddam and the international community throughout late 1990 that he wished to avoid war, these efforts failed to persuade Saddam to withdraw.[2] By January 1991, Congress authorized the use of military force, and Operation Desert Storm was launched shortly thereafter.

1991–1992: Following the conclusion of major combat operations, the Bush administration called on the Iraqi Army and people to overthrow Saddam Hussein. Iraq had accepted UNSCR 687 as the basis for the ceasefire, which included provisions for disclosure of WMD programs, reparations to Kuwait, and a commitment to cease supporting terrorism.[3] However, the Bush administration ruled out combat operations to support anti-Saddam uprisings that emerged in Iraq, though it did deploy troops to protect the Kurds in northern Iraq and issued warnings to Saddam not to attack them. Recognizing the limited nature of American and international support for these uprisings, Saddam crushed the uprisings, restricted the activities of UN weapons inspectors, and began to mobilize both domestic and international resistance to the sanction regime.[4]

1993–1996: By 1993, the nature of the coercive struggle between the US and Iraq openly shifted from forcing compliance with ceasefire terms to a strategy aimed at isolating and crippling Saddam's regime. The US and its coalition partners employed limited military strikes to enforce no-fly zones in northern and southern Iraq, while regional deployments were used to deter new ground offensives by the Iraqi military.[5] Opposition to sanctions grew in the Arab world, and Saddam gradually reasserted control over most of Iraq, including a successful intervention to quell intra-Kurd fighting in the north in 1996.[6] In late 1994, under renewed US military pressure, Baghdad signaled readiness to address Western concerns by recognizing Kuwaiti borders; however, the regime did not receive the sanctions relief it had anticipated from this move.[7]

1997–2000: Saddam grew increasingly bold in his resistance to both sanctions and the no-fly zones, while European allies of the United States became more vocal in their opposition to military action against Iraq. The US shifted further from a focus on isolating and weakening Saddam to explicitly supporting regime change through the Iraq Liberation Act of 1998, though containment, rather than overthrow, remained the official policy.[8] The period is often characterized as a gradually escalating contest, in which Saddam sought to expand his room for maneuver while undermining allied support for intensified US coercion.[9] Russia, China, and France increasingly opposed US coercive efforts during this period.[10]

2001–2003: President Bush introduced the "Axis of Evil" concept during his 2002 State of the Union address,[11] reflecting the elite consensus after 9/11 that war with Iraq was a matter of when, not if. As President Bush increasingly advocated for the use of force against Iraq, he framed the issue as a fundamental choice: either Iraq would accept broad compliance with international limitations and inspectors, or the US would act to remove the regime. US pressure led to the re-admission of international inspectors to Iraq, but the administration demanded further that Saddam provide evidence of voluntary disarmament. The US laid out the case for war at the UN, but given opposition from France, Russia, and Germany, it also prepared to initiate unilateral military operations.[12] In the fall of 2002, Saddam showed some interest in meeting US demands to preserve his regime, but Washington did not view these signals as credible.[13] This coercive episode culminated in the launch of Operation Iraqi Freedom.

2007–2009: The shift in approach to Iraq during President Bush's second term, commonly known as the "surge," can be seen both as a military strategic adjustment and as a new coercive episode aimed at pressuring Shia and Sunni oppositionists within Iraq to align with the US-backed government. Between January and June 2007, Bush announced the deployment of 20,000 more troops to support General David Petraeus's strategy, particularly through the Sons of Iraq, or Sunni Awakening, initiative. Nouri al-Maliki, who became prime minister in 2006, facilitated a meeting between US ambassador Ryan Crocker and Iranian officials in Baghdad—the first such meeting since the Iranian Revolution. At the time, Iran had been steadily arming Shia militias with explosively formed projectiles (EFPs) for use against US forces. Bush EO 13538 in July 2007 targeted individuals aiding insurgents in Iraq. In November 2007, a Bush-Maliki statement of principles outlined a shared vision for strengthening Iraqi sovereignty.[14] The March 2008 Operation Charge of the Knights under Maliki's supervision ended the control of Shia militant groups, particularly the Mahdi Army, in southern Iraq. Bush and Maliki also established a general timeline for Iraqi Security Forces (ISF) to assume the lead, facilitating the eventual withdrawal of US forces. By the time of Petraeus' departure, both Shia Sadrists and Sunni insurgents had been significantly weakened. In late 2008, Maliki and Bush signed a Status of Forces Agreement (SOFA) and Strategic Framework Agreement (SFA), which structured US-Iraqi relations through 2011.[15] With the electoral victory of pro-drawdown Obama over the pro-surge John McCain, US efforts moved from coercing opposition and institution-building to ensuring access for limited counterterrorism operations.

Iran
1992–2000: Clinton-era sanctions constituted the first of several coercive episodes with Iran during the period under study; it stands out as the most consistently coerced target through sanctions and other tools across the study's thirty-year timeframe.[16] While the Bush (41) administration had pursued informal contacts with Tehran to explore the possibility of rapprochement, the Clinton administration's 1992 policy review reaffirmed a coercive response to Iran's nuclear ambitions, regional aggression, and human rights violations. This approach was formalized under the "dual containment" strategy, as reflected in the

Iran-Iraq Nonproliferation Act of 1992.[17] In the spring of 1994, President Clinton permitted Iranian weapons to reach Bosnia via Croatia which may have contributed to the diplomatic opening at Dayton.[18] In his second term, Clinton again sought to engage Tehran, notably by designating the anti-regime group Mujahideen-e Khalq (MeK) as a terrorist organization and removing Iran from the list of illegal drug-producing states.[19] There was also an exchange of letters between Presidents Clinton and Mohammad Khatami, alongside several sympathetic public statements by administration officials about Iran. However, no concessions were made—neither by Washington on sanctions nor by Iran on issues related to its nuclear program, regional conflicts, and human rights record.

2001–2008: President George W. Bush maintained pressure on Iran over its nuclear program and regional aggression. Citing Iran's accelerated nuclear developmental efforts, President Bush in his January 29, 2002, State of the Union address, labeled Iran as part of the "axis of evil" alongside Iraq and North Korea. US and European suspicions were heightened in December 2002 when news broke of two new facilities at Arak and Natanz that were potentially capable of producing weapons-grade fissile materials.[20] In September 2003, the International Atomic Energy Agency (IAEA) Board of Governors issued a statement giving Iran until the end of October 2003 to provide additional information to disprove its involvement in nuclear weapons development. After a visit to Tehran by the foreign ministers of Germany, the United Kingdom, and France, the three countries issued a joint statement with Iran pledging full IAEA disclosure, suspension of enrichment, and approval of additional protocols in exchange for the provision of peaceful nuclear technology. On May 6, 2004, the US Congress passed a resolution with overwhelming support, calling for all parties to the Non-Proliferation Treaty to use "all appropriate means to deter, dissuade, and prevent Iran from acquiring nuclear weapons, including ending all nuclear and other cooperation with Iran."[21] The Bush administration agreed to join talks on a potential compromise (P5+1) in 2006, but Iran did not accept the proffered deal. UNSCR 1696 applied the first Chapter VII UN sanctions, yet Iran expanded enrichment in response. In turn, Bush added oil and gas sanctions and signed the Iran Freedom Support Act of 2006. Iran reportedly viewed the Second Lebanon War as weakening Western threats since Israel, with Western support, failed to dislodge Hezbollah forces out of southern Lebanon. Amid fears that Bush might order military strikes against Iran, the UNSC issued UNSCR 1747 in early 2007. Iran inferred that time was not on its side and sought to quickly demonstrate mastery of the nuclear fuel cycle to avoid more intense coercion. A late 2007 National Intelligence Estimate concluded that Iran had stopped nuclear weapons development in 2003 but could restart at any time. Although Iran maintained a degree of cooperation with the IAEA, more sanctions were applied under UNSCR 1803.[22] Convinced that the pressure was aimed at regime change rather than preventing nuclear weapons, Iran ceased cooperation with the IAEA in March 2008.

2009–2016: The Obama-era coercive approach to Iran softened considerably. In March 2009, President Obama initiated an exchange of holiday messages with Tehran for Nowruz, expressing that change in the relationship was possible; Iranian leader Ali Khamenei made public statements inviting Washington to make the first move if the intent was sincere.[23] In June 2009, Mahmoud Ahmadinejad defeated Mir-Hossein Mousavi in the presidential election, and the Green Movement—composed largely of Tehran-based urban youth protestors—emerged, only to be violently suppressed. Western capitals publicly endorsed the protests but offering no tangible support. In October 2009, Tehran rejected a proposal to exchange 1,200 kg of 3% low-enriched uranium (LEU) for 120 kg of 20% LEU fit for medical purposes, citing a need for further assurances. The West pressed Iran to shutter its Tehran Research Reactor (TRR); in response, Tehran demonstrated its ability to enrich uranium to 20% in February 2010. In April 2010, President Obama sent a letter through the presidents of Brazil and Turkey, recommending that Iran "escrow" the 1,200 kg of LEU until the 120 kg for exchange was prepared. As a result, Brazil, Turkey, and Iran signed the Tehran Declaration of May 17, 2010, meeting all Obama conditions.[24] The next day Secretary Hillary Clinton called on the Senate Foreign Relations Committee (SFRC) to impose more sanctions as a response to the deal —apparently unaware that it had been coordinated at President Obama's behest. IAEA director general Mohamed ElBaradei characterized this as "the United States refusing to take yes for an answer."[25] Congress directed a renewed tightening of sanctions, and from late 2010 onward Israel ramped up cyberattacks and assassinations targeting Iran's nuclear program.[26] In 2011 and 2012, additional executive orders were issued: EO 13590, targeting the petrochemical and energy sectors, and EO 13599, freezing the assets of Iranian financial institution). Meanwhile, P5+1 talks continued during this period. The 2012 National Defense Authorization Act (NDAA) Section 1245 imposed secondary sanctions on third-country banks dealing with the Central Bank of Iran; the scope of these sanctions was later widened through EO 13590 and the Iran Threat Reduction and Syria Human Rights Act. From 2013, President Rouhani appointed Jawad Zarif to lead negotiations with the P5+1, which ultimately resulted in the Joint Comprehensive Plan of Action (JCPOA). In October 2015, Iran and the P5+1 signed the JCPOA, which brought modest economic benefits to Iran in exchange for a temporary moratorium on enrichment, though it imposed no restrictions on regional military activities or missile development. Throughout the Obama administration, increasing unilateral and multilateral sanctions correlated positively with Iran's expanding uranium enrichment capabilities.

2018–2020: The Trump administration ramped up coercive pressure on Iran. In May 2018, the US withdrew from the Obama-negotiated JCPOA and appointed Brian Hook as head of the State Department's Iran Action Group (IAG) to oversee sanctions implementation and coordination within the US government and with allies. Hook had previously helped design the "maximum pressure" campaign at the State Policy Planning Staff (S/P) office.[27] Trump reimposed economic sanctions on Iran, targeting the automotive sector and precious metals in August 2018, followed by the oil and energy sectors in November. In late 2019, Trump approved strikes on Iranian-backed militias in Iraq after those groups attacked US bases in Iraq. On January 2, 2020, Trump authorized the airstrike that killed Quds Force commander Qasem Soleimani in Baghdad.[28] As a result of these sanctions, Iran's economy contracted 4 percent in 2018 and 9 percent in 2019 before modest growth resumed in 2020. Despite the new sanctions, Iran continued its nuclear program and faced clandestine Israeli attacks supported by US intelligence. The maximum pressure effort successfully tightened the US sanctions enforcement and inflicted significant damage on Iran's economy, though this was partially offset by continued economic engagement by Europe, Russia, China, and other actors. According to IMF data, Iran's foreign exchange reserves fell from $70 billion prior to 2017 to $4 billion in 2020. Supporters of the maximum pressure strategy argued that it constrained Iran's power projection in the region, though it did not prevent further development of its nuclear program.[29] Opponents noted that Iran developed a substantial resistance economy under sanctions, based on domestic production and non-oil trade, which may have added 30 to 50 percent to GDP beyond officially measured figures.[30]

Afghanistan

1996–2000: Washington employed military, economic, and diplomatic measures to pressure the Taliban regime in Afghanistan to expel Osama bin Laden. In May of 1996 bin Laden left Sudan for Afghanistan via the United Arab Emirates. By mid-1997, the Department of State was denied access to militant training sites in Afghanistan. In April 1998, Ambassador Bill Richardson visited Kabul to request bin Laden's extradition; the Taliban demurred but offered peace talks.[31] In August 1998 the US targeted but missed bin Laden in Operation Infinite Reach (cruise missile strikes in Khartoum, Sudan, and Khost Province, Afghanistan). In September 1998, Saudi Arabia and Pakistan failed to convince the Taliban to comply with the US request. The Clinton National Security Council (NSC) developed plans for a comprehensive political-military pressure campaign called "Delenda," but the Pentagon considered the military requirement too high, and incomplete intelligence made lower-end options unreliable.[32]

After the US strikes in Khost, Taliban leader Mullah Omar declared that President Clinton should be stoned to death and ruled out negotiations. In August 1999, Executive Order 13129 placed new sanctions on the Taliban, including an asset freeze and flight ban; in response, UN offices were burned and anti-American rallies were held in various Afghan cities. The UNSC approved mild sanctions to encourage the Taliban to expel bin Laden, but the Taliban again refused.

2001: The US escalated diplomatic and military efforts for bin Laden's extradition, culminating in a transition to war in late 2001. Pakistan advised reducing direct pressure on the Taliban to alleviate the suffering of the Afghan people, while the Taliban continued massacres against the Hazaras in February 2001. A Taliban envoy spoke with the US press and delivered a letter to the State Department seeking to improve ties but did not address US concerns over terrorism.[33] President Bush renewed Clinton-era sanctions and vowed to hold the Taliban accountable for any attacks on US interests in the region. After 9/11, Bush demanded in a speech to Congress that the Taliban turn over bin Laden or face severe consequences. A council of 600 Afghan religious leaders called on bin Laden to leave voluntarily, a significant gesture in Afghanistan but insufficient for Washington. In late September, the Taliban ambassador refused to surrender him, offering instead to try him in Afghanistan.[34] The result was war.

Syria
2004–2009: In 2003, Congress passed, and in 2004, President Bush implemented harsh sanctions on Syria due to President Bashar al-Assad's support to Iraqi insurgents. As the insurgency spread in Iraq, some members of Congress described Washington as one step short of war with Syria. Initially, criticism was discrete, but the Syria Accountability and Lebanese Sovereignty Restoration Act of 2003 marked a definitive shift.[35] The law demanded that Syria crack down on Iraqi insurgents operating from or through its territory, disclose its WMD capabilities, and end its interference in Lebanon. Egypt and Lebanon indicated early

on that they would not support sanctions against Syria. Deputy Secretary of State Richard Armitage said that Damascus had not learned from the Gulf War and Saddam Hussein's fate, threatening even greater sanctions. While Secretary of Defense Donald Rumsfeld did not rule out military strikes, Secretary of State Colin Powell explicitly did. Syrian troops formally withdrew from Lebanon in September 2004 and April 2005, though some viewed it as a superficial gesture due to Syria's continued covert influence. The US offered to lift sanctions in return for several concessions, but Syria refused, with analysts attributing the pullout more to pressure from UNSCR 1559 than to economic sanctions. The Bush administration initially opposed the harsh actions mandated by Congress and sent an ambassador back to Damascus. Some analysts believe the five Congressional delegations that visited Damascus to urge compliance watered down the effect of threats.[36] The Obama administration's early Syria policy represented continuity with the Bush 43 approach. Obama sought engagement, arguing that sanctions without diplomatic outreach were ineffective, but Congress criticized this strategy as ineffective, citing Assad's pursuit of a nuclear reactor and continued support to Lebanese Hezbollah as evidence.

2011–2016: This episode included US coercion against Syria's chemical weapons program, with the secondary goal of punishing Assad for his "war against his own people." In August 2011, President Obama declared that "for the sake of the Syrian people, Assad must give up power,"[37] which initiated a campaign of diplomatic isolation and economic pressure. In an SFRC hearing in August 2012, Senator John Kerry described mass atrocities and chemical weapons' use as "redlines," a characterization Obama echoed several times later that year. In September 2013, Obama offered Assad an option by demanding the verifiable turnover of all chemical weapons, accompanied by a threat airstrikes. However, Obama undermined the threat by stating that any military action would first be brought to Congress. The US position was weakened by an asymmetry of motivation, rooted in suspicion of militant groups within the anti-Assad opposition, concerns over allied commitment (Arab League, GCC,

NATO), third-party involvement (Russia and China), and domestic factors, including public opposition in Congress, resistance from think tanks, and the Department of Defense, and general war-weariness. A series of missteps that undermined own message (ruling out military options, equivocating in strategic communications). Assad perceived little menace, given the limited nature of the threats and the high cost of compliance, while the lack of action for clear violations of the "redlines" contrasted sharply with the rapid military response in Libya, where Muammar Gaddafi faced swift consequences for similar defiance. Faced with these complications, Obama narrowed his demand to focus solely on the removal of chemical weapons. After the redline was crossed, Obama publicly mused that "the question now is what are we going to do about it," signaling uncertainty in the response. Assad ultimately continued chemical weapons use into 2014 and beyond.[38]

2017–2020: The Trump administration proved more willing to conduct limited military strikes against Syrian regime targets to deter chemical weapons use, including strikes in April 2017[39] and April 2018.[40] These strikes damaged Assad's remaining military aircraft fleet and coincided with a sharp drop in chemical weapons use in the conflict. From August 2017 onward, Trump accelerated the counter-ISIS campaign in eastern Syria by increasing US ground troops and conducting more frequent airstrikes against ISIS targets. When a combined Russian mercenary and Syrian force tried to contest control of areas where US forces and their Syrian proxies were operating, US aircraft attacked their crossing site on the Euphrates, killing an estimated 200.[41] The Trump administration adopted a policy based on UNSCR 2254 and appointed a senior envoy to coordinate interagency actions related to Syria. The policy rejected regime change in favor of a negotiated settlement to the conflict. By 2020, significant challenges to Assad's regime emerged, including opposition-held territories, currency collapse, and uprisings in regime-controlled areas. The Caesar Civilian Protection Act began to take effect with bipartisan support, imposing strict sanctions on regime officials, their supporters, and secondary targets. The Trump travel ban under EO 13780 was also considered part of this episode. Narrowly construed, Trump's demands on Syria—no chemical weapons use and no obstruction of the counter-Islamic State campaign—were largely met. Viewing the broader US demands still in place through the Caesar Act and the commitment to UNSCR 2254, however, Trump's demands remained unmet.[42]

Lebanon

2003–2008: While Congress passed legislation in 2003 to pressure Damascus over its involvement in Lebanon, direct and concerted pressure within Lebanon itself did not materialize until three years later. Following the February 2005 assassination of Lebanese prime minister Rafik Hariri, the Lebanese opposition unified, and over one million people marched in Beirut, demanding the immediate withdrawal of Syrian forces. In concert, the United States, Europe, and Middle Eastern allies demanded immediate withdrawal of Syrian forces from Lebanon. Syria, which sought Hariri's removal to manipulate the 2008 Lebanese elections, recognized that its military presence was no longer sustainable. On March 8, 2005, Syrian forces began withdrawing, while 500,000 pro-Hezbollah Lebanese demonstrated in gratitude for Syrian help. On March 14, 2005, over one million Lebanese counter-demonstrated for Lebanese sovereignty. A series of UNSCRs related to the assassination, including 1595 (April), 1636 (October), and 1644 (December), passed in 2005, pressing for Syrian cooperation with a tribunal investigating the assassination, under threat of sanctions. In August 2007, President Bush issued EO 13441, which blocked the property of individuals undermining Lebanese sovereignty or attempting to reassert Syrian influence. US military aid to Lebanon increased from $40 million in 2006 to $220 million in 2007.[43] UNSCR 1701, which ended the 2006 Lebanon War, built upon UNSCR 1559 from 2004, encouraging the disarmament of militias, although it lacked the authorization to operate beyond southern Lebanon. Hezbollah rejected what it saw as Western interference in Lebanese politics and forced a domestic compromise, culminating in the election of its preferred candidate, Michel Sleiman. An 18-month political crisis between pro-Western and pro-Iranian factions, as well as militias, ended with Hezbollah seizing new territory in May 2008. Qatar mediated an arrangement under which Hezbollah and its allies obtained veto powers over major policy decisions. In September 2008, President Bush hosted Sleiman at the White House, praising him for reconciliation efforts, even as he and other Lebanese political elites gradually ceded influence to Hezbollah and Iran.[44]

2009–2016: The early Obama administration posited an "unshakable" commitment to an independent Lebanon with strong institutions, advocating for both Syria and Israel, while imposing coercive measures in varying ways to support this policy. In the June 2009 elections, the pro-Western March 14th bloc defeated the pro-Syria/Iran March 8th bloc, though March 14th's momentum waned over time. After the 2011 elections, the March 8th coalition, led by President Michel Aoun, gained control. As the Obama administration increasingly engaged with Iran during negotiations over the JCPOA, CIA director John Brennan signaled a willingness to work with "moderate elements" within Hezbollah.[45] During a December 2009 meeting between Presidents Sleiman and Obama at the White House, discussions reportedly focused more on the "Israeli threat" to Lebanon than on the threats posed by Hezbollah, Syria, or Iran to Lebanese sovereignty. Furthermore, the Obama administration also reportedly curtailed a Department of Justice investigation, known as Project Cassandra, into Hezbollah regional drug-trafficking operations. Simultaneously, it allowed Iran and Hezbollah a freer hand in Syria after initially supporting Sunni resistance to Assad. Under congressional pressure to take a tougher stance against Hezbollah even while easing pressure on Tehran, Obama signed the nearly unanimous Hezbollah International Financing Prevention Act of 2015. From 2010 on, Hezbollah expanded its influence over Lebanese institutions through political agreements, social services, and economic leverage in ports, businesses, and ministries, while continuing to function as a sanctioned "resistance" organization in southern Lebanon and Beirut. As the Obama administration sought to balance relations between Hezbollah and its allies on one side and its opponents, such as Hariri and others, Saudi Arabia withdrew $3 billion in military aid to Lebanon. Ultimately, Hariri was forced to once again accept Hezbollah-aligned candidates, including Michel Aoun, for key positions in the government. By the end of Obama's tenure, Hezbollah had gained substantial control over critical sectors of the Lebanese economy and state institutions, effectively suppressing domestic opposition. Although targeted sanctions were imposed, they were widely regarded as minor setbacks, given Hezbollah's ability to hedge against and mitigate their effects. Washington refrained from implementing broader sanctions, out of concern for their potential impact on the Lebanese civilian population.

Yemen

1990–1997 (and Jordan): Washington imposed secondary sanctions on Jordan for failing to comply with the sanctions regime against Iraq. The US sanctioned Jordan for exporting dual-use technology and for its support of Saddam Hussein during the Gulf War. However, the White House and Department of State significantly softened the enforcement of these sanctions to avoid jeopardizing ongoing peace negotiations between Israel and Jordan. In March 1991, President Bush suspended military aid to Jordan, but this suspension was lifted in September of the same year. After Yemen voted against a UN resolution authorizing military action against Iraq, a US diplomat reportedly told President Ali Abdullah Saleh, "that will be the most expensive vote you ever take." US aid to Yemen remained limited until after the 1994 civil war, and relations only improved significantly after 9/11.[46]

2011–2020: Washington imposed sanctions to penalize those undermining stability in Yemen. During the Arab Spring, a popular uprising targeted President Saleh, who had increasingly aligned with the US following 9/11. The Gulf Cooperation Council (GCC) brokered an agreement for Saleh to end his three-decade rule, but in March 2011 Saleh reneged on the deal, despite a call from CIA Director Brennan, on behalf of President Obama, urging him to comply. In November 2011, under military pressure from both the Shia Houthis in the north and southern secessionists (al-Hirak), Saleh agreed to turn over the presidency to Abd-Rabbu Mansour Hadi. To support the political transition and maintain stability, President Obama signed EO 13611 in May 2012, blocking the property of individuals disrupting Yemen's transition. US military assistance went from $67 million in 2009 to $150 million in 2010, with $250 million planned in 2012 but the implementation suspended at $30 million due to the outbreak of protests. Once Hadi assumed office, Washington resumed security assistance to Yemeni forces, but Saleh increasingly undermined his successor's authority. From 2012 to 2014, Iranian-backed Houthi forces consolidated control over northern Yemen (including Saada, Amran, and other northern governorates), defeating fighters of the Sunni Islah Party, Salafis, and the Ahmar family militia, with some support from Saleh-aligned forces. In September 2014, the Houthis, alongside forces from the General People's Congress (GPC), took control of Sanaa, forcing Hadi to resign and flee in early 2015. In March 2015, a Saudi-Emirati-led coalition intervened in Yemen. While the coalition's intervention inflicted more damage on GPC forces than on the Houthis, it was unable to prevent a joint Houthi-GPC offensive against southern Yemen, including the strategic city of Aden. In 2017, Saleh called upon the GPC to abandon the Houthis and realign with the Saudi-led coalition to oust the Houthis. In response, the Houthis surrounded Saleh's forces and ultimately killed him. The Saudi-led campaign in Yemen grew increasingly controversial in the US Congress as reports of human rights abuses sparked calls to suspend any aid to GCC countries that could be used in the conflict. Throughout this period, Yemen remained mired in civil war, foreign intervention, and a worsening humanitarian crisis. President Trump's travel ban, enacted under Executive Order 13780, is also seen as part of this broader context of instability and foreign policy concerns surrounding Yemen.[47]

Azerbaijan
1991–2001: Following the conflict between Armenian and Azerbaijani forces over the Nagorno-Karabagh (NK) Armenia's occupation and ethnic

cleansing of seven Azerbaijani districts surrounding NK, Azerbaijan and its allies cut off trade with Armenia. In response, Congress enacted the Freedom Support Act (FSA) of 1992, which banned aid to Azerbaijan. The act did not mention the seven districts but instead called on Azerbaijan to lift its "blockade" against Armenia. From 1991 to 2001, Russia continued to supply arms to Armenia, while leaders in both Baku and Washington emphasized the need for closer cooperation in response to threats from Russia and Iran. Section 907 of the FSA specifically prohibited military or other aid to Azerbaijan, but in 2001, the Bush administration successfully sought waiver authority due to Azerbaijan's strategic importance in the Global War on Terror (GWOT). Beginning in 2001, the Bush administration annually granted this waiver, enabling greater counterterrorism cooperation between the two nations.[48]

Kyrgyzstan

2020: The Trump administration imposed a visa ban on Kyrgyzstan due to concerns over the country's lax passport, customs, and border security enforcement, as part of a broader effort to tighten passport and migrant information systems. The ban applied to all types of visas except Special Immigrant Visas (SIVs). Acting Secretary of Homeland Security Chad Wolf stated that the restrictions were imposed on a number of countries to "address concerns in the way the banned countries track their own citizens, share information with the US and cooperate on immigration matters." Kyrgyzstan faced particular challenges, including issues with a counterfeit passport ring, delays in implementing biometric passports, and corruption in the contracts for passport production. The Kyrgyz president Sooronbay Jeenbekov was later ousted following widespread protests driven by economic concerns and corruption. On his first day in office, President Biden reversed the visa restrictions on Kyrgyzstan.[49]

Palestinian Authority (PA)

2017–2020: The Trump administration imposed sanctions and pressure on the PA to compel acceptance of the so-called "deal of the century."

According to a leaked Hebrew version of the Trump Peace Plan, the US threatened to block financial transfers to the PA if it rejected the proposal. Moreover, if the PA accepted the deal but Gaza factions—Hamas and Palestinian Islamic Jihad—rejected it, Washington signaled its willingness to support direct military action against Gaza. The PA firmly rejected the plan, condemning the "deal of the century" as an Israeli land grab by "breaking the legs of the Palestinians" and leaving them with next to nothing. French officials similarly dismissed the deal as "dead on arrival." In response, Israeli prime minister Benjamin Netanyahu and his Likud party announced that they no longer support a two-state solution. In March 2018, Congress passed the Taylor Force Act, halting all US aid to the PA through the US Security Coordinator and Consulate General in Jerusalem. The Trump administration then closed the Palestine Liberation Organization (PLO) office in Washington, DC, and in May 2018, formally moved the US embassy in Israel from Tel Aviv to Jerusalem. In August 2018, the US stopped its contributions to the UN Relief and Works Agency for Palestinian Refugees (UNRWA), which had accounted for roughly one-third of the agency's $1.1 billion budget. The PA severed political contacts with the Trump administration following the embassy relocation and ceased security cooperation with the US government in May 2020. Beginning in 2021, the Biden administration reversed many of these actions, restoring diplomatic and financial engagement with the Palestinians.[50]

Expert and Practitioner Comments

A number of experienced US and international policy practitioners shared their insights on several of the coercive dyads examined in these regions. Several focused on the recent lessons of coercion in Syria. One retired US ambassador noted that American responses frequently hinge on the public mood, with the effectiveness of coercive measures often depending on whether leaders in Washington or the targeted state are better at interpreting and responding to that sentiment.[51]

If the target assesses that US commitment is surficial rather than deep, it makes sense for them to double down and refuse to budge, but not try to provoke further pressure. If the target assesses that real US interests are involved—and thus serious commitment—the better strategy is to start seeking compromise solutions. If they misjudge the seriousness of the US position and ignore it, further escalating pressure is likely to come. Kosovo and Libya are interesting examples—they started out as non-core, surficial interests for the US, but ultimately triggered serious commitment by the core national security community or "deep state" in the US, with both elite and public opinion favoring committed action. Capturing the public imagination requires both immediate and horrific threats or violations by the target. If they are horrific but slowly unfolding, as in the case of Assad's atrocities in Syria, serious US commitment is unlikely. If they are dramatic but not morally egregious, public risk tolerance for action will be limited.

Another senior civilian official involved in crafting sanctions policy contended that the limited effectiveness of US coercion in these regions can be attributed to primarily technical factors[52]:

Sanctions authorities against Assad in 2004–2005 era were not tightly coordinated and were not sufficient—a very leaky sanctions regime. Sanctions enforcement is done "on the honor code," and enforcers never have the personnel and bandwidth to match the evaders. You have to count on vigilance to make the evasion costly; can't economically isolate while you are not politically isolating the regime that runs that economy. When we don't diplomatically isolate, it waters down the pressure and coercive messaging. Sends the wrong message about seriousness, and then decreases intensity of enforcement and resource mobilization by potential partners. It was knowable all along—it was a failure of targeting. The nodes of revenue could have been identified and cut off. If you sanction correctly, the target nation's framing isn't relevant. If you're not doing enough damage, their calculations will be predictably not what we want.

A third civilian official involved with Syria sanctions cited a combination of procedural and analytic factors for the failure to successfully coerce Assad[53]:

> What sounds good to us is not necessarily what sounds good to the regime. There are tons of ways to find this out. Can use intel, back-channels, precedent—there is a fair chance of using these sources to understand where the Zone of Potential Agreement (ZOPA) lies. Did I ever see the ZOPA ever remotely related to the actual roadmap in Syria? No. I did not see our approach lined up to what I thought the regime's calculations might be. Why didn't that happen? How do you force a relationship between the Intelligence Community (IC) and the policy folks trying to shape coercion? You can find people who meet with the leadership of these countries. It is a question whether such people are integrated into or drawn upon by formal IC products that shape conversations. Such people are easily marginalized or suppressed during IC and policy debates. People with contextual knowledge are sometimes seen as threats—people with detailed knowledge make it harder to apply "shellaque" or spin to the policy product.

A former General Officer in an Arab state military offered his view of coercive pressure on Iraq[54]:

> You can impose pressure, but you must provide an exit as well. The dictator will understand the ultimate result. Saddam was ready to cooperate with the US at the end of the sanctions, and wanted to turn a new page—it was a missed opportunity. It was feasible to achieve concessions from a weakened dictator at the end of that period, and perhaps he would have changed his behavior. Because the most important thing for the dictator is to remain in office.

A civilian policy analyst in a European think tank noted the lack of consistent political logic linking coercive measures to expected outcomes in the region[55]:

> The US coercive episodes seem to have lacked a political strategy or dimension at all. All the kinetic actions lack the transactional

element of understanding leverage and tying specific, achievable goals and decisions to the application of pressure. With Assad, the US didn't have a real transactional strategy, but took a Russian offer as a way out. With Baghdad, the whole idea was to avoid a transaction.

A retired Israeli security official argued that the US record in the Middle East has been a mixed bag[56]:

> When Obama pressured Egypt on human rights—freezing a portion of aid until they got better...the Egyptians were steaming, basically saying "we don't need your money...stay out of our politics." They saw it as interference not just in elite but in national life. Did you really think Egypt would change its practices for $100 million? On the matter of Saudi Arabia and Khashoggi...dealing with their future king—do you really think squeezing was going to help? Or would it be perceived as a punishment campaign? The Saudi oil decision (not to increase production) and the Huawei decision (not to ban) were related to the perception of punishment by the US—Washington must learn to factor the response by mid-sized powers and the great complications they can bring.

REGIONAL SUMMARY

The three-decade record of US CD in the Middle East and Central Asia calls to mind the saying that history repeats itself, first as tragedy, then as farce.[57] In the early post–Cold War period, the US successfully coerce Saddam out of Kuwait, created sufficient deterrence to pursue Arab-Israeli peace deals, and played a role in forcing the Syrian army out of Lebanon. However, US missteps in Iraq, Afghanistan, Yemen, Lebanon and elsewhere in the following decade led to a general deterioration of its position across the region, including the erosion of deterrence and the rise of hedging and balancing behaviors, even among US allies. By the end of the third post–Cold War decade, it had become clear that the US was struggling to achieve its regional objectives through open warfare, coercive diplomacy, or traditional negotiation methods, and the widespread perception was that US interest and influence in the region were waning.[58] Structural shifts in regional power dynamics, Great Power Competition, domestic US politics and other factors all contributed to the reduction of US influence over regional events. However, poorly conceived and poorly executed CD also played a role. While Washington failed to achieve its objectives through major wars, it similarly struggled to see the desired results from its diverse campaigns of coercion short of war.

NOTES

1. Office of the Historian, "The Gulf War, 1991," *Milestones in the History of US Foreign Relations,* US Department of State, May 19, 2017, https://history.state.gov/milestones/1989-1992/gulf-war.
2. R. Jeffrey Smith, "State Department Cables on Iraq-Kuwait Tensions, July 1990," *Washington Post,* October 21, 1992, https://www.washingtonpost.com/archive/politics/1992/10/21/state-department-cable-traffic-on-iraq-kuwait-tensions-july-1990/ff97c773-ea84-41ec-8c7c-f811ea61d2e5/.
3. John Goshko, "Iraq Accepts U.N. Terms to End Gulf War," *Washington Post,* April 7, 1991, https://www.washingtonpost.com/archive/politics/1991/04/07/iraq-accepts-un-terms-to-end-gulf-war/9800a4ea-62c1-4215-8119-f21cf4630b78/.
4. Laurie Mylroie, "The US Watches, as Saddam Crushes the Uprisings: 25th Anniversary," Kurdistan24, March 31, 2016, https://www.kurdistan24.net/en/story/4314-The-US-Watches,-as-Saddam-Crushes-the-Uprisings:-25th-Anniversary.
5. Scott Silliman, "The Iraqi Quagmire: Enforcing the No-Fly Zones," *New England Law Review* 36, no. 4 (2002): 767–773, https://scholarship.law.duke.edu/cgi/viewcontent.cgi?referer=&httpsredir=1&article=1775&context=faculty_scholarship&sei-redir=1.
6. Arms Control Association, "Iraq: a Chronology of UN Inspections," *Arms Control Today,* October 2002, https://www.armscontrol.org/act/2002-10/features/iraq-chronology-un-inspections.
7. Rym Brahimi, "Iraq Gambled and Lost When it Formally Recognized Kuwait's Borders," United Press International, December 20, 1994, https://www.upi.com/Archives/1994/12/20/Iraq-gambled-and-lost-when-it-formally-recognized-Kuwaits/5514787899600/.
8. United States Congress, *Iraq Liberation Act of 1998* (105th Congress Public Law 338), Government Printing Office, https://www.congress.gov/105/plaws/publ338/PLAW-105publ338.htm.
9. United States Congress, *Iraq; Are Sanctions Collapsing?* Joint Hearing of the Committee on Foreign Relations and the Committee on Energy and Natural Resources, US Senate, May 21, 1998, https://www.govinfo.gov/content/pkg/CHRG-105shrg49526/html/CHRG-105shrg49526.htm.
10. Barbara Crossette, "France, in Break with U.S., Urges End to Iraq Embargo," *New York Times,* January 14, 1999, https://www.nytimes.com/

1999/01/14/world/france-in-break-with-us-urges-end-to-iraq-embargo. html.

11. President George W. Bush, *State of the Union Address* (2002), Office of the Press Secretary, January 29, 2002, https://georgewbush-whitehouse. archives.gov/news/releases/2002/01/20020129-11.html.

12. Richard Haass, "Revisiting America's War of Choice in Iraq," *Project Syndicate*, March 17, 2023, https://www.project-syndicate.org/onpoint/ iraq-war-20-years-later-causes-misconceptions-and-lessons-by-richard-haass-2023-03.

13. Peter Beaumont and Ed Vulliamy, "World Waits as Saddam Makes a Fateful Choice," *The Guardian* (UK), November 9, 2002, https://www. theguardian.com/world/2002/nov/10/iraq1.

14. Timothy Andrews Sayle, Jeffrey Engel, Hal Brands, and William Inboden, eds., *The Last Card: Inside George W. Bush's Decision to Surge in Iraq* (Ithaca: Cornell University Press, 2019), especially 209–238.

15. Greg Bruno, *US Security Agreements and Iraq,* Council on Foreign Relations, December 23, 2008, https://www.cfr.org/backgrounder/us-security-agreements-and-iraq.

16. E. Mohseni Cheraghlou, "When Coercion Backfires: the Limits of Coercive Diplomacy in Iran" (PhD diss, University of Maryland, College Park MD, 2015), https://spp.umd.edu/sites/default/files/2019-07/When%20Coercion %20Backfires%20-%20Mohseni%20Dissertation.pdf.

17. Harry L. Myers, *The US Policy of Dual Containment Toward Iran and Iraq in Theory and Practice* (Maxwell AFB, AL: US Air War College, April 1997), https://apps.dtic.mil/sti/tr/pdf/ADA399045.pdf.

18. Permanent Select Committee on Intelligence, *Investigation into Iranian Arms Shipments to Bosnia,* US House of Representatives, October 9, 1998, https://www.govinfo.gov/content/pkg/CRPT-105hrpt804/html/CRPT-1 05hrpt804.htm#:~:text=The%20Clinton%20Administration%20failed%20 to,Iranian%20arms%20flows%20constituted%20notification.

19. President William J. Clinton, *Remarks at the Seventh Millenium Evening at the White House*, April 12, 1999, https://www.presidency.ucsb.edu/ documents/remarks-the-seventh-millennium-evening-the-white-house.

20. Julian Borger, "US Accuses Iran of Secret Nuclear Weapons Plan," *The Guardian* (UK), December 14, 2002, https://www.theguardian.com/world/ 2002/dec/14/iraq.iran.

21. Kenneth Katzman, *Iran: US Concerns and Policy Responses*, Congressional Research Service (CRS) Report RL32048, February 11, 2005, https://apps. dtic.mil/sti/tr/pdf/ADA472455.pdf.

22. United Nations Security Council, *Resolution 1803*, March 3, 2008, https://www.iaea.org/sites/default/files/unsc_res1803-2008.pdf.

23. "Ayatollah Ali Khamanei Dismisses Barack Obama's Overtures to Iran," *The Guardian*, March 21, 2009, https://www.theguardian.com/world/2009/mar/21/ali-khamenei-barack-obama-iran.

24. Jillian Macnaughton and Paul Sotero, *A Reflection on the May 2010 Brazil-Turkey Nuclear Initiative Toward Iran* (panel summary) Wilson Center, February 22, 2011, https://www.wilsoncenter.org/event/reflection-the-may-2010-brazil-turkey-nuclear-initiative-toward-iran.

25. Mark Hibbs, "Who Wants Diplomacy on Iran?" *Arms Control Wonk*, December 1, 2011, Carnegie Endowment for International Peace, https://carnegieendowment.org/2011/12/01/who-wants-diplomacy-on-iran-pub-46104.

26. Dan Raviv, "US Pushing Israel to Stop Assassinating Iranian Nuclear Scientists," CBS News, March 21, 2014, https://www.cbsnews.com/news/us-pushing-israel-to-stop-assassinating-iranian-nuclear-scientists/.

27. Andrew Hanna, "Sanctions 5: Trump's 'Maximum Pressure' Targets, *The Iran Primer*, March 3, 2021, https://iranprimer.usip.org/blog/2021/mar/03/sanctions-5-trumps-maximum-pressure-targets.

28. Karen Pinchin, "Qassem Soleimani's Complex Legacy in Iraq," *Frontline*, pbs.org, January 5, 2020, https://www.pbs.org/wgbh/frontline/article/qassem-soleimani-killed-airstrike-iran-iraq-legacy/.

29. Elliot Abrams, "Did the 'Maximum Pressure' Campaign Against Iran Fail?" *Pressure Points*, Council on Foreign Relations, July 12, 2021, https://www.cfr.org/blog/did-maximum-pressure-campaign-against-iran-fail.

30. Reuel Marc Gerecht and Ray Takeyh, "Ayatollah Khamanei's 'Resistance Economy,'" *Wall Street Journal*, July 26, 2022, https://www.wsj.com/articles/ayatollah-khameneis-resistance-economy-austerity-subsidies-gasoline-iran-jcpoa-nuclear-weapons-diplomacy-protests-11658864527.

31. Dexter Filkins, "US Ambassador Receives Promise of Peace Talks in Visit to Afghanistan," *Los Angeles Times*, April 18, 1998, https://www.latimes.com/archives/la-xpm-1998-apr-18-mn-40540-story.html.

32. Barbara Elias, "Bush Administration's First Memo on Al-Qaeda Declassified," *National Security Archive Electronic Briefing Book No. 147*, National Security Archive, February 10, 2005, https://nsarchive2.gwu.edu/NSAEBB/NSAEBB147/index.htm.

33. David Ottaway and Joe Stephens, "Diplomats Met With Taliban on Bin Laden," *Washington Post*, October 29, 2001, https://www.washingtonpost.

com/archive/politics/2001/10/29/diplomats-met-with-taliban-on-bin-laden/15c446d3-0c6e-4429-b8f3-9896951fc444/.

34. Mujib Mashal, "Taliban Offered bin Laden Trial Before 9/11," al-Jazeera.com, September 2011, 11, https://www.aljazeera.com/news/201 1/9/11/taliban-offered-bin-laden-trial-before-9.

35. United States Congress, Public Law 108–175, December 12, 2003, https://www.congress.gov/108/plaws/publ175/PLAW-108publ175.pdf.

36. Jeremy Sharp, *Syria: Background and US Relations*, CRS Report RL 33487, September 14, 2009, https://www.everycrsreport.com/files/20090914_RL33487_4f0595d8826f82a9595cb665b51c7204985cfc5d.pdf.

37. Scott Wilson and Joby Warrick, "Assad Must Go, Obama Says," *Washington Post*, August 18, 2011, https://www.washingtonpost.com/politics/assad-must-go-obama-says/2011/08/18/gIQAelheOJ_story.html.

38. Joshua Schore, "Hollow Threats: Why Coercive Diplomacy Fails" (PhD diss., Maxwell Air Force Base, AL: School of Advanced Air and Space Studies, June 2015), 85–114.

39. "Syria War: Why Was Shayrat Airbase Bombed?" BBC News, April 7, 2017, https://www.bbc.com/news/world-us-canada-39531045.

40. Daniel, F. Arkin, Brinley Bruton, and Phil McCausland, "Trump Announces Strikes on Syria Following Suspected Chemical Weapons Attack by Assad Forces," NBC News, April 13, 2018 https://www.nbcnews.com/news/world/trump-announces-strikes-syria-following-suspected-chemical-weapons-attack-assad-n865966.

41. Julian Borger, "Scores of Russian Mercenaries Reportedly Killed by US Airstrikes in Syria," *The Guardian* (UK), February 13, 2018, https://www.theguardian.com/world/2018/feb/13/russian-mercenaries-killed-us-airstrikes-syria.

42. Howard Shatz, *The Power and Limits of Threat: The Caesar Syrian Civilian Protection Act at One Year*, Rand Corporation, July 8, 2021, https://www.rand.org/pubs/commentary/2021/07/the-power-and-limits-of-threat-the-caesar-syrian-civilian.html.

43. Casey Addis, *Lebanon: Background and US Relations*, CRS R40054, November 2, 2009, https://www.everycrsreport.com/files/20091102_R40054_bfbebb730c2212568a74b33b55309f00a2a57478.pdf.

44. David Alexander, "Lebanese Leaders Presses Bush on Land and Refugees," Reuters, September 25, 2008 https://www.reuters.com/article/uk-usa-lebanon-idUKTRE48O6ZT20080925/.

45. Josh Meyer, "The Secret Backstory of How Obama Let Hezbollah Off the Hook," *Politico*, 2017, https://www.politico.com/interactives/2017/obama-hezbollah-drug-trafficking-investigation/.

46. Phyllis Bennis, "Yemen: Déjà vu All Over Again," Institute for Policy Studies, January 13, 2010, https://ips-dc.org/yemen_dj_vu_all_over_again/.

47. Jeremy Sharp, *Yemen: Civil War and Regional Intervention*, CRS Report R43960, April 23, 2020, https://crsreports.congress.gov/product/pdf/R/R43960/38.

48. Jim Nichol and Julie Kim, *Armenia, Azerbaijan and Georgia: Political Developments and Implications for US Interests*, CRS Report IB95024, January 3, 2002 https://apps.dtic.mil/sti/tr/pdf/ADA474109.pdf.

49. President Joseph R. Biden, *Proclamation on Ending Discriminatory Bans on Entry to the United States*, The White House, January 20, 2021, https://www.whitehouse.gov/briefing-room/presidential-actions/2021/01/20/proclamation-ending-discriminatory-bans-on-entry-to-the-united-states/.

50. Yousef Munayyer, "The Trump Term: An Israel-Palestine Damage Assessment," Arab Center, Washington, DC, November 11, 2020, https://arabcenterdc.org/resource/the-trump-term-an-israel-palestine-damage-assessment/.

51. Author interview, August 9, 2022.

52. Author interview, September 28, 2022.

53. Author interview, October 25, 2022.

54. Author interview, October 24, 2022.

55. Author interview, October 28, 2022.

56. Author interview, November 2, 2022. Note that one episode referenced by the interviewee, coercion against Saudi Arabia over the assassination of Jamal Khashoggi, is not among the 122 cases covered in the study.

57. Michael Rechtenwald, "First as Tragedy, Then as Farce: How Marx Predicted the Fate of Marxism," *New English Review*, January 1, 2019, https://www.michaelrectenwald.com/essays/first-as-tragedy-then-as-farce.

58. Hasim Tekines, "Reality or Misperception: the US Withdrawal from the Middle East," Orion Policy Institute, March 14, 2022, https://www.orionpolicy.org/research/88/reality-or-misperception-the-us-withdrawal-from-the-middle-east.

CHAPTER 6

GOODWILL BURNING: US COERCIVE DIPLOMACY IN EUROPE

The US experience with CD in Europe in some respects mirrors some of the challenges faced in the Middle East and Central Asia, with efforts in both regions proving far less successful than in the Western Hemisphere. In Europe, the US achieved compliance in only 25% of the coercive episodes (3 of 12), while securing alternative concessions in 33% (4 of 12). CD in Europe was generally popular domestically, with 83% of the episodes (10 of 12) aligned with domestic political interests. However, there was a relatively high rate of coercion escalating to war, largely driven by the conflict with Yugoslavia in the 1990s. One striking similarity between coercive outcomes in Europe and the Middle East/Central Asia is the strength of negative trajectories in bilateral relations between the US following coercive episodes. In Europe, a whopping 83% of cases resulted in long-term deterioration of relations with the US, similar to the 82% rate for the Middle East and Central Asia. In the other three regions studied—the Americas, Africa, and South/East Asia, negative trajectories applied in under half the episodes recorded. US standing seems to have suffered the most damage in what could be termed the "middle regions" of Europe and the Middle East—closer and more integrated with the US than Africa or much of south and east Asia, but less so than most Western Hemisphere countries. As was the case with the Middle East, in Europe the record of US CD is also marked by a number of dyads with long-running, multi-episode coercive courses—in this case, Yugoslavia/Serbia, Russia, and Turkey.

The following summary illustrates how three decades of US coercion played out across this subset of cases. Coercive performance scores range from 0 to 4, framing performance 0–1, compliance and other outcome variables (alternative concession or AC, trajectory or T, and domestic satisfaction or DS) 0–1. Detailed episode scoring procedures and results are available in Appendix 1 online.

US coercive performance was stronger in Europe (2.77) than in the Middle East and Central Asia (2.57), while equaling the performance in the Western Hemisphere. The framing score was weaker than in the Americas, and similar to that in the Middle East; this lends support to the idea that Washington struggles to craft messages that resonate with elite and popular audiences beyond its own proverbial backyard. The compliance rate was far below that achieved in the West, though slightly better than in the Middle East and Central Asia. Alternative concessions were obtained at comparable rates to the Middle East and Central Asia, significantly lower than those achieved in our own hemisphere. All three regions showed relatively high scores (0.67 to 0.77) for domestic political satisfaction, but it came at a much higher cost in Europe and the Mideast than closer to home in terms of deteriorating bilateral relations. In the Western Hemisphere, there was a slightly positive trajectory post-episode (0.02), but in the other two regions, it was strongly negative (-0.61 and -0.70). It might be fair to ask how transient this deterioration in bilateral relations or regional standing is in the eyes of experts and practitioners, but the perception that it has occurred and is significant broadly applied to the episodes studied.

COERCIVE DYADS

Yugoslavia

1992–1994: This coercive episode involved pressure over Macedonia. UNSCR 757 (May 1992) targeted trade, travel, and exchanges; UNSCR 787 authorized naval blockades (Operations Maritime Guard and Sharp Guard). The Vance-Owen Peace Plan (VOPP) for a new Bosnia and Herzegovina was offered in 1993, and rejected by Bosnian Serbs; subsequently UNSCR 820 tightened sanctions. The Yugoslav GDP declined by half from 1990 to 1993, resulting in shortages and hyperinflation. These sanctions were lifted after Bosnian elections in 1996. UNSCR 749 established a neutral United Nations Protection Force (UNPROFOR) to protect civilians, which expanded with US and Nordic battalions in North Macedonia in 1993 (Task Force Able Sentry). President Bush reportedly considered airstrikes against the Serbian Air Force and no-fly zones, as well as arming the Bosnians, but was restrained by lack of European support.[1] While sanctions began to hurt Belgrade, the Russians opposed further tightening, and the Serbs became both more self-sufficient economically and more proficient at regional smuggling as time wore on.[2] It is estimated that sanctions on Serbia also cost Macedonia $3 billion between 1992 and 1995, exacerbated by a Greek embargo based on a dispute over official name and flag. [3] Nonetheless, US efforts to deter attacks on Macedonia appear to have succeeded, whereas the coercive effort with regard to Bosnia ended in war.

1992–1996: This coercive episode covers the US-led effort to halt the Serbian war in Bosnia, distinct from the Macedonia case. In June 1992, a coalition of nations led by the US imposed comprehensive sanctions on Yugoslavia, targeting trade, flights, foreign assets, and diplomatic representation, with the objectives of forcing Serbian troops out of Bosnia and Herzegovina and removing Slobodan Milosevic from power. The US spearheaded an international campaign to broaden and enforce these sanctions, despite strong opposition from Russia. Both the US and the EC offered sanctions relief in exchange for a negotiated settlement and territorial concessions favorable to the Bosnian Muslims.[4]

The Serbs survived the sanctions by drawing down foreign currency reserves and smuggling goods, while continuing ethnic cleansing and the siege of Sarajevo despite sanctions and a UNPROFOR. After the massacre of 8,000 Muslims at Srebrenica in July 1995 and Serbian promises to "liquidate" remaining "safe zones," Washington decided to escalate its response by launching more intensive airstrikes and presenting a compromise ceasefire and confederation plan that would safeguard some Serbian gains. Following the NATO air campaign and a Muslim-Croat ground offensive, which reversed many Bosnian Serb advances, Richard Holbrooke's shuttle diplomacy with the Contact Group (including Russia) and Balkan capitals led to the convening of the Dayton Accords.[5]

1998–2001: Sanctions and military pressure were imposed in response to Serbian military operations in Kosovo. The US Department of State raised concerns over Serbian crackdowns in Drenica and, in consultation with the Contact Group (US, UK, France, Germany, Italy, and notably Russia), threatened sanctions.[6] In June 1998, President Clinton imposed sanctions under EO 13088 to end violence perpetrated by the Serbian-dominated Yugoslav federal government and to restart negotiations with the Kosovo Liberation Army (KLA). During the same month, the US and France advocated for harsher measures, including possible military action. The Contact Group proposed a plan that called for Serbian withdrawal from Kosovo, the deployment of 28,000 peacekeepers (including 4,000 US troops), a self-rule framework for Kosovo, and a deadline of February 1999. In negotiations at Rambouillet, the Serbs accepted some terms for self-rule but rejected the presence of a Western peacekeeping force. On January 30, 1999, the NATO Secretary General authorized airstrikes, and NATO forces assembled an armada of 260 aircraft. Secretary of

State Madeleine Albright and the Contact Group warned that if the KLA accepted peace plan and Federal Yugoslavia rejected it, bombing would commence. The KLA, the US and the UK formally accepted the agreement at Rambouillet, but Yugoslavia, with Russia's backing, rejected it. The matter was handed from NATO's political wing to its military command for the use of force in late March 1999, leading to a NATO bombing campaign from March through June of 1999. Milosevic ultimately accepted the terms.[7] A peacekeeping force, Kosovo Force (KFOR), entered the region in June 1999. In April 1999, EO 13121 expanded sanctions against Serbia. President Clinton lifted most sanctions on Yugoslavia and Serbia the day before he left office in 20000, following the election of new leadership in the Federal Republic of Yugoslavia (Kostunica and others).[8]

Russia

2009–2016: The Obama Administration, spurred by Congress, imposed measures to restrain Russian military aggression, especially in Ukraine. Obama's efforts for a "reset" with Russia during his first term faltered as Vladimir Putin blamed the West for a surge in domestic opposition in 2009. Putin formally returned to power in 2012, determined to prevent the West from replicating the regime change approach it had employed in Libya whether in Syria or elsewhere. Between 2012 and 2014, Putin also voiced grievances over US policy, which led to scaled-back missile defense plans for Europe. In 2014, Russia launched a military operation against Ukraine, annexing Crimea in February and March, and initiating conflict in the Donbas region in April.[9] By August, Russian forces had reinforced proxy militias in the Donbas region, and by September, those separatists controlled much of the region. In March 2014, President Obama applied EO 13660 "to impose a cost on Russia" by freezing assets held in US-controlled financial institutions. Subsequent executive orders expanded targeted sanctions to include Putin's inner circle (EO 13661) and key economic sectors (EO 13662). In December 2014, the United States (EO 13685) and EU imposed sanctions on investment in Crimea. Obama publicly urged Russia to change its strategy in Ukraine, grant access to the

MH17 civil airliner crash site, and rein in the separatists. In 2014, Congress passed the Sovereignty, Integrity, Democracy, and Economic Stability of Ukraine Act and Ukraine Freedom Support Act.[10] German Chancellor Angela Merkel and Obama jointly condemned Russian aggression and considered the possibility of providing defensive arms but determined that "military solution prospects are low." Additional sanctions were imposed in response to Russian cyber intrusions (EO 13694) and election meddling (EO 13757) were applied in 2015 and 2016, respectively. In December 2016, the Obama administration expelled Russian diplomats, a move that was met with reciprocal expulsions by Moscow. By the end of the Obama administration, Russia had responded neither to the "reset" nor to sanctions and diplomatic pressure, continuing to act in line with its grievance narrative and strategy to reassert strategic influence in Europe and the Middle East.[11]

2012–2016: The Magnitsky Act is widely regarded as an episode of coercive diplomacy against Russia, though it has since evolved into a norm-setting tool of legal pressure applied to individuals internationally. The Act's origins trace back to the case of Sergei Magnitsky, a Russian tax lawyer who was arrested and mistreated by Russian authorities, later dying in custody. His supporters in the United States pressed Congress for legislation to punish those deemed responsible. The proposal found broad bipartisan support because the corruption and human rights abuse were blatant and "there was no pro-Russian torture and murder lobby to oppose it."[12] President Obama opposed the Act because he wanted to pursue normalization with Russia, but Congress insisted that the Jackson-Vanik amendment, which restricted trade relations with closed economies (especially Russia), would not be repealed unless Obama approved the Magnitsky Act.[13] The law was passed and signed in December 2012. In 2016 Congress expanded the Act into the Global Magnitsky Act, allowing property and visa sanctions against international actors engaged in extrajudicial killings, torture, human rights abuses, or corruption. Over time, many countries have adopted their versions of Global Magnitsky

Act, transforming the legislation from a singular coercive event into a liberal international mechanism for legal accountability.[14]

2017–2020: During the Trump administration, sanctions on Russia were primarily driven by Congress, driven in part by unsubstantiated election-year accusations that Trump was "colluding" with Russia on election interference. These led to stricter coercive measures against Russia, which the Trump administration implemented. Trump signed the Countering Russian Influence in Europe and Eurasia Act of 2017 (CRIEEA) and Countering America's Adversaries Through Sanctions Act (CAATSA) into law in August 2017, codifying earlier EOs and broadening sanctioned activities, with broad secondary sanctions authority. The administration carried out multiple rounds of designations under 2014 and 2016 EOs, as well as CRIEEA and CAATSA.[15] Rosboronexport, the Russian weapons export authority, was blocked starting in 2017 due to its support of Syria, North Korea, and others. In March 2018, the administration expelled 60 Russian diplomatic personnel in response to the Skripal poisoning in the UK, which Russia reciprocated. While Trump sought a more positive tone in bilateral relations, he simultaneously increased deterrent measures. Examples include the 41% increase to the European Reassurance Initiative funding, freer Rules of Engagement for US forces in Syria, and lethal aid to Ukraine (which his predecessor had declined).[16] Trump aimed to establish a "tough on Russia" stance by authorizing an attack on Russian mercenaries in Syria, upping US energy production, pushing NATO partners to increase defense expenditures, authorizing Black Sea naval patrols, and facilitating Israel's anti-Hezbollah strikes in Syria. Additionally, he pursued upgrades to the US nuclear arsenal and supported Montenegro's accession to NATO.[17] Although Trump and Putin met face-to-face five times and spoke on the phone nine times, Trump combined engagement with a firm deterrent approach on Syria, energy markets, sanctions under the Magnitsky Act, and European security.

Turkey

2018: The Trump administration imposed tariffs to pressure Turkey into releasing US pastor Andrew Brunson, who had been arrested in Turkey on allegations of ties to terrorist groups—charges he vehemently denied and which were based on weak evidence. Initially, the administration pursued incentives, including softening Congressional interest in sanctions and dropping charges against Turkish President Recep Tayyip Erdoğan's bodyguards. After months of "fruitless negotiations," President Donald Trump applied economic pressure in what was described as "a bullet a day."[18] Vice President Mike Pence and evangelical groups increased pressure after a religious freedom conference hosted by the State Department in July 2018. Pastor Brunson was placed under house arrest at about the same time, but US officials had expected his unconditional release and were angered. Then Secretary of State Mike Pompeo tweeted that the US has seen no credible evidence for Brunson's detention, while Erdoğan publicly suggested a swap of Brunson for Fetullah Gulen, a US resident whom the Turkish government accused of masterminding a failed 2016 coup. The US responded by imposing asset and visa sanctions on Turkey's Ministers of Interior and Justice.[19] Turkey's Ministry of Foreign Affairs promised retaliation for sanctions and asserted that Erdoğan could not interfere in a judicial case. In August President Trump threatened via Twitter to double tariffs on Turkish steel and aluminum if Brunson remained detained. Some diplomatic observers suggested that the public nature of Trump's threats delayed Brunson's release by several months.[20] The episode concluded in October 2018, when Brunson was sentenced to three years in prison but was released for time served.[21]

2019: Sanctions were imposed in response to Turkey's Operation Peace Spring (OPS) in northeast Syria. The US and Turkey had spent over a year negotiating a compromise regarding the US-backed YPG (People's Protection Units, or Yekîneyên Parastina Gel), which has ties to the PKK (Kurdistan Workers' Party, or Partiya Karkerên Kurdistanê), a group Turkey considers a terrorist organization.[22] After the negotiations stalled over US reluctance to allow Turkish verification patrols to confirm the pullout of YPG forces near the Turkish border, Turkey launched a unilateral military operation to remove the YPG from a border strip.[23] While US and Turkish forces did not engage directly, the US condemned the Turkish operation as a threat to unravel its counter-ISIS operations in northeast Syria and destabilize the region. President Trump sent an open letter to President Erdoğan threatening severe economic sanctions, including tariffs and the suspension of trade talks, if OPS did not halt.[24] He also signed EO 13894, authorizing sanctions against persons or organizations contributing to instability in Syria. Several Turkish officials were designated under this order, and Congress issued a statement of support for the sanctions. In October 2019, a senior-level US delegation, including Vice President Pence, Secretary Pompeo, National Security Advisor Robert C. O'Brien, and a senior-level military delegation, traveled to Ankara to offer a compromise. The proposal involved halting the fighting along current geographical lines, jointly supervising the withdrawal of the YPG, and lifting current sanctions while foregoing new ones.[25] Concurrently, Turkey negotiated with Russia to establish deconfliction measures along parts of the border where US troops were not stationed, while the YPG accepted the presence of Syrian and Russian troops in areas near the newly seized Turkish-controlled area. territory. Despite initial concerns, the US position in Syria did not collapse as a result of this episode.

2019–2020: Washington imposed sanctions related to Turkey's purchase of the Russian S-400 air defense system. Turkey had long been pursuing upgrades to its air defense system and had engaged in discussions with US, Russian, European, and Chinese manufacturers. A key sticking point in these discussions was co-production and transfer of technology, as Turkey sought to develop their own air defense manufacturing capabilities. In 2015, NATO deployed Spanish, German, and US Patriot systems to Turkey due to the threat of Russian air incursions and possible Syrian or Iranian missile attacks on Turkey. In November 2015, Turkish jets shot down a Russian bomber that had violated Turkish airspace, prompting Russia to respond with threats, bombings of Turkish proxies in Syria, and an economic boycott. As part of Russo-Turkish talks aimed at resolving bilateral tensions, Turkey agreed to collaborate more closely with Russia in Syria and in security matters more generally. Following the failed coup against Erdoğan in the of summer 2016, Putin offered moral support and defense equipment, including an August 2017 offer to sell the S-400 system to Turkey. While Congress had never approved a sale of the Patriot system to Turkey, the Russian offer for the S-400s faced no such hurdles.[26] Over the course of 2018, the US government expressed concern but applied little direct pressure to stop the deal. US concerns focused on the technological threat posed by the S-400 operating in close proximity to the F-35 fighter, which Turkey was scheduled to receive. In April 2019, Vice President Pence publicly stated that Turkey had to choose between purchasing the S-400 and remaining a NATO member. Congress and the Departments of State and Defense ramped up messaging to Turkey, linking the purchase of the S-400 to Turkey's possible expulsion from the F-35 program.[27] After Turkey began receiving deliveries of the S-400, the US suspended and eventually expelled Turkey from the F-35 program. Congress also subsequently sanctioned Turkey's Ministry of Defense Industry and several other officials for the S-400 purchase under the CAATSA law.[28]

Belarus

2004–2020: US pressure on Belarus, initiated by President George W. Bush, focused on human rights abuses and undemocratic elections, particularly in 2006. In 2004, Congress had passed the Belarus Democracy Act in 2004, which was updated in 2006 and 2011, discouraging, though not banning, non-humanitarian assistance and requiring reports on arms sales and assets held. Congress favored stronger measures, with earlier bills proposing mandatory travel bans, asset freezes, and trade restrictions. After the fraudulent 2006 election, the European Union, led by the Czech Republic, announced targeted sanctions against Belarusian leaders. In June 2006, President Bush issued Executive Order 13405, which imposed blocking sanctions against President Alexander Lukashenko and several of his cabinet ministers. That same year, Bush referred to Lukashenko's regime as the "last dictatorship in Europe," and pledged support to reformers in Belarus.[29] Following additional designations in early 2007, the Belarusian ambassador to Washington dismissed the sanctions, describing them as "gross deceit" because there were no assets in the US system to freeze. Russia criticized these Western sanctions and strengthened trade and economic ties with Belarus. Despite Lukashenko making symbolic gestures, such as releasing a few prisoners and weakly criticizing Russia's war in Georgia, he conducted another fraudulent election in 2010, followed by a brutal crackdown on protestors and further consolidation of power.[30] The pattern repeated in 2020, with yet another sham election and brutal responses to protests. This time, however, Lukashenko retaliated against European criticism by facilitating the flow of irregular migrants into Europe through Belarus. While this study generally treats coercive campaigns spanning multiple administrations as distinct episodes, there was enough continuity in the approach of the Obama and Trump administrations to consider them together. It is, worth noting, however, that Secretary of State Mike Pompeo did explore a potential shift in strategy during his visit to Minsk—the first cabinet-level visit in twenty-five years—with the goal of returning an ambassador to Belarus. Ultimately, this effort yielded no tangible results.[31]

Hungary

2012–2018: Washington imposed light sanctions on the government of Viktor Orbán in response to increasingly illiberal acts and his promotion of non-liberal (conservative) democracy. In September 2014, President Obama highlighted Hungary, a NATO and EU member, as one of several countries targeting civil society. In October 2014, the US Embassy informed the Hungarian Ministry of Foreign Affairs that six officials were placed under a US visa and travel ban. This action served as a warning against Hungary's growing economic ties with Russia, restrictions on media and non-governmental organizations, corruption, obtrusive outreach to diaspora, and centralization of power.[32] Speakers from the House Foreign Affairs Committee (HFAC) advocated for multi-lateral diplomatic pressure, supporting civil society through grants, condemning racism and anti-Semitism, funding and training journalists, publishing intelligence on corruption and publicly condemning it, and using outreach programs like the International Visitor Leadership Program (IVLP) to engage directly with the Hungarian people. Orbán claimed that the United States was pressuring Hungary over the South Stream pipeline project and a Pakistani nuclear energy upgrade—both projects involving Russia. A group of Congressmen sent Orbán a letter condemning plans for a statue of Balint Homan, an anti-Semitic World War II–era leader. Under the Obama administration, a six-year ban on high-level US government contacts with Hungary was in place, ending when Secretary Pompeo resumed contacts in 2018.[33] NATO remained engaged with Hungary, with General Petr Pavel, then Chairman of the NATO Military Committee, praising Hungary's commitment to the Alliance during a visit to NATO exercises in the country. In February 2019 Secretary Pompeo visited Budapest, and in mid-May 2019, President Trump hosted Orbán in Washington, quipping that "we're like twins."[34]

Germany
2017–2020: Washington applied diplomatic pressure and sanctions to prevent the completion of the Nord Stream II energy pipeline. Nord Stream I had been in operation since 2011, but the parallel second line would double the capacity of Russia-Germany gas sales, bypassing Ukraine. Russian GAZPROM owns the line, with the financial backing of five organizations based in European countries (two German, one French, one Austrian, and one Dutch-British). German leaders, responding to criticism from the Obama administration, characterized Nord Stream II as a business decision that governments should not dictate. Under Section 232 of the CRIEEA of 2017, sanctions were authorized against those investing in Russian energy export pipelines.[35] President Trump intensified pressure on German leaders, highlighting the contradiction of Germany funding a Russian pipeline while the US financed Germany's

national defense against potential Russian threats. Russia hawks in Congress urged Trump to use all available tools to halt the project. In 2017, the German government argued that extraterritorial secondary sanctions violated international law. Trump directed a reduction of US troop levels in Germany, a decision later reversed by the Biden administration. The Protecting Europe's Energy Security Act (PEESA) of 2019 imposed sanctions on maritime activities supporting subsea pipeline construction. In late 2019, President Trump stated that Nord Stream II risked turning Germany and other European states into hostage of Russia, to which the German foreign minister Heiko Maas objected, decrying this as US "interference in autonomous decision-making of Europe."[36] By 2020, some European firms pulled out of Nord Stream II due to the threat of US sanctions. In 2021, the Biden administration effectively ended this episode by reaching an agreement with Germany to avoid further designations if Germany would support Ukraine in the event of Russian threats. As a postscript, parts of the Nord Stream pipeline were destroyed, possibly by Ukrainian forces, during Russia's invasion of Ukraine.[37]

EXPERT AND PRACTITIONER COMMENTS

Several experienced officials involved with shaping, implementing, or assessing these Europe-based coercive episodes reflected on the challenges that resulted in low goal satisfaction and high blowback in the region. A former senior State Department official argued that

> With regard to Russia, it's not a very encouraging story. Desire on the part of the US to see Russia become less corrupt has been legitimate—they have a lot of corruption. But all of our coercive efforts have failed. Since 2010/2011 when the coercion started to gather steam, Russia has become more corrupt. Most other sanctions have been ineffective or counter-productive. The outcome has been pretty disturbing. There is a certain political gain to be had in resisting CD that the US misses. It is designed in part to humiliate. Populations in the target state know this, so resisting has political value. Without corresponding incentive structures,

imposition of CD runs the risk of making US pressure something the target enjoys resisting. The defiance has greater rewards than compliance... it is broadly said in Russia that whatever Russia does, the US will seek to weaken it. The stated aims may be sincere, but there is an ultimate goal. A highly sinister inference even among friendly states has emerged, that the US is pursuing not narrow goals but dominance. So too has the view that CD is generalized competition and antagonism, not a specific or reasonable transaction.[38]

A European financial expert who studies Russia related that

My experience on the Russian case is that it's about communication. Biden turned up, albeit late, on Ukraine, but Russian experience over seven years was that there would not be costs. The cost/benefit calculation was distorted by precedent but also communication. The US didn't adequately align its allies on Russia—French, Germany etc. The message was not constant and coherent. In the period of the first Gulf War, the US had general credibility, and had created political capital through the success of its actions. But that diminishes over time. Obama's Syria "red line" inaction was a negative turning point. Putin didn't take threats seriously, because post-2014 sanctions were fairly light. What we learned in Russia was that Russia was particularly successful in identifying allies within Western countries to undercut or lighten sanctions. There were Russians in academia, business, lobbying effort by Russia's Western allies (Gerhard Schröder, others in UK). We didn't recognize how far we'd been infiltrated. Ironically, Russia has provided its own counter-example in Ukraine. The best way for Putin to win would have been "love and finance". Had he continued "supportive diplomacy," Ukrainians might have willingly aligned with Russia. Russia has provided a catastrophic failure as an object lesson in CD in Ukraine.[39]

A former senior US defense official who shaped coercive efforts targeting Russia in the Pentagon and on the NSC noted one successful instance:

My experience has been primarily with Russia—where we frequently impose sanctions but let them wither away. Sanctions after the Georgia war are an example...after six months, we were almost back to normal. By 2012, we had US firms back in St. Petersburg. We continued investing in the Russian energy sector. My gut says we are OK on balancing threats and demands, but not on follow through. Military force is the bluntest instrument, and when a credible willingness to use it is demonstrated, then even our worst adversaries will generally take us seriously and give us at least part of what we want. [Former Chairman of the Joint Chiefs of Staff] Mike Mullen talked to Valery Gerasimov [Chief of the General Staff of the Russian Armed Forces and First Deputy Minister of Defence] over Georgia—we wanted to bring back Georgian troops from Afghanistan, and we were going to fly them in C5s. We moved some combatant ships off the coast loaded with Tomahawk Land Attack Missiles. We notified Russia they were arriving, Gerasimov said "cannot guarantee safety." Mullen said, "that would be a mistake...here's the tail number and the time they will arrive." Same day the Russians began their withdrawal. They realized the US was willing to lose lives. I don't know of a case where economic coercion had that effect.[40]

Coercive attempts against France did not meet this study's threshold for inclusion as an episode due to the less public nature of the demands and threats, but they offer parallel lessons, which are reflected in the following observations by a senior US national security official and a French strategic educator.

US official: "In the runup to Operation Iraqi Freedom, the French were actively undercutting us in the international community—which enraged Rumsfeld. The French were going after other countries to keep them from providing material support. We decided to go after bilateral defense ties in the interagency—which in turn enraged some in the interagency. We started slow-rolling exercises, defense agreements and the like. Military coercion against an ally. The Marines were starkly opposed. In the end, the French didn't change position, and we failed in the expedition because we didn't have entire US government behind us."[41]

French official: "If I'm the target, it's difficult to push back frequently because of economic reasons; it's hard to retaliate effectively against the US. There's no military power in the world that can equal the US. It's very difficult to have any kind of deterrence or direct pushback. France is an interesting case study of how to push back less directly though. One of the best examples is 2002–2003, which was possible because within the French political assembly, there was consensus. President Chirac took a very clear stance—that there was not enough evidence of Iraqi weapons of mass destruction (WMD) and France would not take part in the Coalition. This would not have been possible without a political unity across the aisle. The only way to stand up to coercion begins with unity. Otherwise, the domestic political risk comes into the equation. It provides an interesting comparison with the European Union; sometimes there are measures passed in Brussels that are not in line with the majority wishes in a given Union state. In France, if there is domestic unity on such matters, the President has the levers to reject it."[42]

A retired senior US intelligence official with extensive experience in Europe and the Middle East addressed strategies for resisting US pressure that applied for Russia and Turkey:

A variety of strategies can be effective, particularly when applied in concert. Countries such as Turkey and Russia that have a) the wherewithal—ideological/nationalistic, religious, institutional— to offer plausible views of world events that compete with the Western narrative; b) strong state traditions; c) leaders who have a significant degree of popular legitimacy, and control over the state military and regulatory apparatus; d) achieved a certain degree of economic independence from the West, and yet retain economic importance to Europe; e) become strategically significant to China, the US peer competitor; and f) the ability to effectively retaliate directly or indirectly against perceived US impositions, are more likely to resist official or unofficial sanctions, or direct or indirect coercion. The Ukraine war appears to be demonstrating the efficacy of resistance via cooperation with countries that are either already at odds with the US or consider themselves likely future targets.[43]

A senior advisor to defense officials in a major NATO military establishment asserted that

The single most important failure of US foreign policy in this region is to understand the context. What is even more surprising is that the people who assess cost and benefit—to include a good number of ambassadors and defense officials—are less than expert in the target countries, and they fail miserably in understanding the calculus in the minds of those who are their counterparts. This creates a dilemma for US foreign policy, because usually those people are big wigs in terms of policy formulation. So, when they fail, they come back with a desire for vengeance. In the case of Turkey, at least one former ambassador misread everything about the country and then became openly antagonistic toward it. To prove that the assessment was not wrong, he sought to portray the actions, the actors, and the target itself problematic, rather than policy. The failure of assessment leads to future failures of analysis and policy. Claims are made that the target is irrational or incapable of understanding, whereas the assessors actually are. There is more than one such case.[44]

In a similar vein, and also referring to Turkey as a target, a long-time Turkish observer of US-Turkish relations with deep ties to the liberal establishment in both countries concluded that

The US has done a terrible job accounting for specific regional and domestic factors. Washington seems entirely oblivious to domestic calculations and constituencies. It's as if these were merger negotiations between two US companies—but that's not how it plays out. In the case of Turkey, not being able to understand how those things factor in is a real weakness. Additionally, we're not working from the same starting point.

US observers say "this is what would be rational for Erdoğan to do..." but don't account for the different factors shaping the viewpoint and analytical starting point. Demands for concession without recompense fail to present a transactional basis for negotiations, and thus place the entire risk on the target. The US is throwing its weight around, but does not look as convincing as it once did. Three allies critical to that notion: Saudi Arabia, Turkey, and Israel. Twenty years ago, when US even leaked something to a newspaper, foreign capitals took note and would seek to toe the line. Even a hint of US punishment or disfavor mattered. Now people sort of roll their eyes. Target countries have become better at excluding US and Western narratives or criticism, so the threats and demands have lost power.[45]

A similar concern was conveyed by a Ukrainian academic who has studied US pressure on Russia, Ukraine, and Turkey:

Very often there is a lack of understanding of local context. First maybe in terms of cultural specifics, and strategic thinking, domestic developments in the target country. In Turkey CD is seen as a very different way than it is perceived in DC. It backfires more often than it helps. There isn't unity in Washington on how to deal with these countries, and domestic debate allows target leadership to argue the lobby effect. Also, the view of unipolar, hegemonic US power—the lack of a specifically articulated message leads to expansive interpretation of threat and demands. The top-down approach of "teaching a lesson" to national leaders misses a host of sensitivities: local security concerns, domestic political campaigns, historical traumas, and such. Lack of local domestic expertise leads to misperception of likely response. In 2014, the Russian bluff and myth of Russian revanchism was taken too seriously, and necessary (though limited) coercion was avoided for an elusive "reset." This shifted the attention in Washington from causes of problems to consequences of solutions. On Russia, diplomatic isolation helps, because it's not just regime but the people who support regime policies. I am very hawkish on Russia—we should ban sports and cultural teams even unless the members are dissident from regime policy. Isolation is important when you have 70-80% of the population supporting the regime, because they will use the platforms for regime propaganda. There has to be a cancelation of the mindset of Russian greatness. Social perception matters. The theory of change sometimes requires pressure to obtain long-term change in social views, not just among elites. If the demand is quite narrow—as with Turkey or Canada—then the diplomatic measures and exclusions are less warranted.[46]

REGIONAL SUMMARY

US CD in Europe generally fell into one of three conceptual categories. The first involved deterring non-allies from regional aggression (e.g., Yugoslavia and Russia), the second focused on democratization of both enemies and allies (e.g., Belarus and Hungary), and the third aimed to modify the behavior of allied states (e.g., Germany and Turkey). When military force was employed, the first set saw some progress; without military force, the targets remained unmoved. The second set of episodes had no appreciable affect, outside of domestic political considerations. The third set led to severe intra-alliance difficulties, often weakening broader multilateral coercive efforts against the antagonistic targets. These cases demonstrate that coercive diplomacy only succeeds under rare conditions, with failed attempts leading to long-term structural challenges to US regional interests.

NOTES

1. Barry Blechman and Tamara Cofman Wittes, "Defining Moment: The Threat and Use of Force in American Foreign Policy," *Political Science Quarterly* 114, no. 1 (1999): 1–30.
2. Raymond Bonner, "How Sanctions Bit -- Serbia's Neighbors," *New York Times*, November 19, 1995, https://www.nytimes.com/1995/11/19/weekinreview/the-world-how-sanctions-bit-serbia-s-neighbors.html.
3. Raymond Bonner, "In Macedonia, Fears of a Wider Balkan War," *New York Times*, April 9, 1995.
4. Elaine Sciolino, "US Backs Bid to Press Peace on Bosnia Foes," *New York Times*, June 9, 1994, https://www.nytimes.com/1994/06/09/world/us-backs-bid-to-press-peace-on-bosnia-foes.html.
5. Leon Hartwell, "Conflict Resolution: Lessons From the Dayton Peace Process," *Negotiation Journal* 35, no. 4 (October 2019): 443–469.
6. "US Deputy Secretary of State Warns Belgrade Over Intransigence," Agence France Presse (AFP), March 16, 1998.
7. Stephen Hosmer, *Why Milosevic Decided to Settle the Conflict Over Kosovo When He Did*, Rand Corporation (Research Brief), January 1, 2002, https://www.rand.org/pubs/research_briefs/RB71.html.
8. "US Lifts Yugoslav Sanctions," CBS News, January 19, 2001, https://www.cbsnews.com/news/us-lifts-yugoslav-sanctions/.
9. Andrew Bowen and Corey Welt, *Russia: Foreign Policy and US Relations*, CRS Report R46761, April 15, 2021 https://crsreports.congress.gov/product/pdf/R/R46761#:~:text=For%20almost%2030%20years%2C%20the,as%20prime%20minister%20from%202008.
10. Corey Welt, Kristin Archick, Rebecca Nelson, and Diane Rennack, *US Sanctions on Russia*, CRS Report R45415, November 28, 2018, https://crsreports.congress.gov/product/pdf/R/R45415/1.
11. Adrian Karatnycky, "The Long, Destructive Shadow of Obama's Russia Doctrine," *Foreign Policy*, July 11, 2023, https://foreignpolicy.com/2023/07/11/obama-russia-ukraine-war-putin-2014-crimea-georgia-biden/.
12. Bill Browder, *Red Notice: A True Story of High Finance, Murder, and One Man's Fight for Justice*. (New York: Simon and Schuster, 2015).
13. Steven Pifer, "Burying the Magnitsky Bill's Message," *Commentary*, Brookings, June 29, 2012, https://www.brookings.edu/articles/burying-the-magnitsky-bills-message/.

14. Michael Weber and Edward Collins-Chase, *The Global Magnitsky Human Rights Accountability Act,* CRS In Focus Report IF10576, October 28, 2020, https://crsreports.congress.gov/product/pdf/IF/IF10576.

15. Rawi Abdelal and Aurelie Bros, "The End of Transatlanticism? How Sanctions Are Dividing the West," *Horizons* 16 (Spring 2020): 114–134.

16. Scott Horsley, "Is Trump the Toughest Ever on Russia?" *Morning Edition,* National Public Radio July 20, 2018, https://www.npr.org/2018/07/20/63 0659379/is-trump-the-toughest-ever-on-russia.

17. Alina Polyakova and Filippos Letsas, "On the Record" The US Administration's Actions on Russia," *Commentary,* Brookings, December 31, 2019, https://www.brookings.edu/articles/on-the-record-the-u-s-administrations-actions-on-russia/.

18. Dion Nissenbaum, "Turkish Turmoil is Tied to Pastor's Fate," *Wall Street Journal,* August 10, 2018, https://www.wsj.com/articles/turkish-turmoil-is-tied-to-pastors-fate-1533942854.

19. Jeremy Diamond, Zachary Cohen, and Elise Labott, "US Sanctions 2 Turkish Officials Over Detention of US Pastor," CNN, August 1, 2018, https://www.cnn.com/2018/08/01/politics/us-turkey-sanctions/index.html.

20. Author interview with senior State Department official, February 14, 2019.

21. Carol Lee and Courtney Kube, "Secret Deal With Turkey Paves Way for American Pastor's Release," NBC News, October 11, 2018 https://www.nbcnews.com/politics/white-house/secret-deal-turkey-paves-way-american-pastor-s-release-n919041.

22. Aaron Stein and Michelle Foley, "The YPG-PKK Connection," *MENASource,* Atlantic Council, January 26, 2016, https://www.atlanticcouncil.org/blogs/menasource/the-ypg-pkk-connection/.

23. Umut Uras, "Turkey's Operation Peace Spring in Northern Syria: One Month On," *Al Jazeera,* November 8, 2019 https://www.aljazeera.com/news/2019/11/8/turkeys-operation-peace-spring-in-northern-syria-one-month-on.

24. "Read Trump's Letter to President Erdogan of Turkey," *New York Times,* October 16, 2019, https://www.nytimes.com/interactive/2019/10/16/us/politics/trump-letter-turkey.html.

25. "Full Text of Turkey, US Statement on Northeast Syria," *Al Jazeera,* October 17, 2019, https://www.aljazeera.com/news/2019/10/17/full-text-of-turkey-us-statement-on-northeast-syria.

26. Roman Goncharenko, "What is S-400 and Why Does Turkey Want It?" *Deutsche Welle* (Germany), July 12, 2019, https://www.dw.com/en/s-400 -missile-system-what-is-it-and-why-does-turkey-want-it/a-49571650.

27. Aaron Mehta, "Turkey Officially Kicked Out of F-35 Program, Costing US Half a Billion Dollars," *Defense News,* July 17, 2019, https://www. defensenews.com/air/2019/07/17/turkey-officially-kicked-out-of-f-35- program/.

28. Mike Pompeo, *The United States Sanctions Turkey Under CAATSA 231* (press statement), December 14, 2020, https://2017-2021.state.gov/the- united-states-sanctions-turkey-under-caatsa-231/.

29. President George W. Bush, *Report on Belarus, the Last Dictatorship in Europe* (Report to Congress), March 16, 2006, https://2001-2009.state.gov/ p/eur/rls/prsrl/63297.htm.

30. Artyom Shraibman,*The House That Lukashenko Built: the Foundation, Evolution, and Future of the Belarusian Regime,* Carnegie Endowment for International Peace, April 12, 2018, https://carnegieendowment.org/201 8/04/12/house-that-lukashenko-built-foundation-evolution-and-future- of-belarusian-regime-pub-76059.

31. Author interview with senior advisor to Secretary of State, October 31, 2022.

32. Gergely Szakacs and Gareth Jones, "Hungary's Tax Chief Says She is on US Travel Ban List: Paper," Reuters, November 5, 2014, https://www.reuters. com/article/us-hungary-usa-corruption-idUSKBN0IP10J20141105/.

33. Patrick Kingsley, "Hungary's Leader Was Shunned by Obama, But Has a Friend in Trump," *New York Times,* August 15, 2018, https://www. nytimes.com/2018/08/15/world/europe/hungary-us-orban-trump.html.

34. Cristina Maza, "Donald Trump Told Hungary's Authoritarian Leader Orban, 'It's Like We're Twins,' According to US Envoy," *Newsweek,* May 15, 2019, https://www.newsweek.com/donald-trump-hungary- authoritarian-orban-twins-1426097.

35. "Nordstream 2: Germany and Russia Decry US Sanctions," BBC News, December 21, 2019, https://www.bbc.com/news/world-europe-50879435.

36. Matthew Karnitschnig, "Germany Blames Trump in Pursuit of Nord Stream 2 Pipeline," *Politico,* August 10, 2020, https://www.politico.eu/ article/germany-plays-trump-card-in-pursuit-of-russian-nord-stream-2 -pipeline-dream/.

37. Mark Bowden, "The Most Consequential Act of Sabotage in Modern Times, *The Atlantic,* December 13, 2023, https://www.theatlantic.com/

international/archive/2023/12/nord-stream-pipeline-attack-theories-suspects-investigation/676320/.
38. Author interview, January 4, 2023.
39. Author interview, October 3, 2022.
40. Author interview, November 21, 2022.
41. Author interview, November 21, 2022.
42. Author interview, November 22, 2022.
43. Author interview, January 25, 2023.
44. Author interview, December 10, 2022.
45. Author interview, February 4, 2023.
46. Author interview, January 12, 2023.

CHAPTER 7

ROAD TO NOWHERE: US COERCIVE DIPLOMACY IN SOUTH AND EAST ASIA

The results of US coercive diplomacy in South and East Asia were mixed, falling between the more successful outcomes in the Western Hemisphere (strong performance, high compliance, low rate of deterioration in regional bilateral relations) and the less effective efforts in the Middle East/Central Asia (poor performance, very low compliance rate, and high degree of deterioration in regional bilateral relations). The US achieved compliance in 14% of episodes (4 of 28), the lowest of any region, though alternative concessions were secured in 36% of cases. Domestic political interest in these efforts was moderate, with 71% of episodes scoring at least .5. Importantly, no coercive episodes in this region escalated into full-scale war. Bilateral relations with targets deteriorated in 39% of cases, lower than in Europe and the Middle East, possibly due to already strained relationships with countries like China, Cambodia, Myanmar, and North Korea. Notably, six countries accounted for 22 of the 28 episodes studied.

The following summary illustrates how three decades of US coercion played out across this subset of cases. Coercive performance scores range from 0 to 4, framing performance 0–1, Compliance and other outcome variables (alternative concession or AC, trajectory or T, and domestic satisfaction or DS) 0–1. Detailed episode scoring procedures and results are available in Appendix 1 online.

The data shows that the performance score for US CD South and East Asia (2.62) was moderate among the five regions studied, while the bilateral trajectory score (-0.23) was low but not the lowest. The framing score —how effectively coercive messages were crafted and resonated— was the lowest of the five regions studied. Domestic political interest in this region was also lower than in most others (0.69). Despite frequent coercive efforts, Washington saw negative trajectory results and low compliance, partly due to the region's hedging options, especially given the presence of a systemic rival like China.

COERCIVE DYADS

Pakistan
1990–2000: Following a decade of generally close relations in the 1980s, bilateral tensions escalated due to Pakistan's nuclear program, aimed at countering India's nuclearization. Sanctions under the Symington Amendment and Pressler Amendment were intensified by the cancelation of all aid in October 1990, including $564 million in proposed aid, $2.7 billion in programmed aid, and the sale of 71 F-16 aircraft.[1] Limited aid and military assistance resumed in 1995, though Pakistan remained subject to far more stringent sanctions than its rival India, which was proceeding apace to nuclear weapons testing. Senior US delegations attempted, unsuccessfully, to persuade Nawaz Sharif not to respond to India's nuclear tests. While trade continued with both India and Pakistan, the aid cutoff affected Pakistan more severely than India.[2] International support for sanctions on Pakistan was limited, due to India's actions

and fears of destabilizing Pakistan, which experienced a coup in 1999. This episode marked the end of the close US-Pakistan alliance from the Cold War era.

2001: Overlapping with the 1990s sanctions on Pakistan, a sharp coercive episode emerged after the 9/11 attacks, centering on US demands for Pakistan's support in the GWOT. Reportedly, these demands included direct military threats, with Deputy Secretary of State Richard Armitage allegedly stating that the US might "bomb Pakistan to the stone age."[3] President Pervez Musharraf complied with US demands in exchange for sanctions relief and a substantial aid package.[4]

2009–2016: The Obama administration gradually shifted away from its predecessor's approach of accommodating Pakistani concerns to obtain counterterrorism cooperation. In May 2009, President Obama praised Pakistan at an "Af-Pak" summit in Washington and expressed hope for a mutually beneficial outcome in Afghanistan. Despite the aid flow, Islamabad complained that Obama did not treat Pakistan as an equal, even as Obama requested roughly $2 billion in Pakistan Counter-insurgency Capability Funds (PCCF) and Coalition Support Funds (CSF), as well as $1.3 billion in Economic Support Funding (ESF) for 2011.[5] Obama recognized the internal support some elements of the Pakistani government provided to the Taliban and al-Qaeda, understanding they would not fully cooperate in counterterrorism efforts. Consequently, he approved the May 2011 strike in Abbottabad that killed Osama Bin Laden, despite the risk of blowback. Relations worsened in November 2011 when a NATO airstrike killed 24 Pakistani soldiers at the Salala border checkpoint, prompting Pakistan to close the Ground Line of Communication (GLOC), a vital supply route for US forces in Afghanistan. In response, Washington suspended 40% of military assistance, described by some as "the end of happy talk" with Pakistan.[6] The GLOC was reopened in July 2012 after Secretary of State Hillary Clinton issued a formal apology. However, tensions remained, with Pakistani officials sensing a growing rift following the death of Richard Holbrooke, a key diplomat who had maintained delicate communication channels with Pakistani officials. The Obama administration, torn between practical situational interdependence and increasing anti-Pakistan sentiment in Washington, struggled to maintain the previous level of engagement with Pakistan. From 2012 to 2014, Congress made CSF conditional on keeping the GLOCs open and improving counterterrorism assistance. In October 2015, Prime Minister Nawaz Sharif visited the White House, where he and President Obama issued a joint statement praising their cooperation on counterterrorism, Afghanistan, and other matters. By the end of the Obama administration, aid to Pakistan continued at reduced levels, with the final budget request including $860 million in military and economic aid, alongside sanctions on missile-related entities.

2017–2020: The Trump administration stepped up sanctions and pressure on Pakistan. After a policy review in the summer of 2017, Trump took a harder line on Afghanistan, calling out Pakistan while stating there was much to gain for cooperation and much to lose without it.[7] The Pentagon reduced CSF for Pakistan by $50 million in 2017 and threatened the entire $800 million of security assistance in early 2018 unless Pakistan took significant action against the Taliban and the Haqqani network. Trump tweeted accusations of Pakistan's "lies and deceit" in aiding militants. In 2018, Russia began accepting Pakistani students at its military schools, coinciding with the US ending funding for Pakistani students in US military schools and removing students from slots for the current academic year. Later in 2018, Congress stripped $500 million from the CSF budget, while the administration reprogrammed the remaining $300 million and terminated Pakistan's CSF program altogether. In late 2018, Presidents Trump and Imran Khan engaged in a Twitter exchange, with Trump claiming Pakistan "hasn't done a damn thing" and Khan asserting that US compensation was insufficient for Pakistan's costs during the Afghanistan war.[8] Following the spat, the two leaders exchanged letters, leading to a reset in relations. Trump enlisted Khan's assistance in facilitating negotiations to end the war in Afghanistan. Khan visited Trump in Washington, where the two leaders resumed positive messaging and set bilateral trade goals, although most bilateral aid remained suspended. A Financial Action Task Force (FATF) designation was also applied to push for further counterterrorism support from Pakistan. By 2020, funding for Pakistani military students to attend US military schools had been restored. However, the US tilt to India and Pakistan's tilt to China (and Russia) had become accepted geopolitical facts in both Washington and Islamabad.[9]

China

1990–1999: The Bush and Clinton administrations imposed a series of sanctions on China following the Tiananmen Square incident and in response to Chinese exports of missile and nuclear technology to Pakistan and Iran. The Foreign Relations Authorization Acts of 1990 and 1991 suspended seven categories of technical trade and cooperation, with waiver provisions. Military-to-military contacts between the US, European Union, and China were suspended from 1990 to 1995. Although the Clinton administration issued many waivers to promote bilateral trade, Congress sought to tighten sanctions. The Cox Committee later concluded that US technology in the 1990s significantly contributed to China's military advancements, particularly in rocket and missile technology.[10]

1990–2000: The Bush and Clinton Administrations applied coercive measures against Chinese intellectual property (IP) theft alongside defense and proliferation demands.[11] Chinese intransigence in the face of sanctions threats, and use of reciprocal tariffs against US goods, led the Clinton administration to pivot toward supporting China's World Trade Organization (WTO) accession, believing it would foster compliance. Throughout the early 1990s, Congress threatened to revoke Most Favored Nation (MFN) trade status, citing issues like IP, human rights, and market access. An IP agreement was reached in 1995, followed by sanctions in 1996 due to poor implementation. Conflicting US government messages hindered coercive success, ending with Chinese accession to the WTO in 2000.[12]

1996–1997: The Third Taiwan Straits crisis was triggered by Taiwan President Lee Teng Hui's US visit to Cornell University, his alma mater, in 1995. Having been denied a visa by the Clinton administration in 1994, Lee was assisted by Congress in obtaining one the following year.[13] China took umbrage at the visit, responding with missile tests and the mobilization of forces in Fujian. President Clinton responded to Chinese coercion with countermeasures, ordering a significant naval display of force, which included two carrier battle groups and amphibious assault ships sailing through the Taiwan Straits. A bipartisan House press conference condemned Chinese bellicosity, emphasizing that China could not prevent US military support for Taiwan. Under pressure from Congress to consider revoking MFN status and WTO accession, Clinton warned China to de-escalate. Administration officials, including Winston Lord, emphasized the need to oppose Chinese intimidation and protect access to the Straits.[14] A de-escalation was achieved with Chinese President Jiang Zemin's 1997 White House visit. Although the visit did not resolve US concerns over Taiwan, it led to a US commitment to support China's WTO accession and an agreement to regularize MFN status, rather than reviewing it annually. Nonetheless, Beijing resumed military exercises near the Straits in 1999.

2017–2020: Trump changed four decades of China policy by opposing their rise as a rival, rather than facilitating it.[15] Trump spoke with Taiwan's president before his inauguration, breaking with prior norms. In late 2016, President-elect Trump questioned the "One China" policy, stating that it made no sense unless it leads to a better trade deal. In late 2017, the Trump administration adopted a Free and Open Indo-Pacific (FOIP) policy to counter China's Belt and Road Initiative (BRI).[16] The NDAA for 2019 contained several anti-China provisions, including Sections 1258 (supporting Taiwan defense capabilities), 1259 (keeping Chinese military out of Rim of the Pacific Exercise (RIMPAC) until China ceased military construction in the South China Sea), and 1703 (preventing Chinese acquisition of US subsidiaries with technologically sensitive assets). In May 2019, Secretary Pompeo called out China for the oppression of

Uyghurs and other Muslims. In August 2019, Trump threatened a 10% tariff on most Chinese goods; while China threatened retaliation, the trade imbalance largely placed the burden on China. The US also labeled China as a currency manipulator. In January 2020, the US and China signed a Phase One trade agreement, aiming for greater reciprocity and stronger intellectual property protections for the US. In 2020, the Congress passed the Uyghur Human Rights Act, imposing property and visa restrictions on those involved in the oppression of the Uyghurs. In July 2020, Trump issued EO 13936, suspending Hong Kong's preferential trade status after Beijing revoked Hong Kong's political autonomy with a "national security" law. Trump EO 13959 introduced sectoral sanctions against companies tied to China's military-industrial complex.[17]

North Korea

1992–2000: The United States, with support from South Korea, Australia, and Canada, conducted a show of force, including military exercises and heightened alerts, in response to North Korea's nuclear program.[18] In September 1991, President Bush withdrew tactical nuclear weapons from South Korea, and the Koreas signed a Joint Declaration on Denuclearization. The IAEA later found discrepancies in North Korea's reports and declared non-adherence, while North Korea accelerated its missile program. In June 1992, the Bush administration imposed "missile sanctions" on North Korean entities. Following bilateral talks in New York, North Korea suspended its withdrawal from the Non-Proliferation Treaty after the United States agreed to forego threats, force, and internal interference in bilateral relations. In August 1994, an "agreed statement" to eliminate North Korean nuclear inventory in exchange for normalization and light water reactors was announced. By May 1996 it was clear that North Korea was facilitating missile and nuclear technology transfer to Iran and Pakistan, and several rounds of new sanctions were adopted. After significant North Korean missile launch progress (Nodong rockets) North Korea agreed to a launch moratorium in exchange for sanctions relief, which occurred in June 2000. In the Fall of 2000 North Korea and the United States issued joint statements on terrorism and missile development; Secretary Albright visits Pyongyang, and a presidential visit was discussed (but never happened). Special advisor Wendy Sherman has described this negotiating effort as "tantalizingly close."[19]

2001–2008: In March 2001, President George W. Bush expressed a willingness to engage with North Korea but emphasized the need for full verification, particularly regarding missile agreements. He expressed concerns about North Korea's commitment to honoring all terms of any agreement. In June 2001, Bush called for serious discussions on a broad agenda with North Korea and improved implementation of the Agreed Framework. During his post-9/11 State of the Union address, Bush included North Korea in the "axis of evil."[20] Despite maintaining a missile flight test moratorium, the US continued funding for Light Water Reactors (LWRs) in North Korea. In October 2002, Assistant Secretary of State James Kelly visited North Korea, proposing a comprehensive settlement on missiles, conventional forces, and human rights. North Korea responded by calling Kelly arrogant and defending its military-focused national policy as necessary. Shortly after, the State Department announced that Kelly's visit had confirmed North Korea's nuclear weapons enrichment program. In response, North Korea unsealed its nuclear reactors, restarted operations, and expelled IAEA inspectors. In 2003, North Korea withdrew from the Non-Proliferation Treaty and declared itself a nuclear weapons state. In 2004, the Six-Party Talks began, producing a Joint Statement in 2005. However, in 2006, North Korea fired seven ballistic missiles, prompting condemnation through UNSCR 1695, and later conducted an underground nuclear test. The Six-Party Talks stalled, as US inducements proved less appealing to North Korean leadership than the perceived security benefits of continuing nuclear weapons development.[21]

2009–2016: The Obama administration faced an early challenge when North Korea announced a satellite launch in violation of UNSCR 1718, prompting warnings from Washington, Tokyo, and Seoul that this would lead to a new round of sanctions. After a failed launch in April 2009,

Pyongyang withdrew from Six-Party Talks and conducted a nuclear test in May, leading Seoul to join the Proliferation Security Initiative (PSI), a US-led campaign aimed at preventing the trafficking of WMD by searching ships suspected of carrying illicit cargo. North Korea declared it would no longer honor the Korean Armistice. Sanctions were broadened under UNSCR 1874. Between April and August 2010, the US applied more sanctions and conducted military exercises in South Korea after the sinking of a South Korean ship. A brief interlude, which involved limited food aid in exchange for North Korea suspending research at Yongbyon and a moratorium on missile and nuclear tests, collapsed after a failed missile test in April 2012. North Korea later succeeded with an orbital launch in December 2012,[22] prompting further UN sanctions under UNSCR 2087. Another nuclear test led to additional sanctions under UNSCR 2094. In July 2013, a North Korean ship carrying weapons was intercepted en route from Cuba. Missile tests continued into 2015 as North Korea indicated progress toward fitting a warhead on an intercontinental ballistic missile (ICBM). In response, the Obama administration levied more sanctions. In 2016, following additional nuclear tests, UNSCR 2270 was passed. In July 2016, the US deployed the Terminal High Altitude Area Defense (THAAD) missile defense system in South Korea. President Obama's Director of National Intelligence, General James Clapper, stated that deterrence of North Korea's nuclear weapons program had failed, with nuclear weapons seen by Pyongyang as a "ticket to survival."[23]

2017–2020: The Trump era began with escalating pressure on North Korean nuclear and missile programs. Two weeks after Trump's inauguration, North Korea tested the Pukguksong-2 missile. In a meeting with Xi Jinping, Trump agreed to work together on North Korean denuclearization. The administration's policy, described as "maximum pressure" coupled with engagement, was outlined by State Department spokesmen. Secretary of State Rex Tillerson stated that the US was open to talks but would increase sanctions and coordinate with allies. In 2017, Kim Jong Un conducted ICBM tests, leading to the adoption of UNSCR 2371. Trump responded, stating "North Korea best not make any more threats...[or they'll see] fire and fury like the world has never seen," with military solutions now fully in place and "locked and loaded."[24] In September 2017, Kim conducted North Korea's largest nuclear test, prompting UNSCR 2375 and additional sanctions. On September 19, 2017, Trump threatened to "totally destroy North Korea" in his "rocket man" speech at the UN General Assembly, following with EO 13810 involving broader secondary sanctions. Kim responded with a speech assuring "corresponding, highest level of hardline countermeasures." Trump vowed greater cooperation with Japan and South Korea, including on ballistic missile defense, and placed North Korea back on the list of state sponsors of terrorism. UNSCR 2397 brought more sanctions. In early 2018, Kim indicated readiness for talks with South Korea; the US and South Korea postponed a military exercise in response. The US also led a summit meeting with twenty nations that fought to protect South Korea during the Korean War, focusing on sanctions coordination. Kim promised no new nuclear or missile tests during prospective talks with the US and agreed to inter-Korea talks at Panmunjom. In June 2018, after Kim "destroyed" the Pungye-Ri test site, Trump and Kim met in Singapore.[25] Wartime remains were returned, inter-Korea talks resumed, and additional military exercises were canceled. In February 2019, Trump and Kim met in Hanoi to continue discussions on sanctions removal and denuclearization. In May 2019, North Korea tested short-range missiles, but Trump stated that he did not consider this a breach, and the two leaders exchanged friendly letters. In June 2019, Trump and Kim met in the Demilitarized Zone (DMZ) between the Koreas. Talks later stalled, though no major provocations occurred, and the main US sanctions remained in place.[26]

Thailand

1991–1993: General Suchinda Krapayoon overthrew Thailand's civilian government in 1991, citing corruption and abuse of power. In response to the Black May incident of 1992,[27] where security forces shot unarmed civilians, the US suspended $39 million of military and economic aid,

demanding the return of an elected government. Thailand was also threatened with sanctions over intellectual property concerns and enforcement
of anti-Khmer Rouge security actions. The US military suspended the
annual Cobra Gold exercise, except for a small humanitarian assistance
event, although pending arms sales and $4 million in counter-narcotics
aid continued. Post-coup, the United States also tightened its scrutiny of
Thailand regarding intellectual property issues, putting the country on
the highest concern listing alongside China and India. In December 1992,
pro-military parties won a parliamentary majority in elections held in
December 1992. While the DoD resumed Cobra Gold, other forms of aid
remained suspended. Military aid resumed, and cooperation deepened
beginning in 1993, though civilian economic aid was phased out. From the
late 1990s onward, Bangkok developed closer relations with Myanmar
and China, a trend that has continued in subsequent decades.[28] It bears
mentioning that Thailand falls into the category of "difficult allies"—
along with Turkey and Pakistan—that are strategically located, tied to
the US by defense treaties, and yet iterative targets of failed US CD.

2006–2008: US aid was suspended after the 2006 coup in Thailand,
and again in 2014 after another coup. Under provisions of Section
508 of the Foreign Assistance Act,[29] military aid—including Foreign
Military Financing (FMF), Peacekeeping Operation (PKO), and IMET—was
mandatorily suspended, but exercises like Cobra Gold never completely
ceased. Approximately $29 million in aid was suspended within a month
of the 2006 coup, although International Narcotics Control and Law
Enforcement (INCLE) assistance continued. The US also suspended
bilateral free trade talks. The interim government agreed to hold elections
and adopt a new constitution by mid-2007. Congressional enthusiasm
for sanctions following the 2006 coup in Thailand was tempered by
the long-standing US-Thai alliance and the desire not to impose overly
harsh penalties. However, some members of Congress advocated for
stronger measures, including removing Thailand's designation as a
Major Non-NATO Ally (MNNA). In the end, sanctions were kept light to
avoid pushing Thailand further toward China. In February 2008, Deputy

Secretary of State John Negroponte certified that democracy had been restored, allowing US military aid to resume. Despite this, Thailand continued strengthening its ties with China, balancing relations to avoid over-reliance on the United States.[30]

2014–2019: A junta led by Army Chief Prayuth Chan-o-cha overthrew Yingluck Shinawatra's government. The US suspended $4.7 million in security assistance, some joint exercises, and visits as mandated by Section 508 of the Foreign Assistance Act. Then Secretary Kerry stated that there was no justification for a coup and urged the rapid return to civilian rule. Some aid was maintained, similar to the 2006 coup.[31] Meanwhile, following a trade deal between the Association of Southeast Asian Nations (ASEAN) and China in 2010, China had become Thailand's top trade partner. Chinese-Thai military ties also deepened during this period. Assistant Secretary of State Scot Marciel described the 2014 coup as more repressive and likely to last longer than the 2006 coup. Prayuth held the first general election after the coup in March 2019 under a constitution that allowed the electorate to choose a House of Representatives while the military to pick the Senate. The two houses then convened to select a prime minister. Following the election, US military aid resumed after this with IMET, FMF, MNNA status, and joint exercises such as Cobra Gold.[32]

Cambodia

1993–1997: The Bush administration lifted the 16-year-old embargo on Cambodia in early 1992, following hopes that the Khmer Rouge would adhere to the October 1991 Paris Accord. However, the Khmer Rouge violated the agreement by launching attacks on a UN peacekeeping force. From 1993 onward, the royal government under Hun Sen began moving in a distinctly authoritarian direction. UN Secretary-General Boutros Boutros-Ghali called for sanctions and the deployment of a peacekeeping force, while Western nations supported Prince Norodom Ranariddh as first prime minister, positioning him in opposition to Hun Sen, who served as second prime minister. The UN determined that the Khmer Rouge was exploiting claims of Vietnamese troop presence in border areas to engage in drug trafficking and illegal trade and pressured the Thai government to allow UN checkpoints on Thai territory. The US tried to cultivate positive relations with the royal government while simultaneously supporting economic and military pressure against the Khmer Rouge.[33] The Khmer Rouge movement was gradually co-opted and absorbed by the Hun Sen government, and it was more or less dissolved by 1999.[34]

1997–2007: After Hun Sen removed Norodom Ranariddh, a new set of sanctions was implemented to pressure the Hun Sen government to reform. This period was marked by another attempt by the Bush 43 administration to incentivize reform. All US aid was suspended from 1997 to 2007. Some aid resumed between 2007 and 2017 before it was suspended again under the Trump administration. Multiple senior-level visits between 2000 and 2001 explored the possibility of renewed aid in exchange for reform. In 2003, the US contemplated cutting off contributions to multilateral efforts in Cambodia due to concerns over Trafficking in Persons (TiP). The US offered $1 million in non-lethal military aid in 2007 to acknowledge progress on TiP and in exchange for a commitment from Cambodia not to file cases against US persons in the International Criminal Court; Cambodia accepted the aid but rejected the conditions. Hun Sen grew increasingly close to China during both periods of entirely suspended assistance and limited assistance.[35]

2017–2020: President Trump reimposed sanctions after Hun Sen's dissolution of opposition parties and his increasing security cooperation with China.[36] The People's Republic of China (PRC) developed industrial zones in Cambodia and other regional states, ostensibly linked to the Belt and Road Initiative, but these zones also hosted "security firms" with ties to PRC military intelligence and organized crime. After suspending military assistance in 2017, Washington passed sanctions provisions under the Asia Reassurance Initiative Act (ARIA) in late 2018. Increased targeted sanctions led Hun Sen to cancel the annual Angkor Sentinel exercise, as well as MIA search activities. In 2018, Vice President Pence sent a letter to Hun Sen expressing concern over an apparent Chinese military base under construction in Cambodia. By 2021, an arms embargo was imposed in response to growing Chinese influence.[37]

India

1992–1993 (with Russia): The Clinton administration applied sanctions against Russia and India to prevent the sale of Russian rocket engines to India, spurred by proliferation fears. In May 1992, the State Department announced the suspension of all US contact with the Russian and Indian space agencies pending reversal of the sale, which affected a $300 million US sale to India. US officials warned that a repeated pattern of such sales could result in the end of US aid to Russia. Russia viewed this as the US and Europe trying to squeeze Russian companies out of potential Asian, African, and Latin American markets, and the Indian Space Research Organization (ISRO) asserted that the threatened sanctions would not affect their research program. A deal for $24 billion of US aid to Russia was conditioned on non-sale of cryogenic engines, and a compromise was eventually reached in which the engines—but not technical know-how—would be sold. By the 2010s, India developed its own cryogenic engines and space launch capacity.[38]

1998–2001: The Clinton administration applied half-hearted pressure on India to forego nuclear weapons tests. After India conducted nuclear tests in May 1998, President Clinton announced mandatory sanctions for proliferation, which included suspending non-humanitarian assistance portion of $142 million aid program, banning the export of defense and high technology products to India, ending US credits and loan guarantees, opposing new lending by multilateral financial institutions, and recalling the US ambassador. The SFRC opposed lifting Glenn Amendment sanctions unless India abandoned "all nuclear ambitions."[39] After a coup in Pakistan and elections in India, Congress called for closer cooperation with India and increased pressure on Pakistan.[40] Important external actors—Russia for India and China for Pakistan—supported the South Asian giants in developing their missile and nuclear programs. In 2000, President Clinton reflected the generally pro-India policy by stating that the United States and India differ on nuclear issues, but Washington respected New Delhi's need to make its own security decisions; the Indians interpreted this as accommodation of their position. In 1999, Congress provided the president with waiver authority for Glenn Amendment sanctions; President Bush invoked this authority after 9/11 to secure greater support from both India and Pakistan in the GWOT.[41]

Myanmar

1992–2000: The Burmese military (Tatmadaw) seized power in September 1988 and began ruling through a military-dominated council known as the State Law and Order Restoration Council (SLORC) from 1988 to 1997, and the State Peace and Development Council (SPDC) from 1997 to 2011. The SLORC ignored the results of the 1990 election and jailed opposition leader Aung Suu Kyi. US sanctions, imposed under the Customs and Trade Act of 1990 and 1994–1995 Foreign Relations Authorization Act, restricted aid and US contributions to multilateral assistance. Although the more severe Free Burma Act of 1995 never passed into law, it was enough to prompt the SLORC to release Aung San Suu Kyi from house arrest. Additional sanctions under Section 570 of the Foreign Operations Appropriations Act and EO 13047 banned new investment from 1997 onward. China, ASEAN, Japan, and most other countries did not join the US in its unilateral sanctions, although some European countries did.[42]

2000–2012: There was no major policy shift during the Bush and early Obama administrations. Additional sanctions bills were introduced but not enacted from 1997 to 2003. After a renewed crackdown on political dissent in 2003, Aung San Suu Kyi was jailed again, leading to further sanctions under the Burmese Freedom and Democracy Act and EO 13310. A protest movement led by Buddhist monks, dubbed the "Saffron Revolution," was violently suppressed in 2007, resulting in new sanctions the following year, including the Junta's Anti-Democratic Efforts Act (JADE) and EOs 13448, 13464, 13619). In 2008, the Tatmadaw allowed the passage of a new constitution, which ultimately led to a new civilian government under its supervision.[43]

2012–2016: The Obama administration attempted re-engagement with Burma following the 2012 parliamentary by-elections, in which Aung San Suu Kyi's party was allowed to run. Although the elections were not considered fair, free, transparent, or inclusive, they were viewed as a positive development and noted as such by the White House. The Obama administration announced a five-step program to "relax and re-engage," which included increased use of sanctions waivers and rescission of EOs where appropriate.[44] In May 2012 the Burmese foreign minister visited Washington, followed by visits from President Thein Sein and Aung San Suu Kyi. Aung San Suu Kyi's party won the 2015 parliamentary elections, earning her the position of "State Counselor," though the Tatmadaw continued to control key policy areas. In December 2016, Obama further eased sanctions at Aung San Suu Kyi's request.[45]

2016–2020: Beginning in late 2016, the Tatmadaw initiated operations against Rohingya rebels in the northern part of Rakhine State, resulting in large-scale atrocities and the displacement of Rohingya civilians. In response, the Trump administration imposed visa bans and asset-blocking sanctions against military officers and units.[46] President Trump was criticized for allowing cabinet officials to lead the condemnation of Myanmar for the 600,00 to 700,000 displaced Rohingya, while he issued a somewhat conciliatory joint statement with Aung San Suu Kyi at an ASEAN summit in Manila. In 2017, the US revoked military travel waivers for Burmese officers and agreed with Congress to provide aid to Rohingya refugees. Reflecting a growing view that Obama's outreach to Yangon had been misguided, Trump appointed Kelley Currie, a staunch critic of the Burmese government, as an ambassadorial-level UN representative. Trump also sought ways to pressure the Tatmadaw to facilitate the safe and dignified return of the Rohingya from Bangladesh to Burma.[47] From 2020 onward, an indigenous democratic opposition began to develop in Burma, but there was another coup in early 2021.

Indonesia

1991–1999: The US suspended arms sales and aid after Indonesian security forces killed 270 East Timorese in the 1991 Santa Cruz Massacre in a territory Indonesia had seized following Portuguese decolonization in 1975. The first step was the suspension of IMET assistance in 1993, which Senator Russ Feingold described as a turning point in the relationship between US arms sales and human rights. The Leahy-Feingold Amendment on Arms Sales to Indonesia (1994) later narrowed the scope of the ban to small arms. In June 1997, President Muhammad Suharto rejected the Clinton administration's conditions for F-16 sales and Expanded IMET (E-IMET), renouncing both and broadening Indonesia's defense acquisition strategy to include the United Kingdom, Russia, and others.[48] Some joint training between Indonesian forces and US forces continued throughout the 1990s, but the 1999 Department of Defense Appropriations Act ended all such training. In 1999, Indonesia launched a full-scale intervention in East Timor, killing 1,500 civilians and destroying 70% of the infrastructure. The Clinton administration suspended all military-to-military contacts and offered support to an Australian-led peacekeeping operation. Indonesia moved toward civilian rule and democratization after 1999, spurred in part by the Asian financial crisis of 1997 and Suharto's resignation in 1998. The US re-engaged militarily, marked by a visit by US Pacific Command (PACOM) Commander Admiral Dennis Blair in September 2000. The EU lifted its weapons ban against Tentara Nasional Indonesia (TNI), the Indonesian military, in 2000; and between 2005 and 2007, the US dropped its ban on non-lethal assistance, followed later by lethal assistance. In the interim, Indonesia made a major purchase of Russian aircraft in 2003.[49]

Fiji

2007–2014: Fiji experienced four coups over a span of twenty years. After the last coup, which was less ethnically driven than the previous three (the first three exploited grievances of the native Fijian majority against the influential Indo-Fijian minority), aid and senior-level visas were suspended. These were not lifted until 2021, following democratic elections. There had been elections previously, such as in 2014, which were won by the coup leader's party. The January 2007 coup resulted in sanctions by the United States, United Kingdom, Australia, and New Zealand. Between 2009 and 2011, coup leader Frank Bainimarama invoked martial law, dismissed judicial branch leaders after they ruled the coup illegal, expelled the ambassadors of Australia and New Zealand, censored news outlets, and was accused of torturing opponents. After 2013, he continued to rule by decree, having directed and then rejected a new constitution drafted by a foreign expert. He eventually directed adoption of a Fijian-drafted constitution, which included broad immunity for coup leaders and broad authority for the president to suspend rights. Bainimarama accused the West of trying to damage Fiji and turning their backs on it, while promising not to "kowtow" to them as he sought improved ties with Russia, China, and North Korea in a "Look North" policy.[50] In October 2014, Bainimarama's party won new elections, and the United States subsequently lifted visa bans, resumed aid, and restarted military engagement and assistance. During the period of sanctions, China became Fiji's largest external donor, providing over half of all external aid and engaging in military engagement, including training some Fijian officials in China.[51] Under the Morrison government, Australia resumed serious re-engagement with Fiji, focusing on training Fijian forces for peacekeeping deployments.

Laos

2018–2020: The Trump administration applied diplomatic sanctions on Laos for failing to facilitate the return of deportees. The Departments of State and Homeland Security suspended visa processing for B1, B2, and B1/B2 non-immigrant visas (NIVs) for officials at the Directorate General level and higher, targeting the Laotian Ministry of Public Security and their family members. A3 and G5 Non-Immigrant Visas were also suspended for official employees. The goal was to pressure Laos into signing a repatriation agreement like other countries in the region, such as Cambodia and Vietnam, had signed after normalizing relations with the United States in the 2000s. Laos hesitated to agree, fearing it would encourage deportations. Laos responded "with regret" to the visa bans, calling them an "unfair act" that should be reversed. Despite the diplomatic tension, the visa sanctions did not affect the relatively small aid relationship between the two countries under the US-Laos Comprehensive Partnership of 2016, which had increased funding for demining and related activities from $5 million to $30 million per year. The US agreed to fund a program for repatriation and reintegration, while negotiations with Laos continued. The program proceeded for the small number of already-deported Lao nationals. In early 2020, several members of Congress introduced a bill to halt the deportation of Laotians, including those convicted of crimes. In April 2020, Laos became the first country to be hit with a second wave of visa sanctions related to deportee returns.[52]

Philippines

2020: Congress pressed for action to punish the Philippines for human rights violations. The Foreign Operations Appropriations Act of 2020 (passed in December 2019) imposed travel bans on certain Filipino officials involved in human rights abuses. Senate Resolution 142 condemned extra-judicial killings (EJKs) and the arrest of Philippine Senator Leila De Lima and human rights defenders, and it called upon President Trump to sanction Philippine officials. In retaliation, the Philippine government implemented visa bans on Senators Patrick Leahy and Richard Durbin, who were vocal about the budget resolution and De Lima's detention. In February 2020, President Rodrigo Duterte announced plans to terminate the Visiting Forces Agreement (VFA), but he suspended those plans in June 2020 and again in 2021. At the same time, public trust in China among Filipinos dropped sharply in 2020, leading the Philippines to view the United States and Australia as more favorable hedging options against China. Leila De Lima remained in detention into 2021. Despite these tensions, US development aid and military assistance to the Philippines continued without interruption.[53]

Expert and Practitioner Comments

One experienced senior national security official summed up the US experience with coercing Pakistan through the lens of asymmetric commitment:

> Pakistan understood that its possession of nuclear weapons was worth resisting coercion for, both because it was a high-priority national commitment and because it complicated US risk tolerance for escalation. Islamabad rightly gauged that US popular enthusiasm or mobilization for counterproliferation underperformed Pakistani domestic commitment to matching Indian nukes. They accordingly understood that the US would not mobilize enough resources to inflict sufficient pain to change Pakistan's core security strategy. It was obvious early on that it wasn't going to work. Pakistan had existential interests that we just blew right through. It is very difficult for the US to adequately gauge target commitment because our power advantage means what is peripheral for us is likely central or existential for them. This leads to the target having a more accurate calculation on relative commitment and risk tolerance. Leaders in Islamabad knew that our risk tolerance for instability in nuclear-armed Pakistan was lower than our risk tolerance for failure in Afghanistan.[54]

A senior Indian national security analyst assessed that the US misunderstood the motives of both South Asian nuclear states during their drive for nuclear weapons:

> The US universal approach to cost imposition generally applied over this period. Washington did not get into the mindset and drivers of specific targets, and thus could not reliably predict their response. On non-proliferation, the US early in the period did not appreciate the motives and imperatives of various sides. It overlooked non-proliferation goals in Pakistan due to grand strategic reasons related to the Cold War. There was nuclear testing in China on behalf of Pakistan. By 1984 India was convinced of this, and so restarted its own nuclear program. The US did not understand the mutual escalatory dynamic, and how to affect the

calculus of both sides. Later in the period, though, this changed somewhat. For example, the ASAT (anti-satellite weapons) test by India in 2019 was received differently, because by then the US and India were aligned. India needed to demonstrate a capability to deter China from thinking it had an advantage. It's not clear whether the US has firm, fixed, and fair criteria for removal. In the case of India, sanctions from 1974 and 1998 went on for too long, in some cases being lifted about a decade ago. Even as the strategic relationship improved, these legacy sanctions continued, and in a sense slowed the development of trust…it sometimes seems the sanctions are forgotten, or become a sort of default.[55]

A former US military officer who served in senior civilian security-related positions addressed Chinese resistance to coercion, and why it might not work for smaller countries:

China proved to other countries that you get your tentacles into the US, especially through business, and develop influence within the political system. Getting any sort of condemnation of China is very hard now, because of the many US corporations that are intertwined with Chinese success. That gives them leverage as well as protection. The National Basketball Association makes millions of dollars in China, and the potential loss of that money has political weight. Mutual dependency is a good strategy, but doesn't work for many smaller countries. For smaller countries, dominating their own internal information channels and using them to stimulate resistance is best.[56]

An experienced foreign affairs correspondent covering geopolitics for a major Asian outlet linked poor outcomes in Myanmar (Burma) to Washington's failure in reading regional context:

Burma is a great example. Clearly the junta sees no benefit in listening to America. They've tried their hand at democracy, and it didn't bring anything to the military. America has to put itself in the shoes of the stakeholders in the country—there is a tendency to see things only from one perspective and way of thinking. That democracy is better than autocracy—this is not a universal assumption. Many in Asia think social order is higher. Blind belief in the American system is clouding judgment. America doesn't have the luxury of making big mistakes any more in an era of Great Power Competition. You can't assume that countries won't tilt toward China based on democratic values alone. If the result of Chinese influence is social order and prosperity as opposed to chaos and external impositions, they may prefer China. But China is not the only path—Turkey and other authoritarian democracies, regional alignments with varying systems and degrees of democracy might be the preferred model in a multilateral system with a more distributed power structure.[57]

An American political advisor to previous Secretaries of State described the obstacles in Washington to carefully crafting coercive efforts:

There is a pure inertia in bureaucratic decision-making—sanctions on Burma as an example- not very effective, but hard for the next guy to say this is doing nothing and that we should lift. It is politically more expedient to just leave measures in place. The prevalence of the word "sanctions" and thinking of sanctions as synonymous with CD shows that it has become reflexive or default. We are disinclined to make focused, concerted efforts that combine various tools (including military pressure). The "sweet spot" for Washington is to impose accountability while not incurring domestic political cost. As the number of targets multiplies, to what extent do we have resources to effectively monitor so many targets? Hard to believe we do that effectively.[58]

REGIONAL SUMMARY

South Asia and East Asia are geographically distant from the United States and close to several rival power centers. These factors impose certain limits to US coercive power. While these limitations are similar in nature to those faced by US policy in other regions, they differ in scale. The region's relatively low degree of integration with, and dependence upon, US power has led to two outcomes. First, states targeted by US CD have strengthened trade and security ties with China. This has occurred with long-time allies of the US such as Thailand and Fiji, as well as less friendly regimes such as Cambodia and Myanmar. Second, there has been a growing integration among states opposed to US policies, forming a kind of resistance bloc—China, North Korea, and Pakistan. US CD has generally not been successful in South and East Asia in terms of punishing adversaries, consolidating alliances, or drawing neutral states into the US sphere of influence. In many cases, it is unclear whether it has significantly influenced the strategic decisions of target states. The case of India, however, shows a hopeful example of rebuilding alliances by adapting or ending CD. This case was unusual for the region during the period under study.

Notes

1. Sabir Shah, "A Chronology of US Aid Suspension to Pakistan," *The News* (Pakistan), July 22, 2019, https://www.thenews.com.pk/print/501777-a-chronology-of-us-aid-suspension-to-pakistan.
2. Daniel Morrow and Michael Carriere, "The Economic Impacts of the 1998 Sanctions on India and Pakistan," *The Nonproliferation Review* 6, no. 4 (Fall 1999): 1–16.
3. Suzanne Goldenberg, "Bush Threatened to Bomb Pakistan, Says Musharraf," *The Guardian* (UK), September 22, 2006, https://www.theguardian.com/world/2006/sep/22/pakistan.usa.
4. Shanthie D'Souza, "U.S.-Pakistan Counter-Terrorism Cooperation: Dynamics and Challenges," *Strategic Analysis* 30, no. 3 (Jul–Sep 2006): 525–561.
5. Susan Epstein and K. Alan Kronstadt, *Pakistan: US Foreign Aid Conditions, Restrictions, and Reporting Requirements* (CRS Report R42116), September 12, 2013, https://crsreports.congress.gov/product/pdf/R/R42116/12.
6. K. Alan Kronstadt, *Pakistan-US Relations* (CRS Report R41832), May 24, 2012, https://crsreports.congress.gov/product/pdf/R/R41832/16.
7. Barkha Dutt, "Trump Gets it Right on Afghanistan and Pakistan," *Washington Post*, August 24, 2017, https://www.washingtonpost.com/news/global-opinions/wp/2017/08/24/trump-gets-it-right-on-afghanistan-and-pakistan/.
8. Alena Sadiq, "Trump and Pakistani Leader Face Off on Twitter," *Politico*, November 19, 2018, https://www.politico.com/story/2018/11/19/trump-pakistan-twitter-osama-bin-laden-1005556.
9. Feroz Hassan Khan, "Russia-Pakistan Strategic Relations," *Journal of Indo-Pacific Affairs*, January 15, 2021, https://www.airuniversity.af.edu/JIPA/Display/Article/2473361/russiapakistan-strategic-relations-an-emerging-entente-cordiale/.
10. Shirley Kan, *China and Proliferation of Weapons of Mass Destruction and Missiles: Policy Issues*, CRS Report RL31555, August 8, 2003, https://apps.dtic.mil/sti/pdfs/ADA478389.pdf.
11. Joseph Massey, "The Emperor is Far Away: China's Enforcement of Intellectual Property Rights Protection, 1986–2006, *Chicago Journal of International Law* 7, no. 1, June 2006, https://chicagounbound.uchicago.

edu/cgi/viewcontent.cgi?referer=&httpsredir=1&article=1241&context=
cjil

12. Nicholas Lardy, "Issues in China's WTO Accession," Commentary, Brookings, May 9, 2001, https://www.brookings.edu/articles/issues-in-chinas-wto-accession/.

13. Phillip Saunders and Kristen Gunness, "Averting Escalation and Avoiding War: Lessons from the 1995–1996 Taiwan Strait Crisis," *China Strategic Perspectives 17* (Washington: National Defense University, 2022), 1–10.

14. Winston Lord, "The United States and the Security of Taiwan," *Statement before the Subcommittee on East Asian and Pacific Affairs,* US Department of State Archive, February 7, 1996, https://1997-2001.state.gov/current/debate/mar96_china_us_taiwan.html.

15. Bethany Allen-Ebrahamian, "Special Report: Trump's U.S.-China Transformation," *Axios*, January 19, 2021, https://www.axios.com/2021/01/19/trump-china-policy-special-report.

16. Lindsey Ford, "The Trump Administration and the 'Free and Open Indo-Pacific,'" Brookings, May 2020, https://www.brookings.edu/articles/the-trump-administration-and-the-free-and-open-indo-pacific/.

17. Maxwell Bessler, "The Drive to Decouple," *New Perspectives on Asia*, Center for Strategic and International Studies (CSIS), January 24, 2023, https://www.csis.org/blogs/new-perspectives-asia/drive-decouple.

18. Kelsey Davenport, "Chronology of U.S.-North Korean Nuclear and Missile Diplomacy, 1985–2022," Fact Sheets and Briefs, Arms Control Association, April 2022, https://www.armscontrol.org/factsheets/dprkchron#1991.

19. Mark Landler, "With US and North Korea, a Repeated History of Hope and Disappointment," *New York Times*, March 6, 2018, https://www.nytimes.com/2018/03/06/us/politics/north-korea-us-history-negotiations.html.

20. David Frum, "The Enduring Lessons of the 'Axis of Evil' Speech," *The Atlantic*, January 29, 2022, https://www.theatlantic.com/ideas/archive/2022/01/axis-of-evil-speech-frum-bush/621397/.

21. Rupert Schulenburg, "A Failure of Coercion: the George W. Bush Administration and North Korea," *e-international relations*, June 7, 2020, https://www.e-ir.info/2020/06/07/a-failure-of-coercion-the-george-w-bush-administration-and-north-korea/.

22. Libby Johnson, "The End of Strategic Patience," *The Strategy Bridge*, September 29, 2017, https://thestrategybridge.org/the-bridge/2017/9/29/the-end-of-strategic-patience.

23. Steve Herman, "US Official: Stopping N. Korea's Nuclear Program 'Probably is Lost Cause,'" Voice of America (VOA) News, October 25, 2016, https://www.voanews.com/a/us-official-stopping-north-korea-nuclear-program-lost-cause/3566044.html.

24. Jeff Zeleny, Dan Merica, and Kevin Liptak, "Trump's 'Fire and Fury' Remark Was Improvised but Familiar," CNN, August 9, 2017, https://www.cnn.com/2017/08/09/politics/trump-fire-fury-improvise-north-korea/index.html.

25. "North Korea's Kim Promises No More Nuclear or Missile Tests," France24, April 21, 2018, https://www.france24.com/en/20180421-nkoreas-kim-promises-no-more-nuclear-or-missile-tests.

26. Kevin Liptak, "Trump Takes 20 Steps into North Korea, Making History as First Sitting US Leader to Visit Hermit Nation," CNN, June 30, 2019, https://www.cnn.com/2019/06/29/politics/kim-jong-un-donald-trump-dmz-north-korea/index.html.

27. Dominic Faulder, "Military's Unkept Promise From 1992 Looms Over Thai Elections," Nikkei Asia, March 24, 2019, https://asia.nikkei.com/Politics/Thai-election/Military-s-unkept-promise-from-1992-looms-over-Thai-elections.

28. Christopher Chivvis, Scot Marciel, and Beatrix Geaghan-Breiner, *Thailand in the Emerging World Order* (Publication 90818), Carnegie Endowment for International Peace, October 26, 2023, https://carnegieendowment.org/2023/10/26/thailand-in-emerging-world-order-pub-90818.

29. The Foreign Assistance Act is a landmark piece of legislation enacted by the United States Congress in 1961 to regulate and consolidate US foreign aid programs. It established the framework for providing economic, military, and humanitarian assistance to foreign countries, with a focus on promoting economic development, democracy, and US foreign policy objectives.

30. Emma Chanlett-Avery, *Political Turmoil in Thailand and US Interests*, CRS Report RL40605, May 26, 2009, https://crsreports.congress.gov/product/pdf/R/R40605.

31. Emma Chanlett-Avery, Wil Mackey, and Ben Dolven, *Thailand: Background and US Relations*, CRS Report RL32593, July 31, 2015, https://crsreports.congress.gov/product/pdf/RL/RL32593.

32. Prim Chuwiruch, "US is Ready to Boost Arms Sales to Thailand After its Elections," Bloomberg, March 4, 2019, https://www.bloomberg.com/news/articles/2019-03-05/u-s-ready-to-boost-thai-arms-sales-after-vote-countering-china.

33. National Security and International Affairs Division, US General Accounting Office Cambodia: Limited Progress on Free Elections, Human Rights, and Mine Clearing (GAO Briefing Report), February 1996, https://pdf.usaid.gov/pdf_docs/PCAAA705.pdf.

34. Elizabeth Becker, "Pol Pot's End Won't Stop US Pursuit of His Circle," *New York Times*, April 17, 1998, https://www.nytimes.com/1998/04/1 7/world/death-of-pol-pot-the-diplomacy-pol-pot-s-end-won-t-stop-us-pursuit-of-his-circle.html.

35. Thomas Lum, *Cambodia: Background and US Relations* (CRS Report RL32986), April 30, 2009, https://apps.dtic.mil/sti/pdfs/ADA501062.pdf.

36. Joshua Kurlantzick, "The Trump Administration Takes Action Against the Hun Sen Government," Council on Foreign Relations blog, December 8, 2017, https://www.cfr.org/blog/trump-administration-takes-action-against-hun-sen-government.

37. Elaine Kurtenbach, "US Orders Arms Embargo on Cambodia, Cites Chinese Influence," Associated Press, December 9, 2021, https://apnews.com/article/business-asia-southeast-asia-foreign-policy-george-w-bush-dcace984dcd5a50bf4e3acde33afde5a.

38. "Joe Biden Once Said Russia Selling Space Rockets to India Was 'Dangerous,'" *The Week Magazine* (India), October 13, 2020, https://www.theweek.in/news/india/2020/10/13/joe-biden-once-said-russia-selling-space-rockets-to-india-was-dangerous.html.

39. John Bisney, "Lawmakers Call for Tough US Response to India's Nuclear Tests," CNN, May 13, 1998, https://www.cnn.com/ALLPOLITICS/1998 /05/13/senate.india/.

40. Dianne Rennack, *India and Pakistan: US Economic Sanctions*, CRS Report RS20995, February 3, 2003, https://crsreports.congress.gov/product/pdf/RS/RS20995/4.

41. Office of the Spokesman, "Sanctions on India and Pakistan," (Fact Sheet), Department of State, September 28, 2001, https://2001-2009.state.gov/r/pa/prs/ps/2001/5101.htm.

42. Peter Baker, "US to Impose Sanctions on Burma for Repression," *Washington Post*, April 22, 1997, https://www.washingtonpost.com/archive/politics/1997/04/22/us-to-impose-sanctions-on-burma-for-repression/b573d8ca-450e-4ae3-913a-602e6af1aa5a/.

43. Michael Martin, *US Sanctions on Burma*, CRS Report R41336, October 19, 2012, https://crsreports.congress.gov/product/pdf/R/R41336/17.

44. Josh Gerstein, "Obama Returns to Myanmar Amid Fading Reform Hopes," *Politico*, November 12, 2014, https://www.politico.com/story/2014/11/myanmar-barack-obama-hillary-clinton-112798.
45. Andrew Selth, "Aung San Suu Kyi and the Tatmadaw," *Australian Outlook*, Australian Institute for International Affairs, June 3, 2017, https://www.internationalaffairs.org.au/australianoutlook/aung-san-suu-kyi-tatmadaw/.
46. Prashanth Parameswaran, "US Myanmar Policy Under Trump in the Spotlight With New Sanctions," *The Diplomat*, July 18, 2019, https://thediplomat.com/2019/07/us-myanmar-policy-under-trump-in-the-spotlight-with-new-sanctions/.
47. "Trump Appoints Policy Specialist on Myanmar to UN Job," *The Irrawady*, June 23, 2017, https://www.irrawaddy.com/news/burma/trump-appoints-policy-specialist-myanmar-un-job.html.
48. Larry Niksch, *Indonesia: US Relations With the Indonesian Military*, CRS Report 98-677F, August 10, 1998, https://www.everycrsreport.com/files/19980810_98-677_ccc717c388e29caae32d5e71103fe52381077691.pdf.
49. Satu Limaye, "Minding the Gaps: The Bush Administration and U.S.-Southeast Asia Relations," *Contemporary Southeast Asia* 26, no. 1 (2004): 73–93.
50. Elke Larsen, "Re-engaging Fiji: The Right Policy at the Right Time," *Pacific Partners Outlook*, Center for Strategic and International Studies, February 27, 2014, https://www.csis.org/analysis/pacific-partners-outlook-reengaging-fiji-right-policy-right-time.
51. Ethan Meick, Michelle Kerr, and Han May Chan, *China's Engagement in the Pacific Islands: Implications for the United States* U.S.-China Economic and Security Review Commission, June 14, 2018, https://www.uscc.gov/sites/default/files/Research/China-Pacific%20Islands%20Staff%20Report.pdf.
52. Dan Cadman, "Beyond Recalcitrant: Laos Incurs a Second Round of Visa Sanctions," Center for Immigration Studies, June 8, 2020, https://cis.org/Cadman/Beyond-Recalcitrant-Laos-Incurs-Second-Round-Visa-Sanctions.
53. Thomas Lum, Ben Dolven, and Christina Arabia, *The Philippines: Background and US Relations*, CRS Report R47055, September 14, 2022, https://crsreports.congress.gov/product/pdf/R/R47055/4.
54. Author interview, August 9, 2022.
55. Author interview, September 16, 2022.
56. Author interview, December 21, 2022.

57. Author interview, November 22, 2022.
58. Author interview, October 31, 2022.

CHAPTER 8

TO WHAT END?
US COERCIVE DIPLOMACY
IN AFRICA

There were more episodes of US coercive diplomacy in Africa than in the other four regions studied, with 40 instances over the three decades in question. Compliance was achieved in 12 of 40 episodes, the second highest rate among the five regions studied, while some form of alternative concessions was obtained in 14 episodes, also near the top of the regional rankings. The number of episodes that resulted in a deterioration of bilateral relations or US regional standing over the long term was lower in Africa than in other regions, occurring in 9 of 40 episodes (23%). Additionally, domestic political interest in these cases was minimal, with only 8 of 40 episodes (20%) garnering significant attention. Only one case of US CD in Africa led to open war—Libya.

The following summary illustrates how three decades of US coercion unfolded across this subset of cases. Coercive performance scores range from 0 to 4, framing performance 0–1, compliance and other outcome variables (alternative concession or AC, trajectory or T, and domestic satisfaction or DS) 0–1. Detailed episode scoring procedures and results are available in Appendix 1 online.

The data shows that, across the African episodes, the US demonstrated its strongest regional performance, with a score of 2.94 on a 4-point scale, the highest among the five geographical regions studied. Washington achieved the second-highest performance in terms of framing its message clearly and effectively, scoring 0.51 on a 1-point scale, trailing only behind coercive efforts in the Western Hemisphere. The compliance score (0.26) was relatively positive—better than the Middle East/Central Asia, South/East Asia and Europe, but lower than in the Western Hemisphere. Notably, the post-coercion trajectory score, while not particularly strong, was the highest among the regions studied (+0.03 on a scale of -1 to +1). However, the score for domestic political satisfaction (0.33 out of 1) was the lowest, indicating that coercive efforts in Africa captured the public imagination in the United States less than in other regions. African target countries, like those in Latin America, appear susceptible to effective US CD. Yet, several cases resulted in outcomes that conflicted with US national interests, such as state fracture in Libya and Somalia, rising Russian influence in central Africa, and the weakening of military-to-military ties in several countries.

Coercive Dyads

Somalia
1992–1995: US coercion aimed at ending predatory clan rule in a failed state. In 1991, the Siad Barre regime collapsed, and brutal clan fighting ensued, with Mohammed Farah Aidid emerging as a major player. At the request of the UN, President George H. W. Bush launched Operation Restore Hope, deploying 25,000 troops to restore food distribution and some degree of stability in Mogadishu. The UN then took over from the US as United Nations Operation in Somalia (UNOSOM), although 1,200 US troops remained. After the deaths of US and Pakistani soldiers in the

summer of 1993, Task Force Ranger was deployed to hunt Aidid, while President Clinton offered negotiations with him.[1] Congressional resistance to the mission grew, with Senator John McCain and others accusing Clinton of mission creep. In October 1993, the "Black Hawk Down" disaster resulted in serious US casualties, leading to the deployment of an additional 3,000 troops. Following this, the UN backed off its goal of disarming militias, and by the spring of 2004, Washington withdrew all remaining US forces; other UN forces withdrew in 1995.[2] Somalia experienced a series of interim governments, conferences, declarations, and multilateral stabilization attempts, but a unified, recognized, and reasonably stable government did not emerge until 2012.

2010–2013: The Obama administration initiated a new coercive effort in Somalia in 2010 to shift the balance of power against al-Shabaab, the al-Qaeda-aligned movement vying for control of the country. Executive Order 13536, issued in 2010, targeted arms transfers, the use of child soldiers, and actions undermining the transitional government. In 2012, EO 13620 expanded these sanctions, which was a significant source of funding for al-Shabaab.[3] The US ban on military aid to Somalia was lifted in 2013, although pressure on al-Shabaab was continued through US support to the African Union Mission in Somalia (AMISOM), an African Union's military operation. By 2019, the Trump administration re-established a US Embassy in Mogadishu and intensified military strikes against al-Shabaab Despite these efforts, the group maintained control over a parallel state in much of Somalia.[4]

2010–2016: In April 2010, the Obama administration began efforts to curb piracy and militia violence in Somalia by blocking the property of individuals and entities threatening peace, security, and stability in Somalia. US forces had already been targeting jihadist groups in Somalia since 2008. UNSCR 2002 (July 2011) and UNSCR 2036 (February 2012), along with EO 13620 (July 2012), banned the import of charcoal after it was determined that al-Shabaab was profiting from its sale. In 2012, the Federal Government of Somalia (FGS) was established, marking the first national government since 1991. While President Obama renewed sanctions despite its formation, he also formally recognized the FGS and restarted an aid program. By 2014, the Obama administration shifted from a more "arms-length" approach to the FGS to engaging and supporting the FGS, while also increasing operational and logistical support to African Union (AU) and FGS troops.[5] By the end of the period of this study in 2020, al-Shabaab remained a disruptive force, the FGS continued to be fragile, and AMISOM was still operational.

2017–2020: President Trump's EO 13769 directed the denial of certain categories of visas due to lax passport and customs controls in several countries, including Somalia. The goal was to pressure these nations to tighten their procedures. Several court battles led to revisions, moving from EO 13769 (issued on January 27, 2017) to EO 13780 (March 6, 2017) and Presidential Proclamation 9645 (September 24, 2017).[6] The visa ban is considered a separate sanctions episode in this study only for those countries not concurrently subjected to a broader set of sanctions.

Sudan

1990–2000: Sudan had a civil government until the 1989 coup led by President Omar al-Bashir. In response, Congress suspended non-humanitarian assistance in 1990, and in 1991 President George H. W. Bush suspended Sudan's preferred trading status. In 1993, the Department of State designated Sudan as a state sponsor of terrorism. In early 1996, the Sudanese defense minister El Fatih Erwa visited Washington to explore options for improving ties and was presented with eight demands. Subsequently, Khartoum expelled Osama Bin Laden, which led to a loosening of restrictions on financial transactions. President Clinton, seeking to preempt harsher Congressional sanctions, implemented additional financial and travel bans in November 1997.[7] After the 1998 embassy bombings in Kenya and Tanzania, Clinton ordered airstrikes against targets in Sudan believed to be linked to al-Qaeda, though the intelligence behind the strikes was later questioned. By 1999, Bashir indicated a willingness to fully cooperate with the United States, offering assurances that Sudan did not support terrorists.[8]

2000–2008: Despite increasing cooperation on counterterrorism issues, sanctions pressure persisted as the focus of US concern shifted from al-Qaeda to conflicts in southern Sudan and Darfur. In 2002 a US chargé d'affaires was appointed to Khartoum for the first time in six years. Yet in the Spring of 2003 two major rebel groups, the Sudan Liberation Movement (SLM) and the Justice and Equality Movement (JEM), joined forces in their fight against Khartoum, and the Bashir government responded with a scorched-earth campaign led by the Janjaweed militia; tens of thousands of deaths were reported. President George W. Bush signed the Sudan Peace Act, which authorized comprehensive sanctions, pending a semiannual waiver report on negotiations with rebel groups.[9] After Khartoum signed an agreement to begin negotiations and hold an autonomy referendum for the south, Bush signed the Darfur Peace and Accountability Act (DPAA), allowing for targeted sanctions on government entities and the easing of sanctions in the south. In 2008, the International Criminal Court indicted Bashir, who protested that the indictment came just as he was in talks with Bush over normalization. The African Union, Organization of Islamic Conferences, and Arab League pressed for the indictment to be dropped.[10] Bashir remained in power until he was overthrown by coup d'état in 2019.

2009–2016: The Obama administration's policy review introduced a balanced approach of incentives and disincentives to address oppression in Darfur, improve counterterrorism cooperation, and encourage the implementation of peace agreements with South Sudan. The multilateral strategy was criticized by hawks in Washington as too lenient. After the secession of South Sudan, Khartoum experienced a "soft coup" led by hardliners and retired generals, after the loss of South Sudan, resulting in a remilitarization of Sudanese government's response to unrest in Kordofan, the Blue Nile, and other hotspots. Despite Sudan's role in the Darfur atrocities, US intelligence agencies continued collaborating with Sudanese counterparts. In 2013, President Obama invited Bashir's deputy to Washington but revoked the invitation when Sudan halted security cooperation with South Sudan.[11] In 2015, after Sudan suspended intelligence cooperation, CIA Director John Brennan recommended a path toward reconciliation, advocating for gradual sanctions relief and removal from the terror designation list in exchange for improved counterterror cooperation and expanded humanitarian access. In January 2017, Obama temporarily suspended comprehensive sanctions, citing progress in five areas of US concern: reduction in military offensives, a pledge to cease fighting, improved humanitarian access, enhanced counterterrorism, and cooperation in resolving regional conflicts.[12]

2017–2020: Bashir was optimistic about President Trump and expressed hope for improved bilateral ties. However, Bashir withdrew from a Saudi-hosted summit after Trump faced pressure and the US Embassy dissented from the invitation.[13] In October 2017, after progress in the five areas of concern, President Trump ended twenty years of comprehensive economic sanctions, though Sudan remained designated as a state sponsor of terrorism, and its economic conditions continued to deteriorate. In 2018, bilateral cooperation on security and intelligence improved at the working level. In April 2019, widespread anti-government protests, met with relative restraint from security services, led to Bashir's overthrow in a coup. By December 2019, the post-Bashir prime minister, Abdalla Hamdok, visited Washington and requested the lifting of the remaining sanctions. Both countries announced plans to exchange ambassadors, and other confidence-building measures were taken.[14] However, a subsequent coup overthrew the Hamdok government, resulting in significant loss of life and military suppression of political opposition. The Trump travel ban, implemented under EO 13780, was considered part of this episode.

Burundi
1996–2003: Coercive measures were taken to restore civilian rule and end the civil war in Burundi. President Pierre Buyoya came to power again in 1996 (he had been president from 1987 to 1993) through a coup

on July 25, 1996, prompting neighboring countries to impose sanctions and foreign donors to suspend aid, demanding the restoration of the National Assembly and a return to the Great Lakes Regional Peace Talks.[15] The United States had warned the warring factions in Burundi that any government seizing power by force would face isolation. However, the US chose not to intervene militarily and instead engaged Buyoya directly. The US offered to legitimize Buyoya's government if he restored the assembly, returned to peace talks within six months, and reinstated the constitution and political parties. After two years of waning regional enforcement, regional leaders suspended the embargo in 1999. Buyoya returned to the Arusha talks and supported Nelson Mandela's efforts to deploy the African Mission in Burundi (AMIB) to help stabilize the region.[16] Buyoya agreed to transfer power to a new government under the Arusha Accords, which ended the civil war. As a result, substantial development aid to Burundi resumed in 2003.

2015–2020: The US imposed sanctions to address the repression by President Pierre Nkurunziza, who had been president since 2005, presiding over a recurring cycle of rebellion, conflict, coup, and repression. The situation worsened in 2015, and in April, demonstrations turned violent after the Supreme Court cleared Nkurunziza to run for another term. Nkurunziza was re-elected in a July election deemed not credible by observers from the EU, AU, and UN. In November 2015, the United States and Germany ended economic assistance to Burundi, and President Obama blocked property and visas for designated individuals. Although the government released prisoners during talks with the EU about aid, violence and repression continued, leading to the suspension of EU aid in March 2016.[17] The AU approved a 5,000-man peacekeeping operation for Burundi, but Nkurunziza rejected it. The Organisation Internationale de la Francophonie (OIF) suspended multilateral cooperation, while the UN established a Committee of Inquiry (COI) to investigate human rights abuses by the government. In May 2018, Nkurunziza received 70% approval in a referendum to extend his presidential eligibility window and term length (from five years to seven), a move condemned the US and Europe. Nkurunziza later announced that he would not seek re-election, and in 2020, he died.[18] His successor, Évariste Ndayishimiye, from the same party, won the subsequent election.

Democratic Republic of Congo (DRC)

1990–1997: Washington implemented sanctions to promote democracy in DRC, then known as Zaire. In 1990, the US Congress ended military aid to Zaire, followed by cessation of economic aid the next year, demanding that President Mobutu Sese Seko resign.[19] In 1991 and 1993, riots by military personnel over unpaid salaries resulted in hundreds of deaths, including the French ambassador, prompting the evacuation of most foreigners. In 1993, Washington and several European allies threatened further sanctions unless Mobuto transferred control of key ministries to the control of Premier Étienne Tshisekedi. For a time, parallel governments were led by Mobuto and Tshisekedi. An armed rebellion in support of Tshisekedi ensued, and Mobuto undermined a Sovereign National Conference attempting political reconciliation. Mobuto's regime was overthrown in 1997 by rebels, including ethnic Tutsi forces, supported by Rwanda, Uganda, Burundi and Angola.[20]

2006–2020: Sanctions were introduced to punish DRC leader Joseph Kabila for his role in regional instability. Kabila had been part of the Rwandan/Ugandan force that overthrew Mobuto in May 1997 at the end of the First Congo War, renaming the country from Zaire to the DRC. In 1998, new fighting broke out, marking the Second Congo War, which pitted the Rally for Congolese Democracy (RCD), which included significant leadership and membership from the Banyamulenge, a Congolese Tutsi community, and the Movement for the Liberation of Congo (MLC), a Congolese organization with an alliance with Uganda, against Kabila's forces, who were supported by Angola, Zimbabwe, and Namibia. Although a peace agreement was signed in 2003, fighting continued, involving the Democratic Forces for the Liberation of Rwanda (FDLR), which were primarily Hutu armed groups, and the National Congress for the Defense of the People (CDNP), which were primarily Tutsi, as well as Joseph

Kony's Lord's Resistance Army (LRA). UNSCR 1533, adopted in 2004, established further multilateral sanctions, including an arms embargo, asset freeze, travel ban, greater customs enforcement, and air control. President George W. Bush implemented targeted sanctions on military and political leaders on various sides.[21] President Obama renewed and expanded these sanctions, and he also sanctioned Kabila insiders after Kabila postponed transfer of power from 2016 to 2018. Following the 2018 elections in the DRC, which resulted in a peaceful transition of power, President Trump reinstated the DRC's eligibility for trade benefits under the African Growth and Opportunity Act (AGOA), a US trade program, in December 2020.[22]

Eritrea

2008–2018: In 2008, President George W. Bush described Eritrea as "not fully cooperative" in the fight against terrorism and imposed an arms embargo on Eritrea for its failure to support the GWOT. In 2009, UNSCR 1907 broadened the arms embargo. The Obama administration elevated the accusations against Eritrea, charging the country with supporting al-Shabaab in Somalia; Eritrea dismissed these claims as baseless. Obama concluded that Eritrea had been arming al-Shabaab in Somalia as a proxy force against Ethiopia, and threatened further sanctions, which were imposed in 2010.[23] In July 2012 the UN Monitoring Group for Somalia and Eritrea (UNMGSE) reported that Eritrea's support for al-Shabaab had decreased but was still contributing to instability.[24] In 2014, the UNMGSE noted that Eritrea was supporting a collaboration between al-Shabaab and Ogaden separatists in opposition to the Ethiopian government. However, by late 2017 the UNMGSE stated that, for several consecutive reporting periods, there had been no evidence of Eritrean aid to al-Shabaab. This shift coincided with a period of rapprochement between Eritrea and Ethiopia. In July 2018, following the rise of Ethiopian prime minister Abiy Ahmed to power in Ethiopia, a peace agreement was signed between Ethiopia and Eritrea. Abiy later received a Nobel peace prize for his role in brokering the peace. In November 2018, UN sanctions were lifted with US approval.

2017–2020: Another case or 243(d) sanctions related to deportee returns occurred during this period. On September 13, 2017, the Departments of State and Homeland Security announced sanctions against Eritrea for its failure to accept deported nationals, in accordance with Section 243(d) of the Immigration and Nationality Act. The deportation orders involved 700 Eritreans, mostly criminals. Eritrea was also subject to visa bans due to lax border and passport security controls, as outlined in Proclamation 9983, issued on January 31, 2020, which expanded the scope of the original travel ban.[25]

Gambia
1994–2002: Sanctions were a response to the July 23, 1994, military coup that ousted President Dawda Jawara, who had ruled for 29 years. The United States demanded that Yahya Jammeh, who led the coup, restore civilian rule. Jammeh agreed but described the coup as "non-violent, not even a dog died." Jammeh won a highly suspect election in 1996; and after his re-election in 2001 and 2002, both marred by irregularities, sanctions were lifted and aid was restored.[26] The Clinton administration courted Jammeh to assist with UN activities regarding Libya and Kosovo in 1999. Jammeh continued winning questionable elections and remained in power through 2016, despite his reputation as abusive, corrupt, and authoritarian.

2016–2017: This period saw the application of the Immigration and Nationality Act Section 243(d) sanctions, similar to those imposed on Guyana in 2001. Both the DHS and Immigration and Customs Enforcement (ICE) briefed Congress on "recalcitrant" countries—those uncooperative in facilitating documentation and travel for their citizens deported from the United States due to criminal conviction or other reasons. Following the briefing, bipartisan support for diplomatic and economic sanctions grew. In 2016, US diplomats approached Gambia repeatedly regarding over 2,000 predominantly criminal deportees. In October 2016, the US embassy and the State Department announced a ban on certain types of visas. In response, Banjul agreed to take the necessary steps to accept the deportees, and the sanctions were lifted in December 2017.[27] This episode coincided with the successful effort by the United Nations, African Union, and the Economic Community of West African States (ECOWAS) to force President Yahya Jammeh to cede power after losing the 2016 presidential election in late 2016, though the United States was not a central actor in that effort.

Libya

1996–2007: Pressure was applied to Libya to end its support for terrorism and cease its pursuit of weapons of mass destruction (WMD). In 1992, the UN adopted the US position on Lockerbie sanctions, blocking financial transfers and oil investment or assistance to Libya. These sanctions were ultimately lifted in 2003. House Resolution 3107 became law in mid-1996, further strengthening US sanctions under the Iran and Libya Sanctions Act (ILSA).[28] However, the EU largely opposed universal or secondary sanctions involving Libya. In April 1999, Muammar Gaddafi agreed to an international tribunal for the Lockerbie bombing suspects and began expelling associates of groups such as the Abu Nidal, Palestinian Islamic Jihad, and Popular Front for the Liberation of Palestine. In mid-2001, Congress reauthorized ILSA, stating that only one of the Lockerbie conditions had been met. After 9/11, Assistant Secretary of State Bill Burns met with Gaddafi's intelligence chief to discuss terrorism and WMD. In December 2003, Libya publicly renounced WMD, opened the country to inspectors, and accepted responsibility for past terror attacks. President George W. Bush lifted previous sanctions and allowed US businesses to enter Libya, although Libyan assets remained frozen and Tripoli stayed on the list of state sponsors of terrorism until 2006.[29]

2011–2020: New coercive measures were applied to get Gaddafi to stop fighting in the Libyan civil war that erupted in 2011.[30] International Criminal Court referrals made regime change the tacit goal of international efforts. In February 2011, President Obama announced the end to limited military cooperation with Libya, closed the US embassy, and stated that Gaddafi had lost the confidence of the Libyan people. The following month, Obama declared that Gaddafi had to step down and leave the country. On March 17, 2011, UNSCR 1973 demanded a ceasefire, a no-fly zone, and authorized "all necessary measures" to protect civilians. On March 19, 2011, Obama demanded an immediate ceasefire and the withdrawal of Gaddafi's security forces from Libyan cities, backed by the threat of direct Western military action. From March 19 through October 31, 2011, a NATO-led military campaign targeted Gaddafi and his aligned forces. What began as a civilian protection mission evolved into a regime change operation, culminating in Gaddafi's death. In December 2011, the Office of Foreign Assets Control (OFAC), a financial intelligence and enforcement agency of the US Department of the Treasury, issued a license unblocking $30 billion in Libyan assets, with promises of assistance to the new government. However, the failure to establish a stable central government hindered the implementation of effective aid programs.[31] Sanctions remained in place through the Obama and Trump presidencies, although the arms embargo was increasingly seen as ineffective. Travel sanctions under Trump EO 13780 were part of this broader episode.

Malawi
1991-1993: Sanctions were imposed to push for multiparty elections, an end to one-man rule, and the release of political prisoners. During a visit to Malawi in September 1991, Vice President Dan Quayle raised concerns about human rights, and the United States joined the European Community in demanding human reforms ahead of the May 1992 donors' consultative meeting. Donors cut 33% of non- humanitarian aid following the meeting. When the financially strained government scheduled presidential and parliamentary elections for May 1994, the US lifted sanctions.[32] The main opposition figure credited the sanctions with progress on political activity and press freedom and called for their continuation during the political transition. Former president Hastings

Banda was tried in 1995, and Malawi became a major aid recipient (receiving nearly $4 billion from 1994 to 2000) and a major contributor to UN peacekeeping operations.

2011–2012: The US and EU imposed sanctions to address corruption and electoral fraud in Malawi. In March 2011, Germany, Norway, the World Bank, the African Development Bank, and the EU suspended development assistance, followed by the UK and US in July. President Bingu wa Mutharika had engaged in electoral manipulation and corruption but died of cardiac arrest the following year. Sanctions were lifted after his death, and IMF loans resumed in July 2012.[33]

Niger
1996–1999: On January 27, 1996, Colonel Ibrahim Baré Mainassara deposed President Mahamane Ousmane and Prime Minister Hama Amadou, proceeding to dissolve parliament, ban political parties, suspend the constitution, and declare a state of emergency. After Mainassara won highly suspect elections in 1997 and implemented a limited program of political normalization, France and the organization of Francophone countries lifted sanctions.[34] Clashes with protestors led to serious violence in 1998, and Mainassara was assassinated in 1999 during another coup. President Mamadou Tandja came to power in new elections later in 1999, but Niger continued to experience cycles of repression and violence, including military mutinies throughout 2002. US military and economic assistance, suspended in 1996, was restored in 1999 despite continued repression and violence under civilian rule.

2009–2011: President Mamadou Tandja altered the constitution to allow for a third term, prompting an opposition boycott of the elections. In response, ECOWAS imposed sanctions in October 2009, while the United States suspended economic aid and imposed travel bans on government officials. In February 2010, a coup led by Major Salou Djibo deposed Tandja, and Djibo subsequently assumed leadership as the head of the interim government.[35] In early 2011, Mahamadou Issoufou was elected president in new elections. US sanctions impacted direct bilateral aid to Niger and included a $23 million reduction in Millennium Challenge Corporation (MCC) funds. Additionally, US funding for the Pan-Sahel Initiative, Trans-Saharan CT Partnership, and other military aid were suspended after the coup.[36] The State Department condemned both Tandja's abuses and the coup that ousted him. After Issoufo took office, US aid resumed, including $65 million in 2011, along with the resumption of military cooperation projects.[37]

Nigeria

1995–2000: The Sani Abacha government ruled Nigeria from 1993 to 1998. After the annulment of the 1993 elections by General Ibrahim Babangida, the Clinton administration suspended foreign aid, implemented a case-by-case review of military sales with a presumption of denial, and decertified Nigeria as a counterdrug partner. In 1995, as Abacha intensified repression—including the execution of nine political opponents in November, all members of the Ogoni ethnic minority protesting oil exploitation and environmental damage—the Clinton administration escalated its response. The US banned all military sales, export financing, and imposed travel restrictions on Nigerian officials. Despite congressional support, US analysts noted that unilateral measures were largely ineffective in Nigeria's case, as European allies were reluctant to impose harsher measures. Abacha died in office in 1998. Following the 1999 elections, retired General and former Nigerian President Olusegun Obasanjo took office, and US sanctions were gradually lifted between 1999 and 2000.[38]

2020: The Trump administration pressed Nigeria to tighten its passport and migrant information systems. A visa ban was introduced due to Nigeria's lax passport, customs, and border security enforcement. The ban applied to all types of visas except SIVs. Acting Secretary of Homeland Security Chad Wolf stated the restrictions were imposed on Nigeria and six other countries to "address concerns in the way the banned countries track their own citizens, share information with the US and cooperate on immigration matters."[39] The measures were reversed by President Joe Biden on his first day in office.

Rwanda

1994–1996: The end of the civil war (1990–1994) in Rwanda was marked by the killing of between half a million and one million ethnic Tutsis, moderate Hutus, and Twi people in a genocide carried out by Hutu militants running the government. In May 1994, an arms embargo was imposed by UNSCR 918, and by July 1994 the Tutsi-led Rwandan Patriotic Front (RPF) seized power. Subsequent UNSCRs expanded the arms embargo to armed groups in neighboring states, although the embargo on the government of Rwanda was removed in August 1995. Washington made clear in early 1994 that it did not contemplate large-scale military intervention in Rwanda, given public distaste over the intervention in Somalia, but called on both sides to return to negotiations in Arusha. The Clinton administration also expelled Rwandan diplomats, froze Rwandan assets, and ordered troops and aircraft to support humanitarian assistance efforts in the wake of the killings. The United States resumed aid programs at the end of 1994 and helped to reopen the Kigali airport.[40]

2006–2020: The US applied pressure on Rwanda and, to a lesser extent, Uganda to withdraw forces and proxy support for the fighting in eastern DRC. The US suspended military aid to Uganda when it failed to remove its forces from eastern DRC after the First Congo War. Uganda ultimately withdrew its forces in 2003, and military aid was resumed thereafter. In mid-2012, the UK suspended general assistance to Rwanda under President Paul Kagame due to its involvement in the fighting in eastern DRC but restored the aid in September of the same year. Washington began sharply criticizing Rwanda for its support of the March 23 Movement (M23) rebel group in mid-2012 and suspended military aid soon after. The US designated M23 and others in January 2013. In May 2013, the United Nations authorized a brigade-sized intervention force (United Nations Organization Stabilization Mission in the Democratic Republic of the Congo, or MONUSCO) to target the M23. By November 2013, the M23 was defeated, with a peace agreement and accountability plan put into place. During the Obama administration, Congress restricted military support to dissuade Rwanda from backing rebels in the DRC and Burundi.[41] However, the Rwandan-supported Democratic Forces for the Liberation of Rwanda (FDLR) continued fighting throughout the period, up to and including 2020.

Cameroon

1990–1998: In November 1992, the US government condemned President Paul Biya's rigging of the 1992 elections and restricted foreign aid. In 1998, US sanctions were lifted, but Biya's Rassemblement Démocratique du Peuple Camerounais (RDPC) party continued election rigging, political killings, and other oppressive acts through 2020. After 2010, a growing Anglophone resistance in northwest and southwest Cameroon, along with unrest in the southern Bakassi region and Islamist anti-government movements such as Boko Haram, significantly impacted security in the country.[42] The RDPC promised political reforms but was slow to implement them. During the Clinton administration, Congress shifted to a system of preferential trade terms under the AGOA to incentivize reform, but this yielded minimal results and was suspended by President Trump in 2017.

Central African Republic (CAR)

2012–2014: In December 2012, the US embassy in Bangui suspended operations due to the Seleka insurgency, a coalition of predominantly Muslim rebel groups seeking to overthrow the government. In March 2013, the Muslim Seleka insurgents overthrew President Francois Bozizé, prompting the emergence of a predominantly Christian counter-movement known as the anti-Balaka. In December 2013, President Obama appealed directly to the people of the Central African Republic (CAR), calling for calm, rejecting sectarian and partisan militias committing violence, and urging support for the forces of France and regional countries as they intervened to restore stability. Beginning in October 2013,

France mobilized under UNSCR 2127 and deployed several thousand troops under Operation Sangaris (through 2016). The anti-Balaka, aided by Bozizé loyalists, forced Seleka from power in January 2014. By March 2014, despite the French-led intervention, the anti-Balaka carried out a series of reprisals against Seleka supporters accused of atrocities the previous year, effectively ethnically cleansing portions of the country. In April 2014, the EU launched a security operation in Bangui and at the airport to reduce the level of atrocities. Obama sanctioned specific transactions involving parties in the conflict; initial targets included Bozizé, three Seleka affiliates, and one anti-Balaka affiliate. In September 2014, the US embassy in Bangui resumed operations with a small military deployment. Elections in 2016 yielded a weak but stable government, with anti-Balaka and Seleka militias exercising de facto control over portions of the country.

Chad
2017–2018: In 2017, a Trump-era travel ban directed the denial of some categories of visas due to lax passport, customs controls in several countries; the goal was to force action to tighten procedures. Several court battles led to revisions of the ban. The visa ban is considered a separate sanctions episode only for those countries not concurrently subjected to a broader set of sanctions. Presidential Proclamation 9723 subsequently found that Chad had tightened its procedures, improved passport security, enhanced fraud detection, and increased information sharing. As a result, Chad was removed from the list of countries visa restrictions under the travel ban.

Egypt
2016–2017: Washington directed reductions in military and economic assistance due to concerns over the suppression of civil society and cooperation with North Korea.[43] In May 2017, the US announced plans to cut economic aid to Egypt from $150 million to $75 million. In August 2017, Secretary Rex Tillerson withheld $195 million (out of over $1 billion

in total aid) and $96 million in economic assistance, aiming to pressure Cairo on civil society issues and its ties with North Korea. Additional funds were reprogrammed away from Egypt. In 2018, President Trump engaged with Egyptian officials to discuss the aid reductions and their underlying causes. During these meetings Trump conditioned the release of withheld funds on Egypt ending military and diplomatic cooperation with North Korea, resolving the legal status of 43 staff members of pro-democracy organizations, and amending or repealing the restrictive NGO law. Despite these tensions, military cooperation continued, and the annual Bright Star exercises resumed, albeit at a reduced scale after nearly a decade of interruption. In mid-2018, Egypt allowed a retrial in the NGO cases following discreet negotiations. The Egyptian defense minister, Sedki Sobhi, visited Seoul and announced that Egypt had ended all defense ties with North Korea. Shortly thereafter, the US State Department reinstated the $195 million in withheld security aid, citing the positive steps Egypt had taken on the areas of concern.[44]

Ghana

2019–2020: Beginning in 2016, Washington engaged with Ghana to resolve the issue of travel documents for Ghanaian deportees from the US. Ghana was notified that there were 7,000 Ghanaians at various stages of deportation hearings and was warned of unreasonable delays in processing. In February 2019, the US imposed visa sanctions on Ghana and raised the possibility of further sanctions if substantive action was not taken. The Ghanaian government disputed the accusations, stating that there were doubts about the nationality of a significant portion of those who had not been issued documents. Opposition politicians in Ghana demanded retaliation rather than deference to the US. In August 2019, Ghana accepted 40 deportees on a flight from the US. By January 2020, the Ghanaian government announced that it had reached an agreement with the US on a procedure to identify, verify, and provide documents to Ghanaian nationals in accordance with the guidelines of the International

Civil Aviation Organization (ICAO), a specialized agency of the United Nations. The US lifted visa sanctions shortly thereafter.[45]

Guinea

2017–2018: On September 13, 2017, the Departments of State and Homeland Security announced sanctions on Guinea for its failure to accept deported nationals in accordance with Section 243(d) of the Immigration and Nationality Act. The deportation orders involved 2,137 Guineans, mostly criminals. DHS threatened further sanctions if no progress was made. However, by 2018, Guinea had demonstrated sufficient progress, and the visa sanctions were lifted.[46]

Côte d'Ivoire

1999–2016: After a coup by notable Ivorian military officer and politician Tuo Fozié overthrew President Henri Konan Bédié in December 1999, General Robert Guéï was called out of retirement to lead the new junta as president. Elections were held in October 2000, but only two candidates were allowed to run: Guéï and Laurent Gbagbo. Opposition leader Alassane Ouattara was barred from running. Street protests brought Gbagbo to power, but by 2002 a civil war broke out between his supporters and rebels who accused him of xenophobia. France led a 2003 peace process, but it failed. US foreign aid to Côte d'Ivoire had already declined in 1998 and 1999 due to increasing corruption and mismanagement, and it was suspended following the coup in accordance with Section 508 of the Foreign Assistance Act, which prohibits non-humanitarian aid after coups. In 2004, when Gbagbo's southern forces broke a yearlong truce and attacked the north, killing French forces in the process, France retaliated by destroying Gbagbo's small air force. The UN applied sanctions in 2004 via UNSCR 1572, which included asset freezes, an arms embargo, travel bans, and the authorization of a French-led UN peacekeeping force. President George W. Bush increased US sanctions in 2006, targeting political figures and militia leaders who blocked the 2003 peace process. In 2010, the US placed travel sanctions on Gbagbo for refusing to step down after losing the presidential election. Sanctions were lifted by President Obama in 2016, following French support for the northern Muslim forces led by Ouattara, who ultimately deposed Gbagbo.[47]

Kenya

1991–1993: Washington applied sanctions to end repression and encourage democracy in Kenya, including the suspension of military and economic assistance. President Daniel Arap Moi had engaged in electoral manipulation to undermine the political opposition, which included the murder of the moderate foreign minister Robert Ouko and the manipulation of multi-party elections in 1991. In January 1990, Secretary of State James Baker discreetly demanded reforms from Moi. Congress members warned Moi that deteriorating human rights conditions jeopardized US aid, to which Moi responded by promising reforms that were not implemented. After consultative meetings between US and European donors in 1991, the World Bank withheld $28 million in aid, and donors agreed not to provide new aid until reforms were made. US sanctions ended in the mid-1990s, but meaningful change in Kenya did not occur until after 2002.[48]

Mali

2019–2020: In 2012, northern secessionists, led by the Tuareg National Movement for the Liberation of Azawad (MNLA), launched an insurgency that precipitated a military coup in March, resulting in the ousting of President Amadou Toumani Touré. France intervened with Operation Serval in 2013, and the African Union, through the African-led International Support Mission in Mali (AFISMA), deployed regional forces to support the Malian government.

In 2015, a peace agreement, known as the Algiers Accord, was signed with some armed groups, and the Carter Center, an international NGO founded by former US president Jimmy Carter, was appointed as an independent observer, supported by the United Nations, to monitor progress. Despite these efforts, the agreement's implementation saw minimal progress over the following five years. Rival northern groups managed to maintain a balance of relative autonomy from the government, with limited fighting between the two sides.

Meanwhile, violence perpetrated by jihadist terror groups escalated significantly. In response, President Trump imposed blocking sanctions on individuals deemed to be obstructing stability, with five individuals designated by the end of 2020. Additionally, the United States provided funding for the multilateral peacekeeping force and supported police training initiatives to enhance security and governance in the region.[49] In August 2020, another coup ousted President Ibrahim Boubacar Keïta, and a transitional government was established for 18 months, with the coup leader as vice president. In May 2021, yet another coup overthrew the transitional government. Following this second coup, the ECOWAS suspended Mali, and the US suspended security assistance. Throughout the sanctions period, humanitarian assistance continued while Russia began providing military aid to Mali.

Mauritania
2008–2009: Following a second coup in three years—in 2005 and again in 2008—the US, along with the EU and the AU, imposed travel restrictions and suspended diplomatic relations. The 2005 coup had overthrown the government of President Maaouya Ould Sid'Ahmed Taya, who, despite his authoritarianism, had been a key ally of the United States in the Global War on Terror. In the 2008 coup, the military, led by General Mohamed Ould Abdelaziz, ousted President Sidi Ould Cheikh Abdallahi, Mauritania's first democratically elected leader. In response, France, the AU, and the World Bank suspended aid, while the United States condemned the coup, terminated financial assistance, and threatened further sanctions to pressure the coup government to relinquish power. In June 2009, rival political factions signed the Dakar Accord, under which Abdelaziz agreed to resign from the military and run for president as a civilian. His election in July 2009 was widely regarded as fair, leading the IMF and the World Bank to resume aid soon afterward. The EU

followed suit in February 2010. Abdelaziz remained in power until 2019, when he was prosecuted by his former deputy for alleged corruption.

Sierra Leone

2017–2020: On September 13, 2017, the Departments of State and Homeland Security announced sanctions against Sierra Leone for its failure to accept deported nationals, as required by Section 243(d) of the Immigration and Nationality Act. The deportation orders involved 831 Sierra Leoneans, mostly criminals. In September 2020, the Department of State expanded the visa ban due to the lack of responsiveness from the Sierra Leonean government. By late 2020, the Sierra Leonean government acknowledged the complexity of the issue, and talks continued. This led to a reduction, though not the complete removal, of the visa sanctions in 2021.[50]

South Sudan

2014–2020: After South Sudan gained independence from Sudan in 2011, President Salva Kiir dismissed Vice President Riek Machar in July 2013, accusing him of plotting a coup. This triggered a civil war largely divided along ethnic lines, with the Dinka supporting Kiir and the Nuer backing Machar. A ceasefire was signed in January 2014 but was repeatedly violated. In May 2014, President Obama sanctioned six individuals from both sides for human rights violations. The US hoped the sanctions would push the parties toward compromise and engaged in regional diplomacy, encouraging neighboring countries to implement visa bans and blocking sanctions, and to consider deploying AU troops.

In May 2014, the two factions agreed to form a unity government but missed the deadline. After seven months of fighting, over 1.5 million people were displaced. Sudan was reportedly supporting Machar's forces, while Uganda deployed troops to back Kiir. In August 2015, the two sides signed the Agreement on the Resolution of the Conflict in South Sudan (ARCSS), and Machar returned as vice president in April 2016. However, fighting resumed in July 2016, prompting a large-scale government offensive that displaced more than 4 million people. Machar fled the country, and President Obama imposed additional sanctions in December 2016.[51] A new transitional government of national unity (TGoNU) eventually assumed power under the 2018 revitalized peace agreement, but localized fighting persisted. Bilateral trade and diplomacy between the US and South Sudan remained extremely limited, and humanitarian aid mostly provided through multilateral channels. Meanwhile, Chinese influence in South Sudan increased during this period.[52]

Zambia

1996–1998: Sanctions were imposed to improve human rights and press for constitutional reform in Zambia. The Clinton administration initially supported Zambia with an ambitious program, which included writing off $118.6 million in debt and rescheduling $69.5 million over twenty-six years, along with significant State Department and USAID programs. However, in June 1996, the Zambian government arrested opposition members, leading to the suspension of aid. President Frederick Chiluba suspended the National Assembly, and new elections resulted in a pro-Chiluba majority. An abortive military rebellion in October 1997 resulted in more arrests. Throughout this period, Chiluba and his supporters rallied resistance to sanctions, defending Zambian sovereignty despite the cost of lost aid. Opposition leader Kenneth Kaunda appreciated the Western sanctions, suggesting that Chiluba was considering reconciliation talks. Meanwhile, Zambia continued to support AU sanctions against Burundi, though it imposed a significant economic cost. In October 1997, Chiluba quashed a coup attempt by Captain Stephen Lungu, suspended intraparty talks, and arrested Kaunda. After these measures were reversed in 1998, donors lifted sanctions. Chiluba stayed in power until 2002.[53]

Zimbabwe

2002–2020: After several years of increasing oppression in Zimbabwe, Congress passed the Zimbabwe Democracy and Economic Recovery Act (ZIDERA), a law to restrict bilateral aid and multilateral lending until certification of functioning democracy. The US and EU sanctioned President Robert Mugabe's government as violence escalated before the March 2002 elections, starting with travel bans. Mugabe responded by accusing the sanctions of being a colonialist tool aimed at regime change. President George W. Bush blocked the assets and travel by individuals and organizations seen as impeding democracy. His 2005 Executive Order 13391 expanded the list of blocked individuals and later broadened both the list and criteria for inclusion. In February 2009, Morgan Tsvangirai joined the unity government as prime minister under Mugabe's presidency and called for the loosening of sanctions. However, President Obama renewed the sanctions. President Emmerson Mnangagwa replaced Mugabe after the military and the Zimbabwe African National Union-Patriotic Front (ZANU-PF) party removed him, but Mnangagwa continued the intimidation of opposition and blamed economic troubles on the opposition and sanctions. After twenty years of sanctions, targeted measures remain in place for only 83 people and 37 entities, yet Zimbabwe continues to face public health crises, deteriorating infrastructure, and a declining per capita GDP.[54]

EXPERT AND PRACTITIONER COMMENTS

An American academic specializing in US CD in Africa shared the view that multilateral pressure campaigns on targets in Africa have better chances of succeeding if supported by regional organizations close to the target:

> One of the few examples that "worked" was Cote D'Ivoire... multilateral sanctions imposed (travel ban, asset freeze, diamonds, arms embargo). The UNSC and US had clear off-ramps for sanctions per African Union standards: join the Kimberley Process, conduct demobilization and security sector reform—once you do that, we'll lift...In Côte d'Ivoire it was multilateral support combined with direct bilateral pressure...In such cases it can be hard to find the money, banking systems can't control the funds or do the

forensics. By the time we impose after threat, they've moved the funds. What turned Gbagbo around was that ECOWAS rescinded his signing authority for government expenses. Did France go in afterwards with UN to arrest? Yes. But ECOWAS Central Bank was the fulcrum.[55]

Yet as a Western military officer with multiple tours in Africa conveyed, without significant buy-in from neighboring states, traction can be evasive during coercive episodes.

I've dealt with three or four countries that have just given the middle finger to Washington and the world. We have very little leverage over them. In the case of Tanzania, they were offered President's Emergency Plan for AIDS Relief (PEPFAR) and Millenium Challenge funds, but they offered nothing in return. Other countries—Zimbabwe included—flipped the middle finger; they were going to go their own way. A country that was thriving suffered greatly and still, they would not bend the knee to the West. Eritrea is the best current example. We levy all sorts of measures and they retain a stubborn independence of action. A major reason we don't have leverage is this: remember, it's not Asia or Europe, there is very limited Western private investment (in relative terms). The Africans have a lot of other investors and partners, in Asia and the Middle East. These countries have a variety of potential partners and they will do what they need... most Africans, in my experience, view CD as neo-colonialism.[56]

A European diplomat noted that Africa has similarly been a hard target for European CD:

In Mali there had been a coup in 2012. The major European military intervention without US backing was and has been Mali. Led by French, without American backbone—there were big plans. But a second coup came in 2021, because the military was not happy with civilian leadership. New leaders not accommodating—French were pushing very hard—and there was a clash of egos. The Russians were there, and they offered support without political conditions.

So, the decades-long French investment in Mali collapsed in a number of days. There was no off-ramp offered for the Malians.[57]

A retired senior African military officer provided the Malian point of view on the same episode:

> When the coup occurred, the US did a few things, including sending back non-essential personnel. They also cut programs, such as Peace Corps. This is an organization very embedded in the society; we could really feel that something happened. And the US stopped military cooperation, saying that Mali was no longer democratic and we cannot engage. That was very important, because at the time Mali was trying very hard to develop relations with the US; after the coup, the leadership tried very hard to repair, including engaging through ambassadors and defense attaches, and explaining the situation. To explain the root causes, that corruption was leading to state failure. It is now that we need you the most—if you leave now, what kind of friend are you? It didn't achieve what the US wanted. It's like building a house over several years, then knocking it down in a day. It destroyed confidence and trust at a time that we had al-Qaeda, separatists, and we needed a strong partner...an important part of CD is the emotional side; if you are talking with us you are respecting us. The reputation now is that the US applies sanctions and pressure without really knowing the situation on the ground...so many African countries are saying "we have sanctions, but this cannot be helped—this is just what the US does." The US will behave this way, but by the way Russia, China, Turkey and others want to do deals with us, and we do, too.[58]

REGIONAL SUMMARY

The record of US coercive diplomacy in Africa presents a notable irony. On one hand, the rate of compliance has been higher, and the deterioration in bilateral or regional ties over time lower, than in other regions. There have been some signal successes over time—Sudan, Malawi, and to a lesser extent, Egypt. Yet, the frequency of episodes, coupled with the low policy priority Washington has historically assigned to Africa, at a time when other Great Power rivals have increased their activity, may have contributed to a decline in US regional influence. The practice of severing ties with coup regimes or conflict-stricken states warrants closer examination. While the initial signal of disapproval may be justifiable, prolonged withdrawal of recognition and incentives risks a loss of leverage (as seen in Mali), sustained instability (as in Libya and Somalia), or creating openings for opportunistic groups like al-Shabaab to expand their influence.[59] A "do no harm" approach in the application of coercive measures and incentives may offer a more effective framework for dealing with fragile states in future US policy.[60]

Notes

1. US Army Center for Military, *United States Forces, Somalia After Action Report and History Historical Overview: the United States Army in Somalia 1992–1994* (Fort McNair, Washington, DC, 2003), 1–14, https://history.army.mil/html/documents/somalia/SomaliaAAR.pdf.
2. Nora Bensahel, "Humanitarian Relief and Nation Building in Somalia," in *The United States and Coercive Diplomacy*, edited by Robert Art and Patrick Cronin (Washington, DC: United States Institute of Peace, 2003), 21–56.
3. Julian Pecquet, "Obama Renews Sanctions Against Somalia Despite New Government," *The Hill*, April 4, 2013, https://thehill.com/policy/international/146653-obama-renews-sanctions-against-somalia-despite-new-government/.
4. Panel of Experts (PoE) on Somalia, *Final Report on Somalia S/2020/949*, United Nations Security Council, September 28, 2020, https://www.securitycouncilreport.org/atf/cf/%7B65BFCF9B-6D27-4E9C-8CD3-CF6E4FF96FF9%7D/S_2020_949.pdf.
5. Abdinur Mohamud, "The Obama Administration's Somali Pivot," Foreign Policy in Focus, June 16, 2014, https://fpif.org/obama-administrations-somali-pivot/.
6. Pete Williams, "Trump Restricts Visas From Eight Countries as Travel Order Expires," NBC News, September 24, 2017, https://www.nbcnews.com/politics/immigration/trump-restricts-visas-eight-countries-travel-order-expires-n804366.
7. Subcommittee on Africa Affairs, *Sudan and Terrorism* (Hearing Transcript 105–223), Committee on Foreign Relations, US Senate, May 15, 1997, https://www.govinfo.gov/content/pkg/CHRG-105shrg40875/html/CHRG-105shrg40875.htm.
8. "Brief Timeline of Key Sanctions Events in Sudan (adapted and updated from Hufbauer et al.)," Center for Global Development, October 6, 2011, https://www.cgdev.org/article/brief-timeline-key-sanctions-events-sudan-adapted-and-updated-hufbauer-et-al.
9. Ted Dagne, *Sudan: Humanitarian Crisis, Peace Talks, Terrorism, and US Policy* CRS Report IB98043, June 9, 2005, https://apps.dtic.mil/sti/tr/pdf/ADA475108.pdf.

10. John Feffer and Hussein Yusuf, "Indicting Bashir is Wrong," Institute for Policy Studies, July 2, 2009, https://ips-dc.org/indicting_bashir_is_ wrong/.

11. "Sudan Says it is Unaware of Suspension of Nafie's Planned Visit," *Sudan Tribune,* June 22, 2013, https://ips-dc.org/indicting_bashir_is_wrong/.

12. Justin Lynch and Robbie Gramer, "How Two US Presidents Reshaped America's Policy Toward Sudan," *Foreign Policy,* April 8, 2019, https://foreignpolicy.com/2019/04/08/how-two-us-presidents-reshaped-americas-policy-towards-sudan-bashir-protests-calling-for-removal-diplomacy-east-africa-us-intelligence-cooperation/.

13. "Sudan's Bashir Withdraws From Saudi Summit, Trump Attending," Hiraan, May 19, 2017, https://www.hiiraan.com/news4/2017/May/1422 18/sudan_s_bashir_withdraws_from_saudi_summit_trump_attending. aspx).

14. Jared Szuba, "Sudan to Recognize Israel After US Rescinds Khartoum Terror Designation," *Al-Monitor,* October 23, 2020, https://www. al-monitor.com/originals/2020/10/sudan-israel-normalization-trump-terror.html.

15. Thierry Vircoulon, "Burundi's Coup From Within," Commentary, International Crisis Group, May 13, 2015, https://www.crisisgroup.org/ africa/central-africa/burundi/burundi-s-coup-within.

16. Paul Nantulya, "Burundi: Why the Arusha Accords are Central," *Spotlight,* Africa Center for Strategic Studies, August 5, 2015, https://africacenter. org/spotlight/burundi-why-the-arusha-accords-are-central/.

17. Paul Nantulya, "Burundi, the Forgotten Crisis, Still Burns," *Spotlight,* Africa Center for Strategic Studies, September 24, 2019, https:// africacenter.org/spotlight/burundi-the-forgotten-crisis-still-burns/.

18. James Tasamba, "Profile - Burundi's President Pierre Nkurunziza Dies at 55," Anadolu Agency, October 6, 2020, https://www.aa.com.tr/en/life/ profile-burundi-s-president-pierre-nkurunziza-dies-at-55/1872101.

19. Human Rights Watch (no byline) "Africa - Zaire," *World Report 1994,* December 1993, https://www.hrw.org/reports/1994/WR94/Africa-10.htm.

20. Mark Baas, "The Collapse of Zaire at the End of the First Congo War 1997," *A Moment in Diplomatic History,* Association for Diplomatic Studies and Training, October 16, 2017, https://adst.org/2017/10/collapse-zaire-end-first-congo-war-1997/.

21. Alexis Arieff and Thomas Coen, *Democratic Republic of the Congo: Background and US Policy,* CRS Report R43166, July 29, 2013, https:// apps.dtic.mil/sti/tr/pdf/ADA590459.pdf.

22. Office of the Spokesperson, "Reinstatement of the Democratic Republic of the Congo to AGOA," Media Notes, US Department of State, December 23, 2020, https://2017-2021.state.gov/reinstatement-of-the-democratic-republic-of-the-congo-to-agoa/.
23. Philip Bovo, "Eritrea: The End of Obama and Clinton Coincides With That of 'Unjust Sanctions,'" *Opinione-pubblica*, November 15, 2016 https://www.opinione-pubblica.com/eritrea-la-fine-obama-della-clinton-coincide-quella-delle-ingiuste-sanzioni/.
24. Aaron Maasho, "Exclusive: Eritrea Reduces Support for al Shabaab - UN Report," Reuters, July 16, 2012, https://www.reuters.com/article/idUSBRE86F0AI/.
25. Ted Hesson, "US Slaps Visa Sanctions on 4 Nations," *Politico*, September 13, 2017, https://www.politico.com/story/2017/09/13/trump-sanctions-immigration-242688.
26. "Observers Endorse Gambia Election," CNN, October 20, 2001, https://www.cnn.com/2001/WORLD/africa/10/20/gambia.elections/index.html.
27. Abdur Rahman Alfa Shaban, "US Lifts Visa Sanctions on Gambian Govt After Deportation Deal," *Africa News* December 13, 2017, https://www.africanews.com/2017/12/13/us-lifts-visa-sanctions-on-gambian-govt-after-deportation-deal//.
28. *Iran and Libya Sanctions Act of 1996,* 104th US Congress, August 5, 1996, https://www.congress.gov/bill/104th-congress/house-bill/3107.
29. Eben Kaplan, "How Libya Got Off the List," *Backgrounder*, Council on Foreign Relations, October 16, 2007, https://www.cfr.org/backgrounder/how-libya-got-list.
30. Joshua Schore, "Hollow Threats: Why Coercive Diplomacy Fails (PhD diss., Maxwell Air Force Base, AL: School of Advanced Air and Space Studies, June 2015), 56–84, https://apps.dtic.mil/sti/citations/AD1015763.
31. US Department of the Treasury Fact Sheet: Lifting Sanctions on the Government of Libya, December 16, 2011, https://home.treasury.gov/news/press-releases/tg1387#:~:text=Prospective%20transactions%20involving%20the%20Government,to%20Section%201%20of%20Executive.
32. Lindsay Carpenter, "Malawians Bring Down 30-Year Dictator, 1992–1993," Global Nonviolent Action Database, February 8, 2011, https://nvdatabase.swarthmore.edu/content/malawians-bring-down-30-year-dictator-1992-1993.
33. Frank Phiri and Mabvuto Banda, "US Freezes $350 million in Aid After Malawi Violence," Reuters, July 26, 2011, https://www.reuters.com/article/us-malawi-usa-idUSTRE76P4OV20110726/.

34. "Military Junta That Seized Niger Gets Some Support," *New York Times*, April 13, 1999.

35. Richard Downie, "A Counter-Coup in Niger," *Critical Questions* February 23, 2010, https://www.csis.org/analysis/counter-coup-niger.

36. The Pan-Sahel Initiative is a US counterterrorism program (2002–2005) focused on training and equipping Mali, Mauritania, Niger, and Chad to combat terrorism and enhance border security. The Trans-Saharan Counterterrorism Partnership is a U.S.-led initiative (launched in 2005) promoting counterterrorism, regional cooperation, and development across the Sahel and North Africa to combat extremist groups like AQIM and Boko Haram.

37. "United States Resumes Aid Program in Niger," *Africa News Analysis*, July 7, 2011, https://www.africanewsanalysis.com/united-states-resumes-aid-program-in-niger/.

38. US Department of State *Nigeria Background Note*, November 2004, https://2 009-2017.state.gov/outofdate/bgn/nigeria/40663.htm#:~:text=Following %20the%20annulment%20of%20the,arms%20sales%20and%20military%2 0assistance.

39. Camila DeChalus and Tanvi Misra, "Trump Administration Adds Travel Restrictions to Six Countries," *Roll Call*, January 31, 2020, https://rollcall. com/2020/01/31/trump-administration-adds-travel-restrictions-to-six-countries/.

40. Howard Adelman and Astri Suhrke, *The International Response to Conflict and Genocide: Lessons from the Rwanda Experience*, Organization for Economic Cooperation and Development (March 1996), 65–75, https://www.oecd.org/countries/rwanda/50189764.pdf.

41. Alexis Arieff and Katherine Terrell, *Rwanda: In Brief* CRS Report R44402 (v8), February 7, 2018, https://crsreports.congress.gov/product/pdf/R/R44402/8.

42. Tomas Husted, *Cameroon: Key Issues and US Policy* CRS Report R46919, September 22, 2021, https://crsreports.congress.gov/product/pdf/R/R4 6919/1.

43. Andrew Miller, "Commentary: Five myths about U.S. aid to Egypt," *Reuters*, August 14, 2018, https://www.reuters.com/article/us-miller-egypt-commentary-idUSKBN1KY1WJ.

44. Tamara Cofman Wittes, *Testimony of Tamara Cofman Wittes*, House Foreign Affairs Committee, September 9, 2020, https://www.brookings. edu/wp-content/uploads/2020/09/Wittes_Testimony_HFAC_9.9.20.pdf.

45. Ismail Akwei, "Ghana Gives in to US Pressure After Visa Restrictions, 40 out of 7,000 Nationals Deported," Face2Face Africa, August 20, 2019, https://face2faceafrica.com/article/ghana-gives-in-to-u-s-pressure-after-visa-restrictions-40-out-of-7000-nationals-deported.
46. Office of the Press Secretary, "DHS Announces Implementation of Visa Sanctions on Four Countries," Department of Homeland Security, September 13, 2017, https://www.dhs.gov/news/2017/09/13/dhs-announces-implementation-visa-sanctions-four-countries.
47. Bureau of African Affairs, *Background Note: Cote d'Ivoire*, July 2008, US Department of State, https://2001-2009.state.gov/r/pa/ei/bgn/2846.htm.
48. Dynamic Analysis of Dispute Management (DADM), *Kenya 1945–Present* (database project), University of Central Arkansas, https://uca.edu/politicalscience/home/research-projects/dadm-project/sub-saharan-africa-region/kenya-1963-present/.
49. Mathieu Pellerin, *Mali's Algiers Peace Agreement, Five Years On: An Uneasy Calm*, International Crisis Group, June 24, 2020, https://uca.edu/politicalscience/home/research-projects/dadm-project/sub-saharan-africa-region/kenya-1963-present/.
50. Lamin Kargbo, "The Government of Sierra Leone Reacts to the Visa Sanction Imposed by the U.S.," Switsalone, September 23, 2020, https://www.switsalone.com/37368_the-government-of-sierra-leone-reacts-to-the-visa-sanction-imposed-by-the-u-s/.
51. Alan Boswell, "South Sudan: Peace on Paper," International Crisis Group, December 14, 2018, https://www.crisisgroup.org/africa/horn-africa/south-sudan/south-sudan-peace-paper.
52. "China's Foreign Policy Experiment in South Sudan," International Crisis Group, July 10, 2017, https://www.crisisgroup.org/africa/horn-africa/south-sudan/288-china-s-foreign-policy-experiment-south-sudan.
53. Dynamic Analysis of Dispute Management (DADM), *Zambia 1964–Present* (database project), University of Central Arkansas, https://uca.edu/politicalscience/home/research-projects/dadm-project/sub-saharan-africa-region/zambia-1964-present.
54. Michelle Gavin, "Zimbabwe's Sanctions Smokescreen," Council on Foreign Relations blogpost, September 22, 2022, https://www.cfr.org/blog/zimbabwes-sanctions-smokescreen.
55. Author interview, October 6, 2022.
56. Author interview, November 7, 2022.
57. Author interview, November 11, 2022.
58. Author interview, November 14, 2022.

59. Usman Tar and Mala Mustapha, "Al-Shabaab: State Collapse, Warlords and Islamist Insurgency in Somalia," in *Violent Non-State Actors in Africa*, edited by Caroline Varin and Dauda Abubakar (New York: Springer International, 2017), 277–299.

60. Gilles Yabi, "How Can the United States Better Engage With Africa's Fragile and Conflict-Affected States?" Carnegie Endowment for International Peace, March 30, 2023, https://carnegieendowment.org/2023/03/30/how-can-united-states-better-engage-with-africa-s-fragile-and-conflict-affected-states-pub-89423.

CHAPTER 9

PRACTITIONER REFLECTIONS

The study of group behavior among humans is a central concern of social scientists. While quantitative measurements and historical cases are important foundations for social scientific inquiry, they provide an incomplete picture. Studies of human behavior must also consider how the individuals involved in a particular activity perceive it, as well as how they understand their own roles within it. This requires researchers to engage in direct conversations with those individuals—in the context of coercive diplomacy, this means speaking with people who have witnessed, studied, or participated in coercive episodes, as coercer or target.

The current study mapped out attitudes on US coercive diplomacy from 1990 to 2020 through interviews with sixty expert witnesses, including diplomats, soldiers, policy advisors, and scholars. Of these, thirty were from the US, and thirty represented a variety of European, Asian, African, and Latin American countries. The interviews were conducted on a non-attribution basis to encourage candid responses and protect certain participants in sensitive positions or from sensitive countries. US respondents included ten former military officers, four diplomats, ten academics, and six "others" (journalists or lobbyists). Of these, thirteen had served in senior roles (such as ambassadors, general officers, other senior executives), eleven had worked as NSC staff or Congressional staff, and fifteen had directly participated in at least one coercive episode. Non-US respondents consisted of eight military officers, six diplomats, eight academics, and eight "others." Of these, sixteen came from Europe, four from Africa, seven from the Middle East/Central Asia, and three from South or East Asia. The interviews were conducted between August 2022 and January 2023.

The interviews consisted of ten open-ended, conversational questions posed to each respondent. These questions were designed to elicit broad, impressionistic views of US CD rather than technically informed answers on specific points. The interviews should be understood as a series of conversations that reflected some trends, rather than a formal survey employing strict modeling and sampling techniques. Taken together, they provide a means to compare and contrast how US policy experts perceive the nation's experience with CD over the past three decades and how those efforts are viewed abroad. The questions are listed in the following section, with a summary of the aggregate responses, broken down by US and international respondents, available in Appendix 1 that is posted online.[1] Illustrative comments from the experts interviewed follow the summary of responses.

QUESTION 1:

There are many sources of "demand" for US coercive diplomacy—Congress, pressure from interest groups or the media, pleas from regional allies, decisions within the US interagency process. Yet effective CD requires broad enforcement coalitions, and as the number of countries targeted by US coercion increases, the greater the presumptive risk to coalition building for future coercive episodes. In your view, did the US balance this risk effectively from 1990 to 2020?

The first question was designed to explore how respondents viewed the frequency and breadth of US coercive diplomacy in terms of sustained effectiveness over time. Majorities among both US and international experts believes the US did not effectively balance the frequency of coercion with the need to build and maintain coercive coalitions during the period under study. Several US respondents attributed the increased frequency of coercive measures to "bandwidth" limitations within the US governmental bureaucracy, which affected its ability to coordinate and follow through on the implementation of coercive measures. International respondents noted that increased frequency and breadth of coercion has spurred adaptive resistance measures by Great Power rivals and heightened allies' concerns that they are potential future targets of coercion.

Illustrative Responses (US):

> We coerce too frequently. We inherited from the Cold War generation the residual habit of managing collective security, but lost the discipline of focusing on serious US interests while doing so. We have the muscle memory of leading an alliance, but have added in additional demands as a result of achieving extraordinary power in the immediate post–Cold War period and developing an exaggerated sense of what can be done through pressure. Both the Left and the Right in the US bought into this for different reasons. They had related goals of transforming the international system and the states within it. The drive to democratize the world had both progressive and hard-power arguments to back it up. There was a competition of sorts between the US and Europe to consolidate post–Cold War gains in democratization; this resulted in a global project to force the pace of many countries' democratic development. But it was largely a sham that inflicted pain on many without real results, because of an inability to follow through on such an ambitious mandate.[2]

> When CD fails, it poisons relations with the target, especially with allies. It creates a reticence to join subsequent sanctions. Balance is trickier with allies than adversaries—it's like showing a gun in the movie, the director knows it will be used. Induces a search for

other options, and hedging. If you think twice about CD, think three times with allies...it will likely change the relationship.[3]

There is an overwhelming pressure for a variety of good reasons to "do something" on foreign affairs, especially given the inter-connectedness of the world. The urge often comes from good impulses and good people. But there clearly has to be a threshold: North Korean nukes, Russia and its war against Ukraine, Myanmar, Venezuela, Iran. These are bad in ways that go way beyond specific disputes or frictions with other countries. So, do you save the measures for the "baddies," for the comprehensive measures? Are there other ways to show displeasure with other countries that displease us? Yes...The question is one of setting thresholds and exercising creative restraint short of that.[4]

We often impose sanctions but then allow them to wither. My gut says we are OK on balancing frequency, but not on follow through. The tradeoff with coercive diplomacy is that we may need the target country down the pike. You may or may not sanction today, but the effects will last, and we don't think enough about the long-term effects on those countries. A country that's been coerced is unlikely to willingly cooperate in future coercion.[5]

It's not the number of times that it's applied that's a problem, but the lack of focus and follow-through with which it is applied. When it is specific enough and focused enough it can be a solvable problem. The breadth of targets can be a problem because it limits focus and exceeds bandwidth. Are the demands and the threats specific, timely, and lifting criteria clear? Does the US bureaucracy follow through? Because the answer frequently is "not really," the number of instances becomes a problem.[6]

Illustrative Responses (International):

You can apply more diplomacy and incentive than coercion and punishment. An alternative that gives something—coercion gives no assurance or guarantees, with assured losses from lost invest-ments. "If you forego" the thing the US demands MAYBE you will receive a benefit, but no assurance. The US needs sustained and constructive approach when dealing with allies. When dealing with adversaries, a heavy hand is warranted...but know and protect the difference. Differentiation must drive the approach in each specific case.[7]

For most of the world, the multilateral route (UN) route is important. It is easier for countries to present a formidable front if an episode has UN endorsement. Multilateral response is more credible, and protects participants from regional backlash. Going it alone or pre-emptively became a doctrine for the US.[8]

We need to look at the difference between destroying capabilities and weakening an opponent, or really trying to get them to change mind. In either case, though, there is an erosion of US standing with third parties due to the overuse of coercion.[9]

The US has its classical allies that follow suit when you coerce, but then you lose the global south, and countries on the other end of the spectrum politically. In Arab countries and other parts of the global south, the historical use and overuse of these tools has lost us potential partners out of fear or memory of coercion in their own case.[10]

QUESTION 2:

Coercive success depends in part on leaders within a target country assessing that the costs of resistance outweigh the cost of compliance, but in practice it can be difficult for the coercer to understand how those leaders frame and calculate costs. In your view, did the US effectively account for differences in target country framing and calculation while engaged in coercive episodes during the period under study?

This question was intended to solicit comments on the psychological aspects of coercion and whether respondents believed the US was adept at considering the specific context of target-country decision-makers when initiating and developing coercive episodes. Negative responses to this question were nearly unanimous among both US and international respondents. A common theme in both groups was that US coercive policy makers frequently fail to consider or operationalize assessments of target psychology, framing, and available options. Metaphorically, Washington tends to deploy coercive tools consistently as a hammer, very rarely as a screwdriver or a wrench.

Illustrative Responses (US):

> The US has a hard time understanding other countries' interests, especially when they don't align with our own. The idea that Obama made popular of the US knowing who was "on the wrong side of history" implied that there was no point in understanding or compromising with the views of other countries, because their regional policies and concepts would clearly not stand the test of time...By discounting or ignoring target countries' view of their own interests and commitment, we overestimate their response to our statements of commitment. But US statements of commitment are not always taken at face value, and can be dismissed as the price to be paid for the target's core interests.[11]

> The difficulty of precisely anticipating the response and interpretation of US policy positions and actions is exactly why coercive diplomacy should be judiciously employed. Analyzing the rationale of a target country is fraught with danger. We project our own values and thinking on adversaries, and this can lead to severe miscalculation and unintended consequences. To the extent that we have a cadre of trained and experienced professionals who deeply understand the psyche of a target country, we can improve the likelihood of effective coercive design. However, this expertise must be deeply involved in the analysis, planning and execution of coercive foreign policy. Obviously, having a skill set or resource that is not sufficiently used is ineffective.[12]

> I think we do a good job of weighing the implications of our actions. We are too risk averse in many cases to initiate or accept the costs of intensification of an episode. My sense is that we have failed to appreciate the extent to which we control the escalation ladder

against various adversaries. We are habituated to avoiding cost...
If we had fewer episodes, we could devote more resources, and
that might lead to better outcomes—but risk aversion in general
is the bigger problem.[13]

Illustrative Responses (International):

You know the step you want to disincentivize, but this is not
tied to finding common ground and resuming better relations
after. It has to be tailored case by case. Trying to draw a line
and apply it everywhere across regional and national lines is not
likely to succeed.[14]

It's not that the US doesn't do it well, but doesn't do it at all. It
seems the US policy establishment is so big that it doesn't need to
study specific rivals or enemies' psychology and specific context.
The personal behavior, character and so forth of the target leader is
not considered, nor the cultural specifics of the regions in question.
The UK during their imperial period spent a great deal of effort to
understand local traditions, actors, and cultures, and had greater
effectiveness in manipulating the power balances. They had rivals,
which spurred innovation and calculation, so asymmetrical US
power in this sense has been a disadvantage.[15]

The question implies that there is a process by which you evaluate
a variety of ways and prefer one. I don't see that sort of evaluation
process going on—the default is always sanctions. There is some
matching between the subject matter (demand) and the type
of sanctions. But because you have no appetite for risk, your
selection of ways is not driven by "map-reading" of the target
or subject matter but by your appetite for risk and knowledge
of own limitations. It is an internal US process—what can I do
without risks and costs—and taking own temperature rather than
that of the target.[16]

The US often ignores the rally-around-the-flag response in coerced
countries and the fact that because half of the financial sources in the
world are not registered, and countries need energy and food sources, they

will find ways to either by-pass it or try to convince the US -in areas with mutual interests- for exemptions. From time to time the US government also ignores that the primary duty of the coerced governments is to protect their own national interest; not the US interests.[17]

The single most important failure of US foreign policy in our region is to understand the context...the people who assess costs and benefits...are less than expert in the target countries, and fail miserably to understand the calculus in the minds of their counterparts...to prove that their assessment was not wrong, they seek to portray the actions, the actors, and the target itself as problematic, rather than the policy.[18]

QUESTION 3:

> What are the most effective strategies for target states to resist US coercive diplomacy? Examples might include retaliation, forming resistance networks with like-minded or similarly targeted countries, domestic nationalist mobilization, and seeking protection from other large states.

Question 3 was included to develop insights into the varying approaches taken by states targeted by US CD beyond the binary response of comply or resist. Several resistance strategies were suggested in the question, but respondents offered additional ones as well, such as waiting out the US administration through strategic patience and manipulating divisions between the ruling party and opposition within the US. A majority of both US and international respondents viewed working with external patrons or resistance networks, mobilizing domestic resistance, or a combination of the two as the most effective strategies. In discussion, none of the respondents indicated that target strategies were not generally viable or relevant, and many within both groups of respondents noted that the US does not have a systematic or consistent approach to evaluating and adapting to target resistance strategies.

Illustrative Responses (US):

If the target assesses that US commitment is surficial rather than deep, it makes sense for them to double down and refuse to budge, but not try to provoke further pressure. If the target assesses that real US interests are involved—and thus serious commitment—the better strategy is to start seeking compromise solutions. If they misjudge the seriousness of the US position and ignore it, further escalating pressure is likely to come.[19]

As the scale of sanctions programs has increased, so have evasion networks. As increasingly large economies have been subject to significant or comprehensive sanctions programs, so have their evasion networks expanded to include finding limited safe haven in peer or near peer economies. Overreliance on blocking and visa denial—not very imaginative. There are some innovative tools.[20]

Military force is the bluntest instrument, and when a credible willingness to use it is demonstrated, then even our worst adversaries will generally take us seriously and give us at least part of what we want.... I don't know of a case where economic coercion had that effect.[21]

Strategic patience works, given our own strategic "attention deficit disorder." Depending on the country, the Iranians and Chinese for instance, they see us as very short-sighted and unable to stick with issues over time. The Cold War is a great historical example of how we can stick with the struggle over time, but that was a case in which we picked the right fight. If it was peripheral, and we couldn't tie it into core interests, it was difficult to justify continued investment. When we are capricious in what we engage in, the risk of walking away is high.[22]

Illustrative Responses (International):

It's very target specific; styles differ. For many Middle East countries, delay, procrastinate, tell stories. It's all about wasting time and promising empty promises; some of it is lying. Bringing the Americans or Europeans back to check and inspect. If it's long and sanctions-heavy, look for work arounds, alternatives, circumvention. Make America think that there is a moderate element with you can work, as with China and Iran. Let the US and the West meet with people that pose as moderates...Playing domestic politics to explain why you can't compromise. Iran shows the way very effectively—undermining the coercer indirectly. Attacking you through proxies, attacking your partners, brinksmanship and harassment. Approach [to resistance] will rhyme with the specific strategic culture.[23]

Ways to resist depends on the nature of the e targeted regime; in the case of authoritarian regimes, the control of national media plays in favor of using the nationalist sentiment, which is very effective when coupled with the support of other large states (prominently Russia and China in the last decade, a s they have a permanent seat at the UNSC, enabling them to disrupt regimes of sanctions and UN formal condemnation). In the case of other, democratic regimes, playing on US domestic internal political divide (including divide between federal and state laws is a workable ploy. So is the use of mutual economic interests in the globalized economy, especially when considered in the framework of regional economic alliances (the EU for instance).[24]

Best strategy is time—more patience than the US Second is to exceed the US risk tolerance. US wants the game played within a box in which costs are unilateral and risks hedged. Ideal case for occurs when target is a small country, they are in pain, no risk of kinetics, you impose your will over time. When the target does not recognize this box—like Iranian escalation in the Gulf—they can spread risk and cost to become mutual. The US triangle of unilateral pain, hedged risk, no escalation—break that, and play it out over time.[25]

There is a track record of "other guy" willing to help targets resist. The difficulty is asymmetric information. The targeted countries know what they're going to do; they have the initiative and a lot of cards that we don't have, leaving us to guess what crazy stuff they're willing to do. In most cases they also dominate local media narrative in their own markets.[26]

QUESTION 4:

In your assessment, when the US issues coercive threats, are its demands generally viewed as sincere by the target and third parties (i.e., generally believed that defiance will be punished, and that compliance will be rewarded rather than generating new demands)?

This question was designed to gather feedback on the clarity of US intent during coercive episodes. Specifically, it aimed to determine whether target and third countries interpret US demands as literal, seriously intended, and limited to the immediate request, with the expectation that compliance or a negotiated solution will bring an end to the coercion. Alternatively, targets and third countries might assess that US demands are vague political signals, subject to expansion over time, or that coercion will continue iteratively even if initial concessions are made. This can be understood as a matter of initial and ultimate credibility: will the US inflict harm predictably and lift harm predictably? Four types of responses were received: that the US is generally seen as sincere in both initial and ultimate terms, that it is generally seen as insincere, that it is viewed as initially sincere but ultimately insincere, or that views greatly vary based on the administration in question. Among US respondents, the most frequent response was that it varies by administration, while among international respondents the most common view was that the US is viewed as insincere both in its willingness to inflict initial harms for specific reasons and in its willingness to cease coercion.

Illustrative Responses (US):

Our being taken seriously depends much on two things: personality is the first...at the end of the day, it's the credibility of the person delivering the message. Do they mean it, are they focused, can they get it through their own system, and do they have longevity in office? Our own divisive politics work against us here, as does our rotation between parties and Presidents. What they've learned, is that the US won't consistently deliver across administrations. We may want and be sincere in the moment, but it is difficult increasingly for our interlocutors to take us seriously and know that punishments and inducements are real.[27]

Those being coerced have learned that they have to be careful, because the Americans can cause both military and economic pain —they will punch in the nose. But they also know we're probably not going to stay long or sustain over the long-term. We have immediate but not long-term credibility. When we start to coerce, it makes potential targets worry. But they have learned to look at how to weather the storm.[28]

There is still a sense that we're sincere, broadly speaking. Are we serious in asking about it? Yes, a lot of times. But, that doesn't mean we won't come back again on another issue later. It may be that targets and third parties think we're sincere, but increasingly unreasonable on demands. A case that comes to mind that is hugely undermining is Libya. We used coercion to get Libya to give up WMD, but then went to war with them several years later. A strong message to other WMD states that you should never give them up—and undermined our own success.[29]

Illustrative Responses (International):

In terms of credibility, most countries do believe that the US will implement sanctions once threatened. A certain amount of effectiveness is expected.[30]

The first part—credibility to give harm—was clearly "yes" up to the Obama redline in Syria. That is not going to go away; it is not an incident, but a trend...Lack of response creates a total lack of initial credibility. As for ultimate credibility...you can lift sanctions, but there is a view (JCPOA as an example) that even if a target compromises you won't reap full benefits in return. The first is a greater problem than the second.[31]

All the examples I have in mind are negative on both sides of the question. Clear that American threats or even messages are taken less seriously than one might think...the feeling I got was that the messages received were not viewed as strong threats. Subjectively, I see a read discrepancy between what Americans think are strong messages and what the peoples of the region perceive.[32]

The first part depends on who is in power. If it's a frantic White House, or one that doesn't reflect mainstream US public or policy views, the ability to cause and sustain hurt is not taken too seriously. A more serious and deliberate White House more so. But the second part is the bigger problem; the general perception is that once targeted, it is really hard to get out of the situation. Sectoral sanctions, terror designations and such are very problematic—if there is no roadmap to reversal that doesn't undermine their own domestic standing, if not done in a politically savvy way, it's a dead end and punitive for life.[33]

QUESTION 5:

In your view, does the US have an effective method to adjust or terminate coercive pressure?

This question aimed to gather views on how the US adapts during coercive episodes by escalating, de-escalating, and interpreting target behavior, and whether it demonstrates the ability to conclude such episodes upon either demand satisfaction, alternative compromise, or failure to achieve coercive success over time. The majority of respondents from both groups indicated that the US lacks such a mechanism. Both international and US respondents frequently noted the absence of a standing process or structure capable of performing the necessary assessments for adaptation and cessation of coercive pressure in a timely manner.

Illustrative Responses (US):

No. There is no campaign planning at the interagency or national level, because each episode is treated in a discrete, incremental manner. There is no playbook that guides toward a strategic end state. A matrix of domestic actors' views, partner views, cost assessments, values and interests are invoked and considered in initiating or adjusting coercive measures, but there is no broad strategy of effect in most cases. Only by exception, when the "Deep State" sees real risk to core national interests, do we really coordinate in a sustained manner across the government. So, we end up with three types of outcomes: real key and core interests in which failed coercion evolves into full-scale military action, peripheral interests in which coercion is less sincere and less complete, so it peters out or continues on with marginal effect, and situations in which the target's reaction pushes us into re-assessment and becomes a core interest, leading to escalation.[34]

No. Sanctions eventually gain a life of their own. The people executing them forget why they were put in place to begin with. Some do not understand our objectives (since they are usually not well defined) so there is no way to achieve them (if you don't know where you are going any road will get you there). Others don't care if we have achieved our objectives. Still others have an ideologically driven dislike for the target.[35]

In theory we have a mechanism through the NSC committees—IPCs, PCs and so forth—to assess. When the Biden Administration came in they were inclined to lift sanctions on Iran and Yemen, but it's almost as if they had a pre-conceived plan to lift sanctions due not to the trends on the ground but due to the position of the Administration. This is part of the consistency problem—reversing what the previous Presidential Administration did regardless of assessment process.[36]

Illustrative Responses (International):

Like Condoleezza Rice and Bush lifting sanctions on India, this must be done from time to time. But this stands out because it was so rare. What it means is that you need a political champion to lift. There is no mechanism for easing or lifting.[37]

My feeling is no, it almost makes me smile. There is not enough calculated strategy behind it, so there is no routine structure to assess and adapt. When the driver is domestic politics, which it sometimes is, it makes it harder to index adaptation to conditions on the ground. This means the coerced also cannot understand the strategy and the transaction—can't see it as credible—and thus has little incentive to comply.[38]

When the pressure does not work well, termination or adaptation of pressure is hard to achieve. And normally what drives the changes or adaptations is not strategic assessment, but political shifts in Washington D.C. There is no clear mechanism to assess and adapt.[39]

You can impose pressure, but you must provide an exit as well. The dictator will understand the ultimate result. Saddam was ready to cooperate with the US at the end of the sanctions, and wanted to turn a new page—it was a missed opportunity. It was feasible to achieve concessions from a weakened dictator at the end of that period, and perhaps he would have changed his behavior. Because the most important thing for the dictator is to remain in office.[40]

QUESTION 6:

Diplomatic sanctions—efforts to reduce contact and isolate a target —are sometimes combined with economic or military pressure. In your assessment, does this undercut the US ability to manage the transactional aspect of coercive episodes?

Question 6 was intended to explore the interaction of diplomatic tools of coercion (e.g., visa bans, reduced diplomatic interaction, and building coalitions to condemn or isolate a target) with other forms of pressure and to determine whether such measures reduce the prospects for effective transactional conclusions to coercive episodes. International respondents expressed slightly higher levels of skepticism regarding diplomatic coercive tools than US respondents, but majorities of both groups agreed that these isolation tactics generally make mutually acceptable transactional outcomes less likely. A significant minority of respondents asserted that such measures do not undermine other tools or successful outcomes, if used carefully and sparingly.

Illustrative Responses (US):

> Blanket diplomatic sanctions do not often produce the desired outcome. It is like a Public Diplomacy nuclear weapon. Also undercuts your own potential base of influence in that country. But carefully targeted sanctions on officials can be more effective. The more discrete—versus blanket—the better. If the system we are sanctioning is democratic and transparent, people will understand that it's about the specific bad actors. Don't target the entire bilateral relationship—that provokes a defensive reaction—but specific actors and actions.[41]

> Completely suspending relations has to have a very high threshold...like the brink of war. We can use protecting powers... like we did with the Czechs in Damascus...but it doesn't really work. We can ramp such measures up or down, but don't breach totally. There can be efficacy up to a point. Why not use minor-league harassment like limiting movement or domestic help?[42]

> Obviously, yes (there is a negative effect). This can be mitigated if there are competent third parties who can provide alternate channels of communication.[43]

Illustrative Responses (International):

> Diplomatic isolation doesn't really work now like it did in the 1990s. Multipolarity and Great Power rivalry mean that there are now "clubs" or "gangs" of states, of which the West is just one, so US isolation matters less. Does not have the same effect as it did two decades ago. There is no real ability to isolate—and China,

for instance, is working consistently to ensure that US isolation efforts don't work.[44]

Reducing intelligence is the key here, and that is what is happening with China. The American reporters have been kicked out of Beijing and fewer Chinese reporters in US This reduces intelligence and creates an echo chamber. This becomes impactful in the wrong way.[45]

This is very bad from my point of view. When you stop talking, this is inferred as disrespect—and it doesn't work. The military juntas don't bank in the US, don't vacation there; you can put travel bans or economic sanctions, but it isn't really relevant for some targets. You will hurt the wrong people.[46]

QUESTION 7:

Polling data has shown in this period (1990-2020) that increasing percentages of foreign publics sees the US as a threat to their national security. This might plausibly stem from big wars such as Iraq and Afghanistan, coercive episodes below the threshold of war, perceived US primacy per se, anti-American narratives, or other factors. Is CD causing reputational problems for the US?

Question 7 aimed to assess whether CD is having an important second-order effect on the US reputation as a global leader. Roughly half of both US and international respondents believe that US CD practices are driving or significantly contributing to reputational problems for the US, portraying America as a global bully. Just under half either agreed that the US faces a reputational problem due to other factors, such as large-scale wars or disinformation campaigns by strategic rivals, or felt that the impact of CD on US reputation cannot be clearly determined.

Illustrative Responses (US):

I think it's partly that we are getting a reputation as the global bully. Can't underestimate the impact of our failed military interventions in Afghanistan and Iraq. Effective military and economic tools, but to what end? We turn the dials on, but do we turn them back off? Reagan sat with Gorbachev, and was quietly threatening while also pursuing treaties and deals at the same time. For most people alive today in the world, there are no similar examples in living memory.[47]

The perception of the us as an aggressive hyperpower feeds this view. We fight too often and win too rarely. Coercion can look like bullying unless we are careful.[48]

...You want to be the hegemon, but not to be seen as the hegemon. You want countries to see you as indispensable. Post-World War Two nearly every country in Asia wanted us present and engaged, and saw us as a positive, stabilizing influence for the region. Now we provide less protection, fewer incentives, and challenge more countries on what they see as their rights and prerogatives. I still think we are a force for good and our objectives are to help the people of these places, but you need to look at the particular circumstances in specific countries.[49]

Illustrative Responses (International):

It is natural to resent the power that enforces or takes upon themselves the role of reinforcing global or regional order. You can see the logic of resentment. But more than a local police force, the US doesn't just protect and serve communities, it also pursues own national interests. Would they like the Chinese or Russians better? No. It's sort of natural to resent the hegemon, and perhaps even ungrateful. Some of these countries are probably in countries that the US saved or reconstructed during the 20th century.[50]

Yes, you have an image problem. In light of the increasing CD, people don't see the US as a protector or "leader of the free world" fighting for values. People see the values as an umbrella behind which the US nakedly pursues its national interests.[51]

I would say yes. The anti-US sentiment is related to the use of force or backing allies who use force, sometimes in limited cases but with large regional impact Iraq is the biggest example: demonstrations against the war in UK, Europe, and the Middle East were the biggest in modern history. The point here would be to account for public opinions in the region and various countries, because ultimately those public opinions can help autocrats consolidate and can mobilize resistance to US coercive initiatives...public opinion has downstream effects.[52]

QUESTION 8:

If we were to characterize US Coercive Diplomacy as motivated primarily by domestic politics, geopolitical and security concerns, or human rights and democratic concerns, which do you view as most frequently the dominant motive?

Question 8 was included to examine whether domestic political factors are viewed as a primary motive for US CD. From a strictly geopolitical perspective, the generally low success rate of CD in achieving its stated demands seems counterintuitive. Why continue with such an approach if it rarely works? Domestic politics may offer a potential explanation. However, the majority of both US and international respondents attributed the primary motivation for US CD to geopolitical and security concerns, only domestic politics or values such as human rights and democracy seen as secondary factors.

Illustrative Responses (US):

Geopolitical and security concerns first, human rights and democracy second, domestic politics last. The obvious geopolitical and security concerns involve Iran, Russia, China, North Korea. Human rights and democratic concerns include all coercion under Leahy,

Magnitsky and similar laws. Domestic cases include steps in Latin America and the Middle East driven by the Cuban lobby and pro-Israel lobbies, respectively.[53]

When we really take the step to coercive practice, I think it's geopolitical first, then human rights, then domestic concerns. Domestic concerns frame decisions, and shape Congressional rhetoric, but don't push us to coercion. Control over foreign policy is of course divided. The Senators respond to domestic constituencies, but not the NSC.[54]

Domestic politics and business first. National security second. Human rights is third. If you decouple domestic politics from wealth, business first. It's almost never the case that we go for oil, gas, resources etc. What this entails is that when businesses in US who fund elections and politics oppose a certain policy, or endorse it, they can shape the policy environment.[55]

Illustrative Responses (International):

Under Trump, geopolitics and security concerns were foremost. But more broadly, democracy and human rights. Of course, that's mostly a DC policy elite concern. People in middle America don't care that much about foreign policy, they are concerned about pocket book issues. So middle America dictates a more pragmatic approach. Trump was more successful at foreign policy because he grounded his approach in geopolitics and an understanding of domestic concerns. He was practical. The US needs a little bit more of that practicality.[56]

A certain amount of domestic politics may be at play but the US has a unique ability, due to its still-relevant position as the primary global power, to turn its domestic priorities into regional or global priorities. Translating domestic priorities into operational international campaigns is the prerogative of the most powerful states.[57]

I think geopolitics is where you should look for coercion in terms of seriously imposing pain. For example, the chip wars with China.

This is where you get most vindictive and effective. Perhaps this is where you are at your best. But being a Great Power means you can use force or power for non-essential reasons: human rights, democratization, punishing bad behaviors. ...Sanctions *du jour* is part of your politics now; "doing something" is why sanctions and pressure are so inflated.[58]

QUESTION 9:

Do you see cumulative negative effects from frequent CD? Does it undercut future prospects for coercive success, or lead to diminishing returns?

This question addresses the issue of diminishing returns: whether the frequent use and frequent failure of coercive diplomacy result in negative second- and third-order effects that complicate and degrade US foreign policy and standing over time. Overwhelming majorities of both US and international respondents expressed the view that US CD is significantly decreasing in effectiveness over time, due at least in part to its frequency of use.

Illustrative Responses (US):

Yes. The more you do it without unambiguous success, without leading to decisive force or decisive pain on the target, the more you dilute the effect. When we move beyond mild or pro forma diplomatic sanctions to isolation campaigns or economic and military coercion and it neither works nor ends in relief of coercive measures, the less effect you have over time. Too many coercive episodes uncarefully executed has weakened our overall diplomacy. Too much surficial coercion on peripheral matters can camouflage the seriousness of our intent on core interests. Then process becomes policy—we measure progress by the number of Deputies Committee or Principals Committee meetings held, rather than changing minds or policies of the targets.[59]

Yes. It has contributed to the emerging China, Russia, Iran nexus. It contributes to the global issue of the US as a bully. There is another negative—the domestic impact. It educates the public to believe that we can virtue signal the world. This miseducates the world as to the role of the US in the world. Increasingly there is the assumption that if a group of Americans sees something wrong in the world, we can expect the US to something about it —coerce—and get results. There needs to be a better education about the arrogance of power, and the limits of what our foreign policy can achieve...Where we do it excessively, the more obvious the limits of our power become.[60]

It is having a negative effect in a huge way...it's like a battery; every time you use power, you lose power. Disciplining the system has some rules: don't threaten unless you can make it stick, and have legitimate reason. We have ruined our brand so much by sallying forth so often—it's not lost on the world that we're willing to kill hundreds of thousands of foreigners to pursue a policy that doesn't work and, in some cases, then just walk away. And it's not just the military. Sri Lanka is an example. Our economic and diplomatic pressure led to changes that ultimately collapsed the government and hurt the people. I think it is lost on policy makers that even though there are no firm and fast Cold War lines (yet), subtle concerts are playing out all the time to oppose us.[61]

Illustrative Responses (International):

Absolutely. It is difficult to stay focused. It's becoming a monstrous architecture of sanctions. It's letting bad guys become comfortably numb because they keep getting beaten. Many times, the threat of a slap—the anticipation—is what you want to do the work. Once you've slapped a number of times, the target knows he can take it. Overuse and proliferation make it difficult to manage.[62]

There is a clear cumulative negative impact that most countries try to avoid being dependent on the US However, there is a cumulative benefit that is overlooked which is that countries avoid taking actions that could potentially attract US reaction even without the

US implying it. I think the US would benefit from using sanctions only when there is no alternative policy and there is a plan to make up with the target state.[63]

In terms of hard power coercion, it never brings a good reputation to the US Soft power and economic measures, even when mixed in with some coercion and interdependence, are always preferable. There is propaganda from other countries about US imperialism...too much CD, especially hard power CD, fuels such views. Economic measures don't confer the same advantage to adversaries. Soft power is preferable to soft coercion, and helps it when needed; too frequent coercion of hard or soft variety undermines the soft power. But in the case of small and isolated countries, frankly the world doesn't care much.[64]

QUESTION 10:

The US continues to rely on frequent CD despite generally low rates of success, the risk of diminishing returns, and manifest long-term complications. Would you attribute this more to institutional structure and political culture, bureaucratic design, misreading the international environment, or some other cause?

Question 10 served as a net assessment question for the respondents, asking them to identify the most convincing explanation for why the US continued, throughout the period under study, to employ CD at a rate and in a manner that yielded disappointing results. By a roughly 2:1 ratio, both US and international respondents attributed the persistence of CD to American political structure and culture, which are relatively immutable factors. A smaller number of respondents pointed to bureaucratic design and process, factors theoretically more open to reform and improvement. A third, smaller group believed the failure to perceive the shifting power balance in the international system explained the failure to adapt the US practice of CD over time.

Illustrative Responses (US):

Yes, because we pay no big immediate price for it. Our tremendous power in military and economic terms means we can get away with the low rate of success. Coercive Diplomacy "scratches domestic itches," is tempting and we can get away with it...so it persists. The urge to transform the international system remains strong, so we go down that road despite its general non-productivity.[65]

This is the "somebody do something" theory of international relations. But it may not be driven by constituents—it may stem from the personality, interests, and values of the legislators. Domestic concerns may not be popular or constituent-motivated, but still comprise a domestic interest. May not be actually domestic, but the exercise of a separate, co-equal branch of government's autonomy in foreign policy. The Presidency has an edge but not monopoly; we have a unitary executive but not a unitary state in foreign policy.[66]

I think a deeper reason CD is used too often with too little benefit stems from low levels of strategic and foreign policy proficiency resident in the national security apparatus at the Congressional and Executive levels...The US government does a good job of educating its soldiers and diplomats on foreign policy issues, theories, and history, and fostering communication among various departments. There are ample opportunities for intellectual cross-pollination to understand the nuances and complexities of our actions and policies overseas. The same is not true for Congress, though. There are classes on legislative process for new members, but as far as I know, none for foreign policy.[67]

Illustrative Responses (International):

When do you revisit and assess? Imposing is easy; it allows you to signal and to show action, and it incurs relatively low up-front costs. But benefits are rare, and no one seems to be measuring reputational costs, opportunity costs, diminishing returns. Or the cost of imposing and maintaining the sanctions and military pressure itself. There is an industry. There are costs that should be quantified, measured, and assessed. The enforcers by training are lawyers and accountants. But this is a use of force—war by other means. The logic of war in the syntax of economy... You need strategic thinking along the execution lines, and campaign design.[68]

It seems to me natural that in the evolution from sole superpower to strategic competition, it's natural to more slowly adapt your methods. But as the rest of the world becomes acquainted with your coercive efforts they learn and adapt to, and each new episode takes more energy on your part to get similar results. "The sign of an unsystematic effort is the need for a bigger dose to get the same cure over time," it has been said about medications, which might apply here. The international system is getting better at dealing with it. Not sure about the alternative.[69]

It's an easy thing to package up and sell. If you sanction you can make an announcement, with little apparent or immediate real-world impact. Traditional diplomacy is harder to package— so you had a meeting or an extended negotiation session. Military threats, sanctions etc. are not boring or slow or gray in the way that traditional diplomacy.[70]

KEY ISSUES RAISED IN THE REFLECTIONS

None of the ten discussion questions elicited responses that dramatically differed between the US and international respondent groups. Both groups of foreign policy practitioners and analysts observed similar patterns and trends within the US practice of CD. Most respondents in both groups of endorsed the view that the US, as a leading power, is expected to employ coercion—but must do so more effectively than it has over the past three decades.

Taken as a whole, the questions and answers highlight three recurring themes related to the research questions motivating this study. First is the generally perceived weakness of the US policy community in conducting contextual target assessment. The US appears to be losing a key framing contest with the leadership of target countries, as it fails to understand the contextual factors shaping those leaders' expectations of cost and benefit during coercive episodes. Second, the US is losing another framing battle in terms of messaging target-nation publics and third countries, as anti-American counter-narratives remains among the most effective tools of resistance to US coercion.

A second key theme is the challenge of adapting US coercion to the evolving international environment since the end of the Cold War. Both American and international foreign policy practitioners perceive that the US is operating from an outdated playbook—one in which it assumes asymmetric and relatively uncontested primacy, and where small and mid-sized target countries had few options for resistance networking or the protection from rival Great Powers. By failing to adjust the breadth and frequency of coercive targeting, the US has committed to too many targets without the necessary resources or attention span to effectively coerce, leading to progressively higher rates of failure.

Finally, the interviews reveal that the US has struggled to reconcile competing objectives within its CD efforts. Geopolitical and security interests often clash with domestic political or values-based interests, and there does not appear to be a systematic approach to resolving or prioritizing these objectives in specific cases. While domestic political concerns can be a legitimate basis for coercive action, how are they weighed against the impact on national interests as they unfold overseas? Short-term achievements, such as capitulation, compliance, or concessions, may not prevent long-term deterioration in US regional standing. Who measures the trade-offs, and what criteria, with which assessors, is the balance struck?

The fact that so many practitioners involved in coercive episodes — both as US executors and as foreign targets —doubt the efficacy of US CD as practiced over the past three decades should prompt concern among policymakers in Washington. It is striking that few question the potential of CD as a tool of statecraft, yet many believe the US has been maladroit in its application. Both theory and practice support the idea that each episode requires contextual analysis, adaptive pressure, escalatory management, and careful signaling. However, the US has a penchant to "fire and forget" in coercive episodes: initiating and escalating coercion but signaling, loosening, and terminating only by exception.

Notes

1. See https://www.cambriapress.com/USCoerciveDiplomacy.
2. Author interview with retired senior US diplomat, August 9, 2022.
3. Author interview with US foreign policy analyst, October 21, 2022.
4. Author interview with US policy analyst and former national security official, October 25, 2022.
5. Author interview with US former national security official, November 22, 2022.
6. Author interview with US policy analyst and former UN official, November 9, 2022.
7. Author interview with Middle Eastern diplomat, October 7, 2022.
8. Author interview with South Asian policy analyst, September 27, 2022.
9. Author interview with retired Middle Eastern senior military officer and policy analyst, November 2, 2022.
10. Author interview with North African policy analyst, November 16, 2022.
11. Author interview with retired US senior diplomat, August 9, 2022.
12. Author interview with US senior military officer, October 22, 2022.
13. Author interview with US senior policy advisor, October 31, 2022.
14. Author interview with Middle Eastern diplomat, October 7, 2022.
15. Author interview with Middle Eastern foreign policy analyst, November 7, 2022.
16. Author interview with retired Middle Eastern senior military officer and strategic analyst, October 12, 2022.
17. Author interview with European foreign affairs journalist, November 12, 2022.
18. Author interview with European foreign policy analyst and government advisor, December 10, 2022.
19. Author interview with retired US senior diplomat, August 9, 2022.
20. Author interview with US sanctions expert, September 23, 2022.
21. Author interview with US foreign policy analyst and former senior security official, November 21, 2022.
22. Author interview with former US senior intelligence official, November 28, 2022.
23. Author interview with retired Middle Eastern senior military officer and foreign policy analyst, November 2, 2022.

24. Author interview with European senior military officer and foreign policy analyst, November 2, 2022.

25. Author interview with Middle Eastern senior retired military officer and strategic analyst, October 12, 2022.

26. Author interview with European financial and foreign policy analyst, October 3, 2022.

27. Author interview with US senior intelligence and policy professional, October 28, 2022.

28. Author interview with retired US senior military officer, November 2, 2022.

29. Author interview with senior Congressional staff member, October 7, 2022.

30. Author interview with Indian foreign policy analyst, September 16, 2022.

31. Author interview with Middle Eastern senior military officer, November 5, 2022.

32. Author interview with European foreign policy analyst, October 28, 2022.

33. Author interview with North African policy analyst, November 16, 2022.

34. Author interview with retired US senior diplomat, August 9, 2022.

35. Author interview with retired US senior military officer, September 5, 2022.

36. Author interview with retired US senior military officer, November 13, 2022.

37. Author interview with Indian foreign policy analyst, October 27, 2022.

38. Author interview with retired Middle Eastern senior military officer, October 30, 2022.

39. Author interview with European diplomat, November 11, 2022.

40. Author interview with retired Middle Eastern senior military officer, October 24, 2022.

41. Author interview with US foreign policy analyst, October 21, 2022.

42. Author interview with US sanctions expert, September 23, 2022.

43. Author interview with retired US senior military officer and NSC official, November 9, 2022.

44. Author interview with Indian foreign policy analyst, September 16, 2022.

45. Author interview with East Asian foreign affairs correspondent, November 22, 2022.

46. Author interview with retired African senior military officer, November 14, 2022.

47. Author interview with US senior intelligence and policy professional, October 28, 2022.
48. Author interview with retired US senior military officer and NSC official, November 9, 2022.
49. Author interview with US NGO leader and former national security official, November 15, 2022.
50. Author interview with Middle Eastern senior military officer, November 5, 2022.
51. Author interview with European military officer, November 8, 2022.
52. Author interview with European foreign policy analyst, October 28, 2022.
53. Author interview with retired US senior military officer and senior State Department official, November 14, 2022.
54. Author interview with US foreign policy analyst and former State Department official, October 19, 2022.
55. Author interview with US senior intelligence and policy professional, October 28, 2022.
56. Author interview with Middle Eastern diplomat, October 7, 2022.
57. Author interview with Indian foreign policy analyst, September 16, 2022.
58. Author interview with retired Middle Eastern senior military officer and policy analyst, November 2, 2022.
59. Author interview with retired US senior diplomat, August 9, 2022.
60. Author interview with US foreign policy analyst, October 19, 2022.
61. Author interview with US strategy professor and retired military officer, November 7, 2022.
62. Author interview with retired Middle Eastern senior military officer and policy analyst, November 2, 2022.
63. Author interview with European defense and foreign policy analyst, October 27, 2022.
64. Author interview with Central Asian policy analyst and diplomat, October 22, 2022.
65. Author interview with retired senior US diplomat, August 9, 2022.
66. Author interview with US sanctions expert, September 23, 2022.
67. Author interview with US senior military officer, October 22, 2022.
68. Author interview with retired Middle Eastern senior military officer and policy analyst, November 2, 2022.
69. Author interview with Middle Eastern senior military officer, November 5, 2022.
70. Author interview with European diplomat, November 17, 2022.

CHAPTER 10

TOWARD MORE EFFECTIVE COERCIVE DIPLOMACY

QUANTITATIVE FINDINGS

Previous studies have generally identified a success rate of around 33% for coercive episodes, but the data in this study shows that US CD from 1990 to 2020 achieved a somewhat lower success rate (27.9%). Policymakers may find some consolation in the fact that there are other forms of coercive success beyond simple acquiescence to the stated demand— some alternative negotiated concession was obtained in over a third of the coercive episodes (39.3%). However, both forms of success fall short of matching or exceeding the primary form of failure: the deterioration of US influence in bilateral or regional relations, which occurred in 45% of the coercive episodes studied. The engagement of domestic political interests and their satisfaction through the use of coercion is an acknowledged, though understudied, outcome of coercion. According to this study, 57% of coercive episodes involved significant domestic political interests, regardless of the geopolitical logic involved. These findings suggest that the assessment of coercive outcomes must go beyond a simple comply/

resist framework, focusing instead on patterns of effects over time and the satisfaction of broader goals beyond the stated demand.

Not all presidential administrations are equal in how they implement coercion or in the results they achieve. President George H. W. Bush had the best record in terms of CD. He conducted public and formal coercion less frequently than his successors, although it is suspected that James Baker and other officials in his administration engaged in a fair amount of behind-the-scenes threats. Of the five presidential administrations from 1990 to 2020, Bush's administration coerced the least but achieved the highest rate of compliance, the highest average performance score, and the lowest rate of negative bilateral trajectory following coercion. The other four administrations coerced more frequently (with the Democrats slightly more than the Republicans) and had comparable average performance scores, compliance rates, and negative bilateral trajectory scores

The location of coercive targets relative to the US clearly plays a significant role in the effectiveness of coercive diplomacy. Compliance from targets in the Americas is much easier to achieve, likely due to economic exposure, distance from rival Great Power patrons, and fewer obstacles to making credible military threats. In contrast, compliance and concessions are much harder to secure in the Middle East and Central Asia. These regions also have higher rates of negative post-coercion trajectories, as do European regions, possibly indicating that allies and partners in these areas have responded negatively to increasing frequency of coercive diplomacy in their neighborhoods.

The duration of coercive episodes also matters. The data shows that short, sharp episodes (lasting less than two years) have the highest compliance rate and lowest rates of negative trajectories. Longer episodes are less likely to escalate into war but are also less likely to achieve compliance, although they occasionally result in alternate concessions.

Credible threats and mutually acceptable off-ramps have a greater impact on compliance than clear demands or urgency through escalation. Some vagueness in demands may actually aid in securing alternate concessions, while clear off-ramps almost certainly contribute to compliance. However, vague demands can also lead to negative post-coercion outcomes, likely because targets perceive a generalized sense of threat and hostility rather than a clearly defined objective. Off-ramps are helpful because they offer an incentive with transactional value for the target. Coercive performance, which is operationalized as a numerical rating based on expert-coded scores for key variables—clear demand, credible threat, urgency, and off-ramp—accounts for 34.4% of the variance in achieving compliance. The strongest relationship existed between credible threat and off-ramp variables and compliance. Performance explained far less (11.4%) of the variance in securing alternate concessions, with off-ramps being most strongly linked to success in that outcome. Coercive performance explained approximately 20% of the variance in bilateral trajectory outcomes, with clear demands and off-ramps playing significant roles. Coercive performance mattered least in achieving domestic political satisfaction during coercive episodes, explaining 5.9% of variance, though clear demands and credible threats were significantly related to this outcome.

The quantitative study reveals a tenuous relationship between coercive performance on key variables —clear demands, credible threats, demonstrable urgency, and feasible off-ramps—and the achievement of domestic political satisfaction. Such satisfaction appears not to stem from high performance on these variables. Instead, the "do something" signaling, identified in expert interviews, may play a larger role in fulfilling domestic expectations than the actual conduct or outcomes of the coercive episode. This could explain the lack of demand across the Executive or Legislative branches for consistent measures of performance or success in coercive diplomacy. Once domestic political appetite is satisfied, there may be a degree of indifference toward the actual outcomes of the coercion.

The study shows a positive and significant correlation between an administration's framing efforts and the success of obtaining compliance while avoiding significant deterioration in bilateral relations. This correlation, however, is less relevant when an administration—or Congress—does not genuinely prioritize either the specified demand or the long-term maintenance of positive relations with the target. In fact, careful framing efforts may even correlate negatively with domestic political satisfaction as an outcome of coercive episodes, though the statistical evidence for this correlation is relatively weak. The importance of careful framing should be reevaluated in the context of renewed Great Power Competition, as the US can no longer afford to alienate as many targets as it could during the "unipolar moment" that preceded the current strategic era.

In summary, the quantitative portion of the study provides an empirical account of thirty years of US coercive diplomacy with significant analytical value. It provides a baseline of "best practices" for a more thoughtful and targeted approach in the coming decades and highlights certain tensions and trade-offs that a coercing power must consider. The design and measurement of both the explanatory and outcome variables also suggest a potential framework for assessing future coercive episodes, should policymakers or analysts determine that such an assessment tool is needed.

Case Study Findings

There are several ways to apply case-based analysis to US CD beyond the approach most commonly used in scholarly literature, which typically treats single episodes as the analytic unit. Linking multiple episodes involving the same target, the same region, or the same presidential administration as cases offers potential insights valuable for policy analysis. The current study has employed each of these as lenses to better understand the drivers and outcomes of CD. The first lesson of the case analyses, then, is that the value of case method for studying US CD is still in its early stages, with considerable room for further valuable research incorporating this approach.

The cases analyzed in this study highlight several long-term negative effects attributable to frequent—and usually unsuccessful—use of CD. First, broad targeting, which includes coercing not only antagonistic targets but also allies and neutral parties, tends to undermine the ability to build coalitions for future coercive episodes. Second, what could be termed the "iterative effect" emerges: when the US unsuccessfully coerces a target, whether in one instance or over multiple episodes, the target and its neighboring states recognize that US coercive pressure can be withstood and develop new strategies for resistance. The shock value of a rarely imposed sanction diminishes, becoming a predictable action that potential targets anticipate and "price in." In some cases, this even serves as a badge of honor for non-compliant leaders. This expectation incentivizes the formation of counter-networks in anticipation of future US coercive attempts. Third, the lack of systematic follow-up in coercive episodes —whether to conclude episodes through escalation or negotiation, or to consistently assess progress—results in reputational damage for Washington.

Viewing the different regions of the globe as cases reveals that coercive dynamics and outcomes vary greatly for the US, depending on where the target is located. US leverage is strongest in the Western Hemisphere, where geographic proximity, economic interdependence, generally friendly regional organizations, and distance from Great Power rivals create opportunities for coercive success. In contrast, the Middle East and Central Asia present unique challenges, with low rates of compliance or alternative concessions and high rates of negative bilateral trajectory following coercion. South and East Asia stand out for their very low rates of compliance but significantly lower levels of negative trajectory. Europe and Africa fall in the middle in terms of compliance and concessions but differ sharply in terms of negative trajectory—Europe being the highest, and Africa the lowest. These patterns suggest the need for coercive strategies crafted with the specific region of the target.

Cross-regional comparison also reveals recurring "target types" with shared characteristics and outcomes—recur in each region. Serially targeted countries that band together with other frequent targets to deepen coercion-resistant economic and political cooperation—such as China, Russia, Iran, and Cuba—might be called "Antagonistic Network Targets," and they rarely comply with coercive demands. Other targets that are not fully aligned with this antagonistic network but are shielded from coercive effects by the support of a non-coercing Great Power, their economic or military power, or factors such as size and geography, can be termed "Buffered Neutral Targets." There are "Fractured Targets," which are in the grip of war, unrest, or state failure and may lack the ability to coherently respond to coercive demands. "Pre-War Targets" are those targeted with a view toward impending hostilities or in the hope of collapsing them without conflict. "Proximate Wobbly Targets" are the most promising for coercion due to their dependency, coherent response capacity, and vulnerability within the same timeframe demands are issued.

Although these categories are imperfect and subjective —other typologies might be more rigorous or useful—the point is that cross-comparison and analogical reasoning can yield valuable typologies for policymakers or scholars interested in evaluating prospective targets before a coercive episode, assessing strategies during an episode, or conducting retrospective analysis. Examining coercive dyads, target typologies, regional analysis, and other comparative approaches helps overcome the limitations of single-episode analysis and creates opportunities for greater understanding into CD as a broader phenomenon.

Practitioner Findings

The interviews with 60 experienced policy practitioners and analysts from the US and other countries provide deeper insight into the empirical record of US CD during the period under study. Both US and international respondents largely view American CD practices as increasingly problematic. Clear majorities in each group believe that Washington has undermined its ability to assemble coercive coalitions by coercing too broadly and too frequently over the past several decades. Neither group, in aggregate, believes that the US has accounted for target nation framing and differential cost/benefit calculations during coercive episodes. Most respondents agree that Washington lacks a sufficient mechanism or process to adapt or terminate coercive episodes effectively. Nearly all believe that the US is facing diminishing returns and reduced effectiveness of coercive tools due, at least in part, to their over-frequent use.

The experts were divided on whether networking with patrons and other target states, retaliatory coercion, domestic mobilization, or strategic patience was central to resistance strategies, but all agreed that belief in the feasibility of resistance is becoming increasingly widespread. The US is perceived as unlikely to follow through on most coercive attempts in the long term, as unpersuasive with elites and the public in target states, and as likely to use rhetoric about human rights and democracy as cover for geopolitical interests. Most respondents felt that US domestic political incentives and political culture hinder adaptive behavior in signaling during coercive episodes or in terminating them altogether.

There are three key takeaways from the interviews that unite the perspectives of domestic and foreign expert communities. First, Washington lacks a rigorous approach to conduct contextual assessments of targets, both before and during coercive episodes. This limits the ability to prioritize targets, adjust pressure, measure progress, or understand and influence public opinion in target countries. Second, the prevailing mindset in Washington appears dated, reflecting views of American power, target resilience, and the competitive capabilities of rival powers that align more with the realities of the 1990s rather than the 2020s. Substantial evidence suggests that CD may impose costs on specific countries for extended periods, sometimes destabilizing them (intentionally or not), and prompting hedging and balancing behaviors among target states that undermine US influence in the long run.

Finally, the interviews reveal that the US has several goals embedded within its approach to CD but lacks a demonstrated ability or mechanism to deconflict and prioritize them. Tensions between domestic and geopolitical concerns, between Congress and the Executive, and between the will to lead and a limited willingness to commit resources and bandwidth are inherent in nearly every coercive episode. While rare cases of wobbly targets, unity of effort, broad coalition support, and alacrity in implementation are generally successful, the broad coercive net is usually frustrated by these tensions and limitations. Furthermore, the logic of using coercive pressure to undermine adversaries in an open-ended manner may be justified in certain cases but conflicts with the logic of employing coercive pressure to elicit specific responses and change specific target behaviors. When coercive pressure becomes habitual and predictable, more effective hedging networks emerge in response, making compliance with specific policy demands or alternative policy concessions becomes less likely. Without a more effective mechanism to distinguish between CD to signal and CD to overthrow, Washington risks developing and reinforcing the worst possible reputation for CD: that of a power that attempts to coerce reflexively against friend and foe alike, lacks the capacity to manage coercive campaigns and coalitions carefully, and shows little flexibility or sincerity in seeking negotiated termination of episodes.

Recommendations

Drawing from this study's findings and analysis, several practical recommendations emerge for both scholars and practitioners of coercive diplomacy. The first five are particularly relevant for the academic community:

- Determining whether a policy tool—be it military, diplomatic, or economic—"works" or is "effective" is only meaningful from a policy perspective if it is tied to the broader policy objectives it is designed to achieve. Future studies should address not only financial losses and tactical reactions to coercion but also long-term achievement of policy goals.

- The cyclical and long-term effects of CD—such as timing in execution, iterative effects, duration effects, second- and third-order outcomes—remain understudied. Study focused on crisis periods or single episodes must be complemented by research that examines the long-term consequences occurring ex post facto over several years.

- The proliferation of CD by the US and other states offers significant opportunities for comparative study across regions, time periods, targets, and modalities to identify recurring patterns in the phenomenon. While this study has focused on US CD, other coercing states and their target sets also present a valuable field for inquiry.

- Comparative studies of this nature require more precise working definitions and measures—such as the scope of coercion, what constitutes an episode, the variables involved, and the outcomes. The theoretical gaps identified early in the study need to be addressed through the development of a common vocabulary and concepts shared across various social science disciplines and researchers.

- These observations stem primarily from underdeveloped theory. Given the empirical reality of the increasing use of coercive tools short of war by numerous international actors, and the serious effects on international relations and human communities, this phenomenon warrants higher prioritization in academic programs and institutions that focus on economics, political science, strategy, conflict resolution, public policy and related fields.

The second set of recommendations are intended for those who shape and manage coercive campaigns:

- The US government needs a net assessment mechanism that tracks ongoing episodes, targets, modalities, policy progress, and trajectory management. This mechanism need not rely on the same measures used in this study, but it should be comprehensive, interagency, cross-administration, and coordinated with Congress.

Given how pervasive coercive diplomacy (CD) is as a policy approach, our current understanding of its effects—whether positive or negative—remains very partial and episodic.

- The US government needs a stronger mechanism for coordinating coercive messaging between executive and legislative branches. There are numerous examples where Congress and the Executive have undermined the effectiveness of coercion through contradictory messaging—sometimes intentionally.

- Better crafting of measures tailored to the specific target context is needed, taking into account domestic politics, regional framing, and prior US experience. A careful balance of carrots and sticks should be maintained, along with a clear reputational effect and the offer of two paths forward. There is a critical moment when the end of an episode seems within reach, and targets may adapt in unhelpful ways if that moment never materializes. Target-specific measures are particularly crucial with fragile targets, which may yield partially and in the desired direction when pressed, but also risk collapsing entirely (as in the case of Libya).

- More attention should be paid to the termination of CD. The study highlights multiple valid reasons for termination: preserving coercive resources, rebuilding coercive coalitions, restoring credibility regarding both assurances and punishments, improving bilateral trajectories after an episode, and capitalizing on the psychological opening that occurs when a foreign leader given the opportunity to demonstrate statesmanship.

- Treat allies, partners, and neutrals differently, and more discreetly, than truly antagonistic regimes. If "black knight networks" are emerging, they should be kept as narrow as to allow coercing coalitions to remain as broad as possible. This requires a form of triage: if engaged in a serious struggle with deeply antagonistic targets, it is crucial to conclude (or avoid) disputes with neutrals and difficult allies. These relationships can often be managed through compromise or quiet, even if forceful, diplomacy to prevent public conflicts and avoid dealignment from or counteralignment against the US.

CONCLUDING THOUGHTS

In the current global and informational environments, CD serves as an important method of diplomatic and strategic signaling, Diplomatically, it communicates concerns, sensitivities, and incentives—transient effects that, in theory, can adapt fluidly to convey evolving positions and responses. Strategically it demonstrates something less transient— coherence, serious intent, resource commitment and commitment to alliances, prioritization—or, conversely, the absence of those elements. These strategic messages change more slowly but often carry more weight with the targets and third countries. The cumulative effect of frequent coercion is the establishment of a lasting set of strategic signals and perceptions rooted in adversarial, rather than transactional or friendly, relations. While this may be entirely appropriate for truly antagonistic targets, it becomes problematic with difficult allies, neutrals, rival—but not antagonistic—Great Powers (e.g., India), and emerging mid-sized powers (particularly in Africa and Asia).

It has been said that states have no friends, only interests. However, they have partners with whom they can conduct trusted transactions— or not. The frequent application of CD undermines trust and fosters its opposite: structural suspicion. If the US is to effectively deter or punish truly pernicious targets when necessary, American decision-makers must shift or de-escalate in other cases with speed and maintain transactional trust with others by being clear, discreet, and sub rosa when possible.

CD remains enigmatic. It is a potentially powerful tool that leverages military, economic, and diplomatic assets to create conjunctural, shifting a target's calculations in favor of the US However, this approach works best—perhaps only—when applied sparingly and judiciously, as shock, fear, and the assurance of either harm or repair are deeply intertwined in each episode. The more the US resorts to coercion, the more CD becomes "priced in" and hedged against, making it increasingly difficult to build coalitions for leverage. While overuse may be subjective, without better empirical assessment of performance and results, Washington cannot even begin to estimate the true extent of the issue.

The results of this study support and build upon the main conclusions from the recent works by Sisson, Siebens, and Blechman, as discussed in chapter 2. These authors, along with others, have noted that the post–Cold War period of asymmetrical advantage for US CD has ended. The tools available for both coercion and resistance are now broader, more adaptive, and more widely distributed, making coercive competitions less predictable. However, the current era of international competition will still present situations where CD is preferable to war or accommodation and, under certain conditions, feasible. Accurately identifying these opportunities, carefully initiating, sustaining, and terminating coercive episodes, and adapting policy to both success and failure will be critical in determining the quality of outcomes. Achieving this will require a level of discipline and theoretical rigor not demanded in the more permissive environment from 1990 to 2020. This study provides data and analysis that may prove valuable for scholars, analysts, and practitioners engaged in these efforts.

The Washington policy community might find it prudent to reexamine several assumptions that have been treated as received wisdom in recent decades. These include the belief that imposing costs translates to policy progress; that coercive tools come without significant cumulative costs; that US coercive policy gets a reset in the minds of targets and third parties with each new presidential administration; that episodes can be allowed to drag on without evidence of positive benefit due to presumed low cost; and that there is a well-conceived plan for managing these efforts. It is quite possible that none of these assumptions hold true. In light of the results of this study, the national interest would be better served by adapting our coercive approach and praxis to a more realistic foundation.

INDEX

About the Author

Richard Outzen is a geopolitical analyst and a non-resident Senior Fellow at the Atlantic Council. A retired colonel who served thirty years in the US Army, Dr. Outzen served on tours in Iraq, Afghanistan, Turkey, Israel, and Germany. He has taught at the National Defense University and has served as policy advisor in the Office of the Secretary of Defense and the State Department's Policy Planning Office. He has researched and published extensively on policy and strategy, primarily on the greater Middle East and Central Asia.

CAMBRIA RAPID COMMUNICATIONS IN CONFLICT AND SECURITY SERIES

General Editor: Thomas G. Mahnken
(Founding Editor: Geoffrey R. H. Burn)

The aim of this series is to provide policy makers, practitioners, analysts, and academics with in-depth analysis of fast-moving topics that require urgent yet informed debate. Since its launch in October 2015, the RCCS series has the following book publications:

- *A New Strategy for Complex Warfare: Combined Effects in East Asia* by Thomas A. Drohan
- *US National Security: New Threats, Old Realities* by Paul R. Viotti
- *Security Forces in African States: Cases and Assessment* edited by Paul Shemella and Nicholas Tomb
- *Trust and Distrust in Sino-American Relations: Challenge and Opportunity* by Steve Chan
- *The Gathering Pacific Storm: Emerging US-China Strategic Competition in Defense Technological and Industrial Development* edited by Tai Ming Cheung and Thomas G. Mahnken
- *Military Strategy for the 21st Century: People, Connectivity, and Competition* by Charles Cleveland, Benjamin Jensen, Susan Bryant, and Arnel David
- *Ensuring National Government Stability After US Counterinsurgency Operations: The Critical Measure of Success* by Dallas E. Shaw Jr.
- *Reassessing U.S. Nuclear Strategy* by David W. Kearn, Jr.
- *Deglobalization and International Security* by T. X. Hammes
- *American Foreign Policy and National Security* by Paul R. Viotti

- *Make America First Again: Grand Strategy Analysis and the Trump Administration* by Jacob Shively
- *Learning from Russia's Recent Wars: Why, Where, and When Russia Might Strike Next* by Neal G. Jesse
- *Restoring Thucydides: Testing Familiar Lessons and Deriving New Ones* by Andrew R. Novo and Jay M. Parker
- *Net Assessment and Military Strategy: Retrospective and Prospective Essays* edited by Thomas G. Mahnken, with an introduction by Andrew W. Marshall
- *Deterrence by Denial: Theory and Practice* edited by Alex S. Wilner and Andreas Wenger
- *Negotiating the New START Treaty* by Rose Gottemoeller
- *Party, Politics, and the Post-9/11 Army* by Heidi A. Urben
- *Resourcing the National Security Enterprise: Connecting the Ends and Means of US National Security* edited by Susan Bryant and Mark Troutman
- *Subcontinent Adrift: Strategic Futures of South Asia* by Feroz Hassan Khan
- *The Next Major War: Can the US and its Allies Win Against China?* by Ross Babbage
- *Warrior Diplomats: Civil Affairs Forces on the Front Lines* edited by Arnel David, Sean Acosta, and Nicholas Krohley
- *Russia and the Changing Character of Conflict* by Tracey German
- *Planning War with a Nuclear China: US Military Strategy and Mainland Strikes* by John Speed Meyers
- *Winning Without Fighting: Irregular Warfare and Strategic Competition in the 21st Century* by Rebecca Patterson, Susan Bryant, Ken Gleiman, and Mark Troutman
- *US Coercive Diplomacy and the Global Order: A Critical Analysis of Post–Cold War Strategies* by Richard Outzen

For more information, see **cambriapress.com**.